# The Buddha

## A SHORT BIOGRAPHY

## OTHER BOOKS IN THIS SERIES

*Buddhism: A Short History*, Edward Conze, ISBN 1–85168–221–X
*Buddhism: A Short Introduction*, Klaus K. Klostermaier, ISBN 1–85168–186–8
*Hinduism: A Short History*, Klaus K. Klostermaier, ISBN 1–85168–213–9
*Hindu Writings: A Short Introduction to the Major Sources*, Klaus K. Klostermaier, ISBN 1–85168–230–9
*Hinduism: A Short Introduction*, Klaus K. Klostermaier, ISBN 1–85168–220–1
*Islamic Philosophy, Theology and Mysticism: A Short Introduction*, Majid Fakhry, ISBN 1–85168–252–X
*Muhammad: A Short Biography*, Martin Forward, ISBN 1–85168–131–0
*Islam: A Short History*, William Montgomery Watt, ISBN 1–85168–205–8
*Jesus: A Short Biography*, Martin Forward, ISBN 1–85168–172–8
*Christianity: A Short Introduction*, Keith Ward, ISBN 1–85168–229–5
*Judaism: A Short History*, Lavinia and Dan Cohn-Sherbok, ISBN 1–85168–206–6
*Judaism: A Short Introduction*, Lavinia and Dan Cohn-Sherbok, ISBN 1–85168–207–4
*Judaism: A Short Reader*, Lavinia and Dan Cohn-Sherbok, ISBN 1–85168–278–3
*The Old Testament Prophets: A Short Introduction*, E.W. Heaton, ISBN 1–85168–277–5
*Sufism: A Short Introduction*, William C. Chittick, ISBN 1–85168–211–2
*The Bahá'í Faith: A Short Introduction*, Moojan Momen, ISBN 1–85168–209–0
*The Bahá'í Faith: A Short History*, Peter Smith, ISBN 1–85168–208–2
*The Psychology of Religion: A Short Introduction*, Kate M. Loewenthal, ISBN 1–85168–212–0
*Pluralism in the World Religions: A Short Introduction*, Harold Coward ISBN 1–856168–243–0
*Scripture in the World Religions: A Short Introduction*, Harold Coward, ISBN 1–85168–244–9
*Confucianism: A Short Introduction*, John and Evelyn Berthrong, ISBN 1–85168–236–8
*Global Philosophy of Religion: A Short Intrduction*, Joseph Runzo, ISBN 1–85168–235–X
*Inter-religious Dialogue: A Short Introduction*, Martin Forward, ISBN 1–85168–275–9

## RELATED TITLES PUBLISHED BY ONEWORLD

*Buddhist Texts through the Ages*, translated and edited by Edward Conze, I.B. Horner, David Snellgrove and Arthur Waley, ISBN 1–85168–107–8
*A Concise Encyclopedia of Buddhism*, John Powers, ISBN 1–85168–233–3
*What Buddhists Believe*, Elizabeth Harris, ISBN 1–85168–168–X
*What the Buddha Taught*, Walpola Sri Rahula, ISBN 1–85168–142–6
*The Wisdom of Buddhism*, compiled by Mel Thompson, ISBN 1–85168–226–0

# The Buddha

## A SHORT BIOGRAPHY

John S. Strong

ONEWORLD
OXFORD

THE BUDDHA:
A SHORT BIOGRAPHY

Oneworld Publications
(Sales and Editorial)
185 Banbury Road
Oxford OX2 7AR
England
http://www.oneworld-publications.com


A CIP record for this title is available from the British Library

ISBN 1–85168–256–2

Cover design by Design Deluxe
Typeset by LaserScript Limited, Mitcham, UK
Printed and bound in the United Kingdom by Bell & Bain Ltd, Glasgow

*For*

*Robbins Strong (1912–99)*

*and*

*Kitty Strong (1917–99)*

# CONTENTS

# TABLES

# ILLUSTRATIONS

# PREFACE

Over two thousand years ago, in what is now Southern Nepal, a person was born who came to be known as "the Buddha," an epithet which means "the Awakened One." Today, he is honored throughout the world as one of the great religious figures in the history of humankind. His greatness lies in his doctrine, and in the religious community which he founded, but also in his lifestory, in the tales that were told about him.

Every author of a biography of the Buddha – especially a *short* biography of the Buddha – faces choices. Which episodes in the Buddha's lifestory should one include? Which should one pass over? What sources should one use in presenting a particular episode? Should one confine oneself only to so-called canonical texts, or should one include also later, more developed, traditions? Should one limit oneself to sources in a particular language (say Pali, or Sanskrit), or to texts reflecting a particular Buddhist sectarian bias, or should one strive for inclusivity, even when such comprehensiveness may lead to confusion or degenerate into obsession with detail?

I have tried to resolve these problems by adopting, in the time-honored Buddhist fashion, a "middle way" approach. On the one hand, I wish to avoid the extreme of getting bogged down in the nitty gritty details of variants and of philological niceties. On the other hand, I feel it is important to give the reader some sense of the richness of the biographical traditions about the Buddha, to compare and contrast different versions of the same tale so as to reflect the many layers of meaning that different Buddhists came to find in the life of their founder.

For there is no *one* biography of the Buddha, and each Buddhist telling and retelling of stories about him has been influenced by historical recollections, doctrinal emphases, ritual concerns, political allegiances, social and cultural factors, or simply the desire to weave a good tale.

This book is intended for the interested generalist rather than the specialist, for the "student" rather than the "scholar," but that does not mean that she or he should be sheltered from exposure to some of the complexities of the biographical process that went into the Buddhist formulations of the lifestory of the Buddha. For this reason, I have not hesitated to present various versions of certain biographical episodes. Where Buddhists differ on their own presentations and interpretations of the life of their founder, readers should be aware of the options.

On the other hand, I have not attempted to be totally thorough in doing this. I have not tried to present *all* versions of each tale, as I proceed with my narrative, and no doubt some readers will find certain stories or favorite points missing altogether. They are encouraged to consult the section entitled "Sources and Further Reading," which stands in lieu of footnotes (within the text I provide citations only for direct quotes). The paragraphs in "Sources and Further Reading" contain references to texts and secondary studies that were used in writing the different chapters and sections of this book, or that may provide leads for persons interested in pursuing particular topics further. But they are not supposed to be an exhaustive bibliography on any subject. Thus references are given only to texts that have been translated into English (or, in the absence of that, into French or German). There are no citations of editions of texts in their original language of composition (for example, Pali, Sanskrit, Chinese), except in a few cases when I felt an important point could be found only in a passage from an untranslated text.

Finally, I would like to thank students of my Buddhist Tradition class at Bates College who were subjected to an earlier version of this work, as well as a number of individuals who read it in manuscript form and made encouraging comments and insightful suggestions: Rupert Gethin, Steven Kemper, Trian Nguyen, Frank Reynolds, and Donald Swearer.

*John S. Strong*
*Auburn, Maine USA*
*August 2000*

# PRONUNCIATION AND TRANSLITERATION OF TERMS

For place-names, personal names and technical terms, I have generally chosen to use Sanskrit forms, even when talking about a non-Sanskrit (e.g. Pali) source. Thus, for example, I speak of *nirvāṇa* instead of *nibbāna*, of "Gautama" instead of "Gotama." On occasion, at the first appearance of a term, I have added the Pali in parentheses when it is better known or when it differs significantly from the Sanskrit. In the Glossary of Personal Names at the back of the book, I include both Sanskrit and Pali forms. In the pronunciation of both Sanskrit and Pali, the following guidelines may be kept in mind:

1. A bar (called a macron) over a vowel makes it long. Thus:
   **ā** is sounded like the *a* in "barb"
   **ī** like the *ea* in "eat"
   **ū** like the *u* in "rhubarb."

2. Short vowels are pronounced rather differently:
   **a** like the *u* in "but"
   **e** like the *ay* in "tray" (only more clipped)
   **i** like the *i* in "is"
   **o** like the *o* in "so"
   **u** like the *u* in "full."

3. **c** is always pronounced like the *ch* in "chest," while **ch** is sounded similarly but more emphatically and accompanied by a strong breath pulse, like the *ch + h* in "witch hunt."

4. **th** is always pronounced like the English letter *t* but also more emphatically, like the *t* + *h* in "hot house." It is never sounded like the English *th* in "this" or "thing."

5. Similarly, **ph** is like the *ph* in "shepherd" and never like the *ph* in "telephone."

6. **ñ** is like the *ny* in "canyon."

7. Retroflex dots under letters (e.g. **ṭ**, **ḍ**, **ṇ**) mean those letters should be pronounced with the tip of the tongue curled back up into the mouth. For Westerners unaccustomed to Indic sounds, it may be easier simply to read them as an English *t*, *d*, or *n*.

   **ṣ**, however, should be pronounced like the *sh* in "sheep"
   **ṛ** like the *ur* in "urge"
   **ḷ** like the second *l* in "little."

8. **ś** is difficult to differentiate from **ṣ** and may, for practical purposes, also be pronounced like the *sh* in "sheep," while plain **s** should be pronounced like the *s* in "silly."

9. Finally, **ṃ** may be thought of as a completely nasal sound, somewhat like the *m* in "hum" when you are, in fact, humming, but more in the nose and the back of the mouth than on the lips.

10. All other letters may be pronounced as in English.

*Bronze image of Śākyamuni Buddha from Vietnam (Ho Chi Minh City [Saigon]). Photo courtesy of Professor Trian Nguyen.*

# INTRODUCTION
# THE LIFESTORY OF THE BUDDHA

Historically speaking, we know very little for certain about the life of Siddhārtha Gautama, the man who came to be known as "the Buddha." Although no one today seriously questions his actual existence in ancient India, debates still rage over the dates of his life, with the year of his death now being set anywhere between 486 and 360 B.C.E. And though few would doubt that his charisma had something to do with the formation of the religion we call "Buddhism" there is still much disagreement about the contents of his teachings and the nature of the religious community he is said to have founded.

To be sure, we can place what we do know about the Buddha and early Buddhism into reconstructions of the social, political, economic, and cultural contexts of ancient India, and we can set this into the still broader framework of the history of religions. We know, for example, that the India of his day was caught up in a period of religious ferment and questioning, spawned by the rise of new urban centers and the breakdown of old political systems. This context saw the ongoing emergence of groups of renunciant questers (*śramaṇas*), as well as the formation of founded "heterodox" religions such as Jainism and Buddhism. As two prominent contemporary scholars put it, at this time,

> A significant number of people, cut off from the old sources of order and meaning, were open to different ways of expressing their religious concerns and were quite ready to support those engaged in new forms of religious and intellectual endeavor. The historical Buddha responded to this kind of situation. . . . He was a renouncer and an ascetic, although the style of renunciation and asceticism he practiced and recommended was,

> it seems, mild by Indian standards. He shared with other renunciants an ultimately somber view of the world and its pleasures, and he practiced and recommended a mode of religious life in which individual participation in a specifically religious community was of primary importance. He experimented with the practices of ... begging, wandering, celibacy, techniques of self-restraint (yoga), and the like – and he organized a community in which discipline played a central role. Judging from the movement he inspired, he was not only an innovator but also a charismatic personality. Through the course of his ministry, he gathered around him a group of wandering mendicants and nuns, as well as men and women who continued to live the life of householders. (Reynolds and Hallisey, 1987, p. 321)

There is nothing inherently wrong with this portrait, and I am happy to espouse it. But it must be realized that this is not the way Buddhists tell the story of the Buddha. Instead, they narrate many tales that have been remembered and revered, repeated and reformulated over the centuries, and whose episodes have been accepted as inspiring and worth recalling, whatever their grounding in history. Together these stories make up a sacred biography, or rather, several sacred biographies, for we shall see that there are many versions of tales about the Buddha. These narrations may contain "fictions" about the Buddha – legends and traditions that have accrued around him – but these "fictions" are in many ways "truer," or at least religiously more meaningful, than the "facts." They are certainly more plentiful, more interesting, and more revelatory of the ongoing concerns of Buddhists. We may know very little about the "Buddha of history," but we know a great deal about the "Buddha of story," and the purpose of this book is to present the life of this Buddha of story.

The study of this lifestory commenced in earnest, in the West, in the first half of the nineteenth century. As scholars began to read Sanskrit and Pali biographical materials about the Buddha, they found themselves facing traditions they deemed to be unbelievable exaggerations or ridiculous superstitions. In light of these, some of them concluded that the Buddha was a mythic being and denied his historicity. At first, accepting the Hindu theory that portrayed the Buddha as an incarnation of the god Viṣṇu, they proclaimed him to be a divinity, the particular god of the Buddhists whom they saw simply as belonging to a sect of Hinduism. Alternatively, tracing out complex and dubious etymological connections, they compared the Buddha to more familiar divinities of Western "paganism," among them the Roman god Mercury and the

Scandinavian Woden. Then, in the second half of the nineteenth century, with the popularity of solar mythology, they read his biography as a great allegory recounting the saga of a sun god, giving solar twists to virtually all of the details of his life. Thus, for example, they viewed the Buddha's mother as a goddess of the dawn and interpreted her death soon after the birth of the Buddha as the dissipation of the matutinal mists in the light of the rising sun (her son); or they saw the Buddha's rival, his cousin Devadatta, as the moon, trying to contest with a solar hero. This was not only viewing the Buddha as a mythic being, but remythologizing his story in the process, making him into something the tradition probably did not intend.

Other scholars, however, took a different tack. Dismissing the exaggerations of the biographies as hyperbole, they sought to strip them away so as to demythologize the tradition and come to an understanding of the "real Buddha." In this, they mirrored to some extent the rationalist, positivist quest for the historical Jesus being undertaken by some of their contemporaries in Biblical studies. In some instances, however, the "real historical Buddha" they discovered tended to appear in peculiar guises, depending on their own enthusiasms and inclinations. He was sometimes seen as a reformer of the "evils" of the Hindu system, a sort of Protestant opponent of Hindu papism; or he was clothed in the mantle of one of Thomas Carlyle's Heroes, a great individual who changed the course of history; or he was viewed as a socialist, a radical revolutionary who sought an egalitarian society; or, if that was disturbing, he was praised as an intelligent, loving, and predominantly moral man, "an ideal Victorian gentleman" (Almond, 1988, p. 79).

In this book, I shall follow none of these leads. As Alfred Foucher has pointed out, to make the Buddha into a myth is "to dissipate his personality into thin air," but to take away that mythic ambiance is to arrive at an "equally grave misapprehension" (1987, p. 13). What is needed is a middle way between remythologizing and demythologizing, between myth-making and history-making, between seeing the Buddha as a god and seeing him as "just a man," In reading and in presenting the life of the Buddha, I shall, therefore, try to respect the extraordinary supernatural elements in the tales told about him, to understand them without explaining them away; and I shall try at the same time to honor the ordinary down-to-earth elements that root him in humanity, in a given time and place.

## TEXTUAL SOURCES FOR THE STUDY OF THE LIFESTORY OF THE BUDDHA

A few words should be said here about some of the sources that I will use. The full formulation of the biographical traditions about the Buddha took some time to develop and, in some ways, it is still an ongoing process since, even today, Buddhists continue to retell and rethink the significance of the life of their founder. Scholars have much debated the issue of when a continuous narrative of the whole of Gautama's life was first composed. Some have thought such a biography was written relatively soon after the Buddha's death. Others have claimed it was centuries before such an account was finally put together. The question of chronology is a very complicated and tricky one. Even when we know when a particular text was written or compiled, that does not mean that the tradition or story it incorporates originated at that time; it may, in fact, be far older, or it may, in some cases, be a later addition to the text.

Nonetheless it is possible to establish a rough relative chronology of sources. Adapting and simplifying a scheme presented by Etienne Lamotte, I would like to suggest that we distinguish three "layers" of tradition, without actually dating any of them.

First, there are biographical fragments found in canonical texts, presenting particular episodes of the life of the Buddha. These, for the most part, were written in Pali or Sanskrit although they may presently exist only in Tibetan or Chinese. For example, the "Discourse on the Noble Quest" (*Ariyapariyesana-sutta)* is a sermon in which the Buddha himself is said to recall his departure from home and his early meditative endeavors culminating in his enlightenment and his decision to preach. It is part of that portion of the Pali Canon known as the *Middle Length Sayings (Majjhima Nikāya)*, but it also has parallels in a number of other Sanskrit and Chinese texts. André Bareau and others have made a career from comparing and contrasting parallel versions of such biographical texts in an attempt to identify layers of traditions, much as Biblical scholars might compare versions of the life of Jesus found in the Gospels of Matthew, Mark, Luke, and John. In "Sources and Further Reading," I have listed some of the canonical biographical fragments used in this book.

Secondly, there are fuller, more autonomous lives of the Buddha. These were also written, for the most part, in Sanskrit or Pali. Some of them may have been incorporated into the Buddhist canon, or into commentaries on canonical texts, but, in all cases, they also enjoyed separate existences as biographical compositions in their own right. Unlike the biographical fragments their purpose is not to recount a sermon, but to narrate a life. Some of these biographies (e.g. *The Great Story [Mahāvastu]*) are incomplete, in that they do not trace the Buddha's life to its end but stop at an earlier point, such as his enlightenment or one of the early conversions made by him. Others (e.g., the *Acts of the Buddha [Buddhacarita]*) are "complete" in that they extend their narration to his death and beyond. Again, a listing of all such biographies used in this book may be found in "Sources and Further Reading."

Finally, there are a host of comparatively late lives of the Buddha, composed in Sri Lanka, Southeast Asia, Tibet, and East Asia, sometimes in one of the so-called canonical languages (Sanskrit, Pali, Tibetan, Chinese) but often in local vernaculars (for example Sinhalese, Burmese, Thai, Khmer, Mongolian, Korean, Japanese). These all tend to be "complete." Some of them are simple narrative biographies; others are hymns of praise based on episodes of the Buddha's life. Some are stylistically very straightforward; others are tremendously ornate. In general, however, these sources are interesting for the local twists they give to stories about the Buddha, and also for the way in which they attempt to resolve certain problems and questions about the Buddha's life left unanswered (or not even posed) in more "classic" sources. I shall not hesitate to turn to some of these late materials as the occasion arises, and, again, translations of those used may be found in "Sources and Further Reading."

## LIFESTORY AND PILGRIMAGE

In all of these sources – both canonical and post-canonical – it is possible to distinguish a number of factors at work in the ongoing formulations and reformulations of the Buddha's lifestory. One of these, clearly, was the development of the practice of pilgrimage in Buddhism. By all accounts, the Buddha at least began his career as a peripatetic teacher, occasionally stopping to give teachings in a place for a while, but before long, moving on. Perhaps as a result of this, in his lifestory, "where" something happened is as significant as "what" happened there. Each of the major events of the Buddha's life was associated with a distinct site which, of course, was also a place of pilgrimage. Early on, four of these places, in particular, were featured: the garden of Lumbinī, just over the North Indian border in what is now Nepal, where the Buddha was born, and the nearby town of Kapilavastu where his father was a ruler and where he grew up. The Bodhi tree at Bodhgaya, in what was the land of Magadha and is now the province of Bihar, in North India. This is where the Buddha attained enlightenment. The Deer Park at Sarnath near the city of Benares on the Ganges River. This is where the Buddha preached his first sermon. And the village of Kuśinagarī, the present town of Kasia, where the Buddha, lying between two trees, passed away, never to be reborn again, an event known as his *parinirvāṇa* (complete extinction).

The Buddha himself is said to have advocated visits to these four places. As time went on, however, four "secondary" pilgrimage sites were added to this list to form a group of eight; these were listed and described in texts, and depictions of them on stelae came to be very popular in Indian Buddhist art. The identity of these four additional sites varies somewhat, but they all appear to be places commemorating "supernatural" events, and they all were fit into the Buddha's biography in between his first sermon and his death. The following are usually included: Śrāvastī, the capital of the kingdom of Kosala, where the Buddha put on a great display of magical powers; Sāṃkāśya, upstream on the Ganges, where he descended from heaven after spending a rainy season preaching to the gods and to his mother who had been reborn there; Rājagṛha, the capital of Magadha, where he is variously thought to have tamed a wild elephant, put an end to a schism, and converted such luminaries as King Bimbisāra and Indra, the lord of the gods; and Vaiśālī, where among other things, he received an offering of honey from a monkey, and is said to have announced his decision not to remain in this world. It should be noted that these four "secondary" sites are all situated in major cities or towns, in contrast to the four "primary" sites located in groves of trees in rather out-of-the way places. It would seem that as Buddhism spread to new urban centers, the lifestory of the Buddha grew in tandem, and there was a desire to incorporate those places into it.

It is also clear that each of these centers became a locale where pilgrims could recall not just a single event in the life of the Buddha but a whole set of stories. This has prompted scholars such as Alfred Foucher to speak of the Buddha's biography in terms of "cycles" of events located in particular places – the cycle of Kapilavastu (concerning his birth and youth); the cycle of Magadha, featuring his enlightenment and its aftermath; the cycle of Benares (the first sermon), and so on. This development and amplification of the pilgrimage areas coincided, of course, with a further expansion of the biography. The cycle of Lumbinī-Kapilavastu, for instance, was now no longer limited to just the event of the Buddha's birth but to a whole set of episodes relating to his infancy and youth. Thus one text, speaking of Kapilavastu, specifies the following places as being on the pilgrimage "circuit": the site where the baby Buddha was shown to his father and where the latter fell down to worship him; the place where he was presented to the gods of his clan and where the statues of those deities all broke and fell down at his feet; the place where the infant Buddha was shown to the brahmin soothsayers, and where they, seeing the signs on his body, predicted that he would become either a Buddha or a great wheel-turning monarch (*cakravartin*); the place where one soothsayer named Asita more accurately predicted that he would, for certain, become a Buddha; the place where the infant Buddha was suckled by his aunt and foster-mother, Mahāprajāpatī; the place where the young Buddha was taught how to write; the place where he trained and excelled in the arts appropriate to his royal lineage: how to ride a horse, how to drive a chariot, how to handle a bow, grasp a javelin, goad an elephant; the place where, somewhat later, he enjoyed himself in his harem with his wives; the place where, still later, he saw the signs of an old man, a sick man, and a corpse – signs that inspired him to quest for an answer to life's sufferings; the place where he sat under a jambu tree and watched his father plowing a field and where he first entered into a meditative trance; finally, the place of his great departure, where he left Kapilavastu, and set out on his quest for enlightenment.

This kind of detail reflects the simultaneous and symbiotic growth of both biographical and pilgrimage traditions. On the one hand, sites became established as the places where certain stories happened; on the other hand, stories came to be told to explain the existence of certain sites. This was a process that could easily feed on itself, for, once a site was considered sacred, any unusual topographical feature in the area could be enough to give rise to a new story. Indeed, Alfred Foucher speculates that the authors of some biographies must have had available to them pilgrims' manuals – guidebooks reflecting local oral traditions and topography. Thus, in the biography entitled the *Living out of the Game (Lalitavistara)*, one reads of how an arrow shot by the young Gautama struck the ground with such force that it caused water to gush forth where it hit. One suspects that this was spawned by the existence in

Kapilavastu of a particular spring, described in fact as the "Spring of the Arrow" by the Chinese pilgrims, Faxian (Fa-hsien) (fifth century) and Xuanzang (Hsüan-tsang) (seventh century).

As a result of this kind of intimate connection between place and event, in the course of time, biographical and pilgrimage traditions became more or less fixed, and the boundaries of the area in which the Buddha lived and preached, in Eastern and Central North India, were more or less defined. This, however, did not prevent Buddhists living outside of that region – in Northwest India, Sri Lanka, Southeast Asia, and beyond – from claiming that their lands too had been visited by the Buddha and from establishing pilgrimage centers at those sites. These extra-Indian journeys are often called "apocryphal" by scholars, and they are obviously of a different nature than the North Indian events recounted above. The Buddha's grand tour of sites in what is now Afghanistan and Kashmir, for instance, is said to have been made during the course of a single night, while he was in a meditative trance. Alternatively, the accounts of his journeys to Sri Lanka have him flying through the air in order to get there and show him using his supernatural powers to tame various non-Buddhist forces (*yakṣas* and *nāgas*) on the island. Nonetheless, the hagiographers who made up these traditions saw fit to insert them into existing biographies; thus the Buddha's three journeys to Sri Lanka are specified as having taken place in the ninth month, the fifth year, and the eighth year after his enlightenment.

## LIFESTORY AND ART

Another important factor in the development of the legend of the Buddha was the influence of art. Some of the earliest narratives of the Buddha's life were not literary texts, but sculpted bas-reliefs, and these works of art and the moments they capture could easily influence the biographical tradition. If there is symbiosis in the relationship between the Buddha's biography and pilgrimage traditions, the same is true about its relationship to art. Simply put, what is recounted in story may affect what is sculpted in stone, just as what is sculpted in stone can influence what is recounted in story. There is nothing surprising in this; the impact of art on narrative is well-known. In Western culture, one need only think of how artistic depictions of, say, Jesus's nativity (e.g. crèche scenes) or of his crucifixion have influenced the reading, imagining, and rewriting of those moments in his lifestory.

Etienne Lamotte has detected no fewer than thirty-four episodes from the life of the Buddha in the first century B.C.E. bas-reliefs at the Sanchi *stūpa*, in Central India. A number of these, significantly, appear to predate any literary account of the same event. For instance, on one of the pillars of the North Gate at Sanchi, there is a representation of a monkey making an offering of a bowl of honey to the Buddha, whose presence is symbolized by a tree and an empty throne. (At Sanchi, the Buddha is represented only by symbols such as a tree, a wheel, or a set of footprints.) This recalls an event that is supposed to have taken place in the town of Vaiśalī; the episode is commonly found in art, but it does not figure in literary accounts of the Buddha's life until centuries later. Clearly, alongside the biographical tradition there existed a sculptural tradition which interacted with it in sometimes complex ways. Etienne Lamotte (1988, p. 666) has described the process as follows:

> Before laying hands on a chisel, the ... artists undoubtedly consulted one or other biography of the Buddha in order to refresh their memories and ascertain this or that detail of the scene to be reproduced. It is no less certain that they questioned their employers and tried to meet the demands and preferences of their clients. Alongside the literary tradition recorded in the "Lives" of the period, there was also an oral tradition, publicly widespread, which had to be taken into account. There was necessarily much interaction between the two. The artists drew inspiration from the texts, but the texts in turn were influenced by the works created by the sculptors.

In this give-and-take, the technical exigencies of the artistic medium could sometimes be a factor (just as topographical facts could sometimes influence pilgrimage traditions). Thus, the statement in certain texts that the Buddha had "webbed hands" comparable to the feet of a swan probably stems from a misunderstanding due to a particular sculptural practice. At least according to Lamotte, the word "web" (*jāla*) originally meant the "network" (*jāla*) of lines on the skin, the visibility and particular configuration of which on the hands and feet were one of the physical signs of the Great Man (*mahāpuruṣa*) (for a list of these signs, see Table 2.1 page 42). The fact that, in time, this original meaning was forgotten can be explained by the technical artistic practice of leaving a web of stone interconnecting the spread fingers of the Buddha's hand so as to reinforce them and keep them from breaking. The texts were thus reread and interpreted in light of the sculptures.

## LIFESTORY AND RITUAL

In addition to the influence of the artistic tradition, it is also important to keep in mind the relationship between the developing biography of the Buddha and the practice of Buddhist rituals. Just as accounts of Jesus's Last Supper are linked to the Christian rite of Holy Communion, or just as the celebration of Passover involves a reading of the events of the Exodus, so too stories about the Buddha's life were to be recited and reenacted on ritual and festival occasions. In Southeast Asia today, for example, the consecration of a new Buddha image involves "infusing" or "programming" it with the lifestory of the Buddha. This must be ritually recited in front of the image so that it will know what it is to "be" a buddha. More specifically, as we shall see, certain events in the life of the Buddha were directly correlated to particular ritual acts. For instance, the bodhisattva's "Great Departure" from his home in Kapilavastu provided the model for the Buddhist rite of ordination of new monks. Still today, candidates for the monkhood ritually dress up in their finery, and ride forth from their homes as "princes," sometimes to be opposed by friends or relatives acting out the part of Māra, the "Evil One" (who opposed the Buddha's going forth), before arriving at the monastery where they exchange their "royal" garb for monastic robes and have their heads tonsured. Such ritual ordinations, of course, were not without their own repercussive influences on the biography. One suspects, for instance, that the whole literary account, at least in one text, of the bodhisattva being dressed up and adorned magnificently by the gods just prior to his departure at midnight on his Great Renunciation is an infusion of the ritual tradition back into the lifestory. We shall see that similar symbioses may be found in other events and episodes.

## LIFESTORIES AND BUDDHOLOGY: THE DEVELOPMENT OF A BUDDHA-LIFE BLUEPRINT

Finally, it is important to remember that not all Buddhist schools were in agreement about the nature and identity of the Buddha. Doctrinal developments, as well as other contextual considerations, could thus affect presentations of the Buddha's lifestory. I have, so far, spoken of the biography of the Buddha as though it were limited to his life as Gautama. That is, of course, nonsense. Buddhist acceptance of the doctrines of karma and rebirth made possible, perhaps even mandated, the extension of the Buddha's biography to include his many previous births (*jātakas*), during which he was a bodhisattva, a buddha-to-be. Thus, we find a text such as the Pali "Introduction" (*Nidāna-kathā*) to the *Jātaka Commentary (Jātakaṭṭhakathā)* beginning its account of the Buddha's life, "four incalculable world periods plus one hundred thousand aeons ago" (Jayawickrama, 1990, pp. 3ff.) when, in a previous life as the brahmin Sumedha, the bodhisattva first made the determination that he wanted to become a buddha someday. In the hundreds and thousands of births subsequent to this embarkation on the path, he was then variously reborn as a human, as a god, and as an animal. In these guises, he did good deeds, made merit, and strove in a variety of ways that eventually resulted in his finally attaining buddhahood as Gautama. Buddhahood thus was a long time in coming, but in achieving it, Gautama at last put an end to his rebirth process. This did not mean the end of his lifestory, however, since, in significant ways, it is possible to think of the Buddha's relics – the remains of his physical body as well as the "body" of teachings which he left behind – as continuing his life and biography, even up to the present. As we shall see, it is only some time in the future, with the expected loss of the Buddha's doctrine and the disappearance of his bodily relics, that his lifestory will truly finally come to an end.

After it does, however, it will in a sense be taken up again, to be lived once more by another buddha and then another and another and another. It is important to realize that, even in the earliest Buddhist traditions, the Buddha Gautama was not thought to have been unique. He had predecessors, the buddhas of the past whom he periodically encountered over the aeons during which he was striving for buddhahood; and he will have successors, some of whom are, right now, bodhisattvas walking the same lengthy path to buddhahood that he did. Gautama is important because he is "our" Buddha, i.e., the most recent one from our perspective, but his lifestory should not be limited to him alone.

Such a message is made clear in the "Discourse on the Great Legend" (*Mahāvadāna-sūtra*) which exists in both Sanskrit and Pali versions. It narrates at some length the life of the Buddha, from birth through enlightenment, but it is not the life of the Buddha Gautama that it recounts but that of the past Buddha Vipaśyi, who is said to have lived ninety-one aeons ago. In all its details, this lifestory is exactly like the lifestory of Gautama, except that the names – of his disciples, his family members, the places where he dwelt, etc. – have all been changed. The young Vipaśyi does not grow up in Kapilavastu but in Bandhumatī; he was not of the Gautama clan but of the Kauṇḍinya; he attained enlightenment not under a fig tree but under a trumpet-flower tree; his two chief disciples were not Śāriputra and Maudgalyāyana but Khaṇḍa and Tissa, and so on. It is clear to scholars that this tale has been patterned on the life of "our" Buddha, Gautama, but the text, in fact, points us towards the opposite conclusion: that the life of "our" Buddha has been patterned on that of Vipaśyi, or more accurately that both of their lifestories reflect a biographical paradigm, a Buddha-life blueprint, which they, and all buddhas, follow.

In time, the particulars of this bio-blueprint became quite detailed and specific. One Sanskrit text, for example, enumerates ten "indispensible actions" which every Buddha must necessarily accomplish in order to "be" a buddha. No buddha, we are told, can pass away into final *nirvāṇa* until he has predicted that another person will become a buddha some day, has inspired in someone else an unswerving resolve for buddhahood, has converted all those whom he should convert, has lived more than three quarters of his potential lifespan, has clearly drawn distinctions between good and evil deeds, has appointed two of his disciples as most prominent, has descended from Heaven at Sāṃkāśya, has held an assembly of his disciples at Lake Anavatapta, has brought his parents to a vision of the truth, has performed a great miracle at Śrāvastī.

The Tibetan tradition favored instead a quite different list of the "Twelve Great Acts" of a buddha, starting with his existence in Tuṣita Heaven, his descent from that Heaven, and his entrance into the womb of his mother. It then goes on to narrate his birth, his skill at various arts, his life in the harem, his great departure from the palace, his practice of asceticism, his defeat of Māra, his attainment of *nirvāṇa*, his first sermon, and his death and *parinirvāṇa*.

But it was the Pali commentarial tradition that was to present the longest and most detailed list, expanding the number of obligatory deeds and facts to thirty. Here, it is clearer than ever that what makes a buddha is living the buddha-life. We are told that: on descending into his mother's womb, the bodhisattva must be aware that this will be his final birth; within his mother's womb, he should assume a cross-legged position facing outwards; his mother must give birth to him while in a standing position, in a forest grove. Immediately after his birth, he should take seven steps to the north, survey the four quarters and roar the lion's roar; his Great Departure occurs only after he has seen the four signs and the birth of his son; he must practice austerities for at least seven days and wear the yellow robe; on the day of his enlightenment, he must first have a meal of milk-rice. Then he should sit on a seat made of grass, concentrate on his breathing, defeat the forces of Māra, and attain full enlightenment in a cross-legged position. After enlightenment, he should spend seven weeks in the vicinity of the Bodhi tree; and the god Brahmā must ask him to preach the Dharma, which he first does in the Deer Park at Sarnath. He should recite the rules of the community to an assembly of monks, reside mostly at the Jetavana monastery, perform the Twin Miracle at Śrāvastī, teach the *Abhidharma* in Indra's Heaven, and descend from that Heaven at Sāṃkāśya. He should constantly abide in the attainment of fruits, survey the capacities of others during two nightly meditational trances, lay down new monastic rules only when necessary, recount *jātakas* when appropriate, and recite the *Buddha-Chronicle* in an assembly of his kinsmen. He should welcome monks who visit him, spend the rains-retreat where invited to do so, and daily carry out his duties prior to and after eating and in the three watches of the night. He should eat a meal containing (pork) meat on the day of his death, and pass into *parinirvāṇa* after myriads of attainments.

Given such standardization and establishment of a "Buddha blueprint," it is perhaps not surprising that some schools of buddhism should come to think of Gautama and other buddhas as mere embodiments or projections of a transcendent pattern. This, of course, was not without its effect on the presentation of their lifestories. The biography known as the *Great Story (Mahāvastu)*, for instance, belongs to a school of Buddhism that emphasized the supramundane nature of the Buddha. In that work, Gautama is seen as conforming to the ways of the world but as basically being unaffected by them. Thus, he may seem to exert himself, but he feels no fatigue; he may sit in the shade, but he is not tormented by the heat of the sun; he may eat and drink, but he is never hungry or thirsty. Much the same kind of thing can be found in *Living out of the Game (Lalitavistara)* which never fails to magnify and glorify events in the life of the Buddha, emphasizing his purity and transcendental qualities.

Both of these texts reflect tendencies that came to be associated with the rise of Great Vehicle (Mahāyāna) Buddhism. This is not the place to embark on an analysis of the changes in Buddha doctrine that came about in the Mahāyāna tradition. Suffice it to point out that, in the Mahāyāna, the lifespan of buddhas in general, and of Śākyamuni in particular, was greatly extended to the point of being more or less eternal in duration. The notion developed that the Buddha had always been enlightened, that his life on earth was but a manifestation of a transcendent, unchanging, eternal Body of Truth, the *Dharmakāya*. Consequently, the Buddha's life-events – his birth, quest, enlightenment, and death – came to be seen not as transformative personal existential processes for him, but as a manifestation of his compassionate attempts to teach others and to be a model for them. In this context, the Mahāyāna schools also saw the opening up of the way to buddhahood for all beings. Inspired by the model of the Buddha and guided by his compassion, devotees began to think not just of their own salvation, but of the path to a realization of buddhahood that would help others. The description of that path was sometimes greatly elaborated, but at some point it still tended to incorporate the tradition of the Buddha's lifestory.

Enough has been said to make it clear that the lifestory of the Buddha is many-faceted, in some ways embodying and reflecting the whole history of the Buddhist experience. It is not without reason that we may speak of the "many lives" of the Buddha, not only to take note of the countless *jātakas* that are part of his lifestory, but also to do justice to the often striking divergences between different biographical traditions. In doing that, however, we must avoid the risk of obscuring the unitive function that the Buddha's lifestory has played throughout much of the Buddhist world. Of course, there are variant versions of different episodes, and we shall pay attention to some of them in the chapters below, but the overall outline of the story remains the same.

In this book, then, I propose to examine and discuss, chapter by chapter, the following topics: previous lives of the Buddha; his ancestry, birth, and youth as Gautama; his spiritual quest and enlightenment; his decision to preach and to establish a community; the growth of monasticism and his further spread of the doctrine by means of miracles and distant journeys; and finally his last days, complete extinction (*parinirvāṇa*), and ongoing existence in his relics.

# 1 PREVIOUS LIVES OF THE BUDDHA

From early on in the Buddhist tradition, it was thought that Gautama's buddhahood was not simply the result of a few years of meditation and striving but the end-product of hundreds of previous lives that are recounted in stories known as *jātakas*. During this time, as a bodhisattva ("buddha-to-be"), he was variously reborn as a human being, as an animal, and occasionally as a divinity, and he performed a variety of meritorious actions, gradually perfecting himself. The Buddha, in fact, is said to have remembered these lives during the first watch of the night of his enlightenment experience, and subsequently to have related them to his disciples. These birth-stories thus form an important part of the Buddha's life experience. At the same time, it is safe to say that they are among the most popular forms of Buddhist literature. Especially in South and Southeast Asia, they often provide the stuff of sermons, and are featured both in art and in ritual.

It is not possible here to deal with the *jātakas* in anything more than a summary fashion. The Sri Lankan recension of the basic Theravāda anthology (the so-called *Jātaka Commentary* [*Jātakaṭṭhakathā*]) recounts 547 previous lifestories at some length, and still more are to be found in other collections (see "Sources and Further Reading"). Moreover, many biographical texts, which are not themselves primarily anthologies of birth-stories, often recount *jātakas* to illustrate some point or another, or to act as "flashbacks" in the narrative.

Scholars have long been aware of the affinities between certain *jātakas* and well-travelled fables of classical Western literature (e.g. Aesop) as well as Indian collections of stories. T.W. Rhys Davids, for example, starts his study of the Pali *jātakas* with a translation of the *Sīhacamma Jātaka*, the tale of the "Ass in the Lion's Skin" which he relates to parallels in Ancient Greece, Medieval Europe, the Near East, China, and India. Similarly, the *jātaka* of the bodhisattva's adventures as a clever thief, in which the future Gautama eludes all the traps that are set for him, bears close resemblance to a tale that is found not only in brahmanical collections in India, but in China, and in Tibet, as well as in Herodotus's account of the Egyptian tale of the Treasure of King Rhampsinitus. Even more striking is the *Jātaka of King Dasaratha* which appears to be a Buddhist reworking of part of the story of Rāma found in the well-known Hindu epic, the *Rāmāyaṇa*. In the *jātaka*, the bodhisattva is identified with Rāma, and Gautama's future wife, Yaśodharā, is identified with Rāma's wife Sītā.

In this way, the *jātakas* served to amplify and popularize the lifestory of the Buddha by associating him – in his previous lives – with many folk heroes and divinities in India and beyond. At the same time, as Buddhism expanded, they provided opportunities for accommodating local cultural and religious beliefs. For example, in the Pali telling of the *Dasaratha Jātaka*, one of the themes is acceptance of the facts of impermanence in family relations. In a Chinese collection of Buddhist tales, however, the same story is reworked so as to emphasize the ethic of filial piety, and no mention is made of Rāma's wife Sītā at all.

While recognizing the fact that *jātakas* belong to world literature, I will look at them here as Buddhist stories. More specifically, I want to focus on what they can tell us about the lifestory of the Buddha, on what images they project about him. Viewed in this light, it is possible to talk about the *jātakas* as having several "biographical thrusts." They add karmic depth to the events of the Buddha's life; they help clarify the structure of the bodhisattva's path to buddhahood; they serve to emphasize the Buddha's perfections; and finally, they allow the tradition to explain some of the Buddha's shortcomings or imperfections, to say certain "taboo" things about the Buddha-as-bodhisattva that it might not want to say about him were it focussing only on his last existence as the Buddha.

## ADDING KARMIC DEPTH TO THE BUDDHA'S LIFESTORY

Typically, *jātakas* follow a given format. A "story of the present" sets up a situation which calls for elucidation or amplification. The Buddha responds to this by recounting a "story of the past," the *jātaka* proper. When that is done, he concludes by identifying various characters in the story of the past with various persons in the present such as himself, members of his family, particular disciples, or others. This gives karmic depth to events and relationships in Gautama's life, and it also gives a *déja-vu* quality to the narrative that helps color the Buddha's lifestory with a tinge of eternality. A relatively straightforward example may be found in the Pali *Somanassa Jātaka*. The Buddha's disciples, learning of the attempt on his life by his jealous cousin, Devadatta, ask him the reasons for that, and he obliges them with a story of the past, explaining that "this is not the first time" that such a thing has happened.

Once, long ago, a king was distressed that he had no sons and he confessed his concern to a passing holy man. Sometime later, after the holy man had gone back to his hermitage, he saw, using his clairvoyance, that the king would soon have male progeny, and he happened to mention this to some of his own disciples. One of them, a dishonest disciple named Dibbacakkhuka, decided to use this information to his own profit. Quickly returning to the city, he ingratiated himself with the king by saying that he, Dibbacakkhuka, could see the future, and by predicting that the queen would soon become pregnant with a son. When she did, and gave birth to a boy, the king was very grateful to Dibbacakkhuka and gave him a position of wealth and authority as a high-ranking minister. In time, the boy, who was named Somanassa, grew up. He turned into a particularly perceptive young man, who was able to see through the fraud and false credit taken by Dibbacakkhuka and realize that he was a charlatan. Fearing that the boy would denounce him, Dibbacakkhuka quickly trumped up false charges against the lad, and even managed to convince his father, the king, to condemn him to death. At the last minute, however, the plan backfired; the wiles of Dibbacakkhuka were uncovered and Somanassa's life was spared. The *jātaka* then ends with the following identifications: Somanassa was the bodhisattva in a previous life; Dibbacakkhuka was Devadatta who sought to do him harm; Somanassa's mother, the queen, was Mahāmāyā (the Buddha's mother); the holy man was one of the Buddha's disciples, etc. The "moral" of the *jātaka* is then drawn when the Buddha points out to his disciples that Devadatta tried "to slay me in former days, as now."

Numerous other such stories could be cited. In the Pali *Jātaka Commentary* alone, no fewer than seventy tales feature past karmic relationships between the future Gautama and the future Devadatta.

Even more feature his karmic connections to his wife, his mother, or his chief disciples. All of these stories add karmic depth and breadth to the lifestory of the Buddha. They explain not only why certain events happened, but why they happened to involve certain people. In other words, they show not only the karmic history of the future Gautama, but its interaction with the karmic histories of others with whom he participates in a sort of collective karma.

At the same time, these *jātakas* serve to add psychological complexity to that karmic history. It is very interesting, for instance, that the queen in the above story is said to be having a hard time conceiving a son, who turns out to be the future Buddha. To my knowledge, no mention of such a difficulty is ever made in the accounts of the Buddha's mother, Mahāmāyā, conceiving him in his final life as Gautama, and yet the Somanassa tale causes us to think again about that final life. In light of it, it perhaps becomes more noteworthy that, in certain Pali commentaries, Mahāmāyā is presented as being in her mid-forties when she gives birth to the Buddha, a very advanced age, especially in ancient India, for becoming a first-time mother and one possibly indicative of difficulties in conceiving. Such a thing, of course, is never spelled out in the lifestory of Gautama, and I do not want to overemphasize a detail which, in the *jātaka*, may serve no more than a narrative function, but, as we shall see, the *jātakas* can sometimes act as a sort of reservoir for subconscious feelings about the Buddha, members of his family, or members of the *saṃgha*.

There are other ways, however, in which *jātakas* may render relationships more psychologically complex. For example, in the story just recounted, the bodhisattva gets the better of Devadatta (as he does in his final life as Gautama). But that is not necessarily always the case; in a number of other *jātakas*, Devadatta is "the winner" in that he succeeds in doing harm to the future Buddha, so much so that the tradition itself later raised questions about this. One of the dilemmas that is posed in the semi-canonical *Questions of King Milinda (Milindapañha)*, for instance, is precisely why should Devadatta, who was so wicked, have occasionally been superior in power to the bodhisattva? The answer given is that Devadatta, in fact, was not "all bad" – that he did do several good deeds in other past lives, such as building bridges, resthouses, courts of justice for the poor, and so on, and that these resulted in his occasional superiority over the bodhisattva. Ongoing karmic relationships are thus not always utterly straightforward, and in exploring them, the *jātakas* can add new dimensions to them – by suggesting (in this case) that the relationship between the Buddha and Devadatta is more complicated than it might first seem to be. *Jātakas* allow the tradition to tell the same story several times, exploring it from many angles. Clearly one life was not enough to say all that needed to be said about the Buddha.

## GAUTAMA'S PATH TO BUDDHAHOOD: WHEN DOES IT START?

Another of the biographical thrusts of previous lifestories is to present and clarify the path that the bodhisattva takes in order to become the Buddha. The Buddha was not always the Buddha; he was once a more ordinary kind of being whose ambition was to reach buddhahood, and his achievement, though remarkable, is something that is open to others. Often, to be sure, he is portrayed as having been a king in one of his past lives, or even a divinity, but he is also commonly presented as having been an ascetic, or a courtier, or a merchant, or various sorts of animals. Less frequently, he is said to have been reborn as an artisan of one kind or another, or even as a slave. He is almost never portrayed as having been a female, a blatant prejudice which, as we shall see, bothered some in the tradition. Nonetheless, it is possible to think of the variety of statuses he did hold in past lives as serving to "open up" somewhat the path to buddhahood, to make it clear that beings of several kinds could and did tread it.

That does not mean that the bodhisattva's path was easy or that it was short; the Buddhist tradition, in fact, developed several ways of describing it, all of them emphasizing its length and arduousness. For instance, in a Pali canonical text called the *Buddha-Chronicle (Buddhavaṃsa)*, it is presented as a series of encounters which "our" Buddha, Gautama, had with previous buddhas in different past lives, spread out over a long period of time. Chapter by chapter, this text tells of various births of the bodhisattva – sometimes as an animal, sometimes as a divinity, but usually as a human being. During these lives, he meets no fewer than twenty-four past Buddhas, and, inspired by each of them, he repeats in their presence some sort of devotional meritorious act. Sometimes, this consists of a great offering, such as the sacrifice of all of his wealth; at other times it is a relatively small act, such as the proferring of a piece of fruit. The details may be studied in Table 1.1.

*Table 1.1 The future Gautama under 24 past buddhas*

| | Time period in ages and aeons | Birth as | Past buddhas met | Acts of the bodhisattva |
|---|---|---|---|---|
| 1 | 4 incalculable ages plus 100,000 aeons ago | Sumedha, a brahmin become an ascetic | Dīpaṃkara | Makes resolve for buddhahood while lying in the mire |
| 2 | Over 3 incalculable ages ago | A *kṣatriya* named Vijitāvin | Koṇḍañña | Great gift of food to the Buddha and community |
| 3 | Over 2 incalculable ages ago | A brahmin named Suruci | Mangala | Gift of perfumes, garlands, and a meal to the Buddha and community |
| 4 | During the same aeon as # 3 | A serpent-king (*nāga-rāja*) named Atula | Sumana | Gift of music, a meal, and robes to the Buddha and community |
| 5 | During the same aeon as # 3 and 4 | A brahmin named Atideva | Revata | Took refuge in the Buddha, praised him and gave him a robe |
| 6 | During the same aeon as # 3, 4 and 5 | A brahmin named Sujāta | Sobhita | Gift of food and drink to the Buddha and community |
| 7 | Over 1 incalculable age ago | A protective divinity (*yakṣa*) | Anomadassi | Gift of food and drink to the Buddha and community |
| 8 | During the same aeon as # 7 | A lion | Paduma | Bowed to the Buddha, roared three times, and attended him for a week |
| 9 | During the same aeon as # 7 and 8 | A matted-haired ascetic | Nārada | Gift of food and drink and sandalwood to the Buddha and community |
| 10 | 100,000 aeons ago | A district governor named Jaṭila | Padumuttara | Gift of food and cloth to the Buddha and community |
| 11 | 70,000 aeons ago | A brahmin youth named Uttara | Sumedha | Gift of 80 crores of wealth to the Buddha and community |
| 12 | Also 70,000 aeons ago | A world-ruling monarch (*cakravartin*) | Sujāta | Gift of kingdom and 7 treasures to the Buddha |
| 13 | 1,800 aeons ago | A brahmin named Kassapa | Piyadassi | Gift of monastic park (*ārāma*) to the Buddha and community |
| 14 | Also 1,800 aeons ago | A matted-haired ascetic named Susīma | Atthadassi | Gift of heavenly flowers to the Buddha |
| 15 | Also 1,800 aeons ago | Indra, lord of the gods | Dhamma-dassi | Gift of heavenly perfumes, garlands and music |
| 16 | 94 aeons ago | An ascetic named Mangala | Siddhattha | Gift of fruit from rose-apple tree |

*Table 1.1 The future Gautama under 24 past buddhas (continued)*

| | Time period in ages and aeons | Birth as | Past buddhas met | Acts of the bodhisattva |
|---|---|---|---|---|
| 17 | 92 aeons ago | A *kṣatriya* turned mendicant named Sujāta | Tissa | Held three heavenly flowers over the Buddha's head |
| 18 | Also 92 aeons ago | A *kṣatriya* named Vijitāvin | Phussa | Gave up his kingdom and became a monk under the Buddha |
| 19 | 91 aeons ago | A serpent-king (*nāga-rāja*) named Atula | Vipassin | Gift of music and a golden seat to the Buddha |
| 20 | 31 aeons ago | A *kṣatriya* named Arindama | Sikhin | Gift of food and drink, cloth, an elephant, and other items to the Buddha |
| 21 | Also 31 aeons ago | A *kṣatriya* named Sudassana | Vessabhū | Gift of great value, food, drink, and cloth to the Buddha and community |
| 22 | In the present aeon | A *kṣatriya* named Khema | Kakusandha | Gift of bowls, robes, and medicines to the Buddha and community |
| 23 | In the present aeon | A *kṣatriya* named Pabbata | Koṇāgamana | Gift of valuable cloths and sandals to the Buddha and community |
| 24 | In the present aeon | A brahmin youth named Jotipāla | Kassapa | Became an exemplary monk under the Buddha |
| 25 | In the present aeon | A *kṣatriya* named Gautama | – | Becomes "our" Buddha, Śākyamuni |

The text begins with the "first" of these encounters – the story already mentioned of the future Gautama's life as the brahmin, Sumedha, who meets a past Buddha named Dīpaṃkara. Seeing the Buddha approach a muddy section of a road, Sumedha is inspired to throw himself down on the ground and spread his matted hair out so that Dīpaṃkara can walk over it (and him) rather than in the mire. At the same time, Sumedha makes a firm resolve to become, himself, someday, a fully enlightened buddha like Dīpaṃkara, so that he can cause others to cross over the sea of suffering, and he later spells out the ten perfections that he knows he will have to accomplish on his way to buddhahood (see below). Hearing him utter this resolution, and recognizing his determination, Dīpaṃkara responds by publicly making a prediction that, innumerable aeons later, Sumedha will indeed become the Buddha Gautama. And he goes on to describe who his mother and father will be, how he will wander forth from his home and attain enlightenment, who his chief disciples will be, and so on.

Much the same story is found in Sanskrit biographies of the Buddha, although Sumedha is known there by other names, such as Megha or Sumati. In all of these texts, this meeting with Dīpaṃkara is crucially important, for it marks the start of the bodhisattva's quest, his embarkation on the path that will eventually result, many lives later, in his achievement of buddhahood. Three factors come to be seen as crucial markers of this embarkation: the bodhisattva's actual physical act of devotion (in this case, his lying down in the mire), the expression of his resolve to become a Buddha, and Dīpaṃkara's consequent prediction of his future buddhahood. With some variations, these three factors will be repeated as the bodhisattva makes his way through the aeons, encountering other past buddhas, being inspired by them to renew his resolve, and receiving from them reassurances of his still being on track.

These repeated encounters with buddhas are important, for, if one thing is evident from Table 1.1, the road to buddhahood is no short-term enterprise. The *Buddha-Chronicle* dates Sumedha's all important meeting with Dīpaṃkara as having taken place "four incalculable ages plus one hundred thousand aeons" ago. An "incalculable" (*asaṃkheyya*) age is a very long period of time, often left unspecified, but sometimes defined as $10^{140}$ years. An aeon (*kalpa*), or world-cycle, is shorter than an incalculable age, but is nonetheless still very long; it is sometimes said to be 4,320 million years, the time it takes for the world to evolve and then return to dissolution again. Several buddhas – anywhere from one to five – may appear during the course of a single aeon, but an aeon can also be empty, with zero buddhas. Thus, there can be great gaps of time, aeons and aeons, between Gautama's past-life meetings with his various predecessors. Gautama's road to buddhahood is therefore an unimaginably long one, lasting aeons and aeons. And yet, in time, the Buddhist tradition was not satisfied even with this scenario, and was to push back the beginnings of the bodhisattva's path even further.

In the Pali tradition, the whole period of time charted in Table 1.1, from the bodhisattva's previous life as Sumedha up through his life as Gautama, is divided into three periods. The first, and by far the longest, is called the period of the "distant cause" (*dūre-nidāna*) of his buddhahood, and it comprises all of his previous births under buddhas 1–24. This is followed by the much shorter period of the "near cause" (*avidūre-nidāna*) of his buddhahood (the thirty-five years from his birth as Gautama up to his enlightenment at Bodhgaya), which in turn is succeeded by the period of the "proximate cause" (*santike-nidāna*) of his buddhahood (the time after his enlightenment, during which he preached the Dharma).

Eventually, some texts were to push the beginning point of this whole process back and extend the saga of the bodhisattva-path to a time earlier than the period of the "distant cause," i.e., to previous births *prior* to his life as Sumedha. For instance, a fifteenth-century Pali text from Northern Thailand, as well as a fourteenth-century Sinhalese vernacular life of the Buddha from Sri Lanka, specify that before the period of the "distant cause" there was a period of the "very distant cause" (*atidūre-nidāna*). This lasted nine incalculable ages, during which the bodhisattva is said to have met no fewer than 387,000 past buddhas (*sic*). Even prior to that, however, was a period of the "great cause" (*mahānidāna*) of his buddhahood, which lasted seven incalculable ages, during which he met 125,000 past buddhas.

During this first period of the "great cause", the bodhisattva made only a "mental resolve" (*manopraṇidhāna*) for buddhahood, whenever he met a past buddha. During the next period of the "very distant cause," however, he also expressed that mental determination orally and so this is sometimes called the period of the "verbal resolve" (*vākpraṇidhāna*) for buddhahood. Finally, during the period of the "distant cause" (which starts with his life as Sumedha), he added a physical expression to his determination, undertaking acts that featured the use of the body. Since they also involved speech and mind, however, this is called, at least in one text, the period of the "great," or perhaps better the "total resolve" (*mahāpraṇidhāna*) for buddhahood. Importantly, it is only after he enters this period of "great resolve," under Dīpaṃkara and his successors, that he starts to receive confirmatory predictions of his future buddhahood from those past buddhas. This is summarized in Table 1.2.

Several comments can be made about the scenario set forth in this table. First of all, we can see the tradition struggling here with a new and important question: Given the possibility of an infinity of previous lives, when did Gautama's aspiration for buddhahood actually begin? When he first *thought* about becoming a buddha? When he first *said* that that was his intention? When he first actually *did* something physically and had that action confirmed by a past buddha? At the same time, within this very questioning there is a recognition of a down-to-earth pattern. For all of its traipsing through incalculable aeons, there is a simple message in

*Table 1.2 The future Gautama under 512,024 past buddhas*

| Time period | Number of births | Number of past buddhas met | Acts performed |
|---|---|---|---|
| Period of the "great cause" of buddhahood (from over 20 to over 13 incalculable ages ago) | 125,000 | 125,000 | Made mental resolves for buddhahood but received no confirmatory prediction |
| Period of the "very distant cause" of buddhahood (from over 13 to over 4 incalculable ages ago) | 387,000 | 387,000 | Added verbal resolves for buddhahood but received no confirmatory prediction |
| Period of the "distant cause" of buddhahood (from over 4 incalculable ages ago to his birth as Gautama) | 24, beginning with his life as Sumedha and identified in Table 1.1 | 24, beginning with Dīpaṃkara and identified in Table 1.1 | Added physical resolves for buddhahood and received a confirmatory prediction |
| Period of the "near cause" of buddhahood (from his birth as Gautama up to his enlightenment) | The bodhisattva Gautama | n/a | Quests for enlightenment |
| Period of the "proximate cause" of his buddhahood (the time after his enlightenment) | The Buddha Gautama | n/a | Preaches the Dharma |

this scheme for ordinary Buddhists who might be interested in embarking on the Buddhist path: first you think about it, then you talk about it, then you do something about it.

Things, however, are not as simple as this, for we can also see, in this table, that whatever the mode of aspiration – mental, verbal, and/or physical – the *inspiration* for it can only come from encountering a buddha in person. And this is true regardless of whether or not that past buddha actually makes a prediction declaring or confirming one's future attainment. And here we come to a potential problem when this conclusion is applied to Buddhism today (or at any point since the death of Gautama): since there is, actually, no buddha in the world, it would seem impossible, at present, for anyone to resolve to attain buddhahood, or even to renew such a resolution.

The Buddhist tradition developed a number of ways of dealing with this dilemma, but, in the present context of describing the path to buddhahood, it seems to have had two reactions. One may be characterized as the hard-line, orthodox position. According to the "Introduction" to the *Jātaka Commentary*, there are eight necessary conditions that must be met in order for anyone to make a resolve for buddhahood. Among these are the specifications that one must be a human being – a male human being – and that one must make one's resolve in the actual presence of a living buddha. Doing it in front of a substitute for the Buddha, such as a relic or a bodhi tree, is not acceptable. Accordingly, given the present absence of a buddha, it is no longer possible, today, to embark on the path of buddhahood. The best one can do is to seek to be reborn at the time of the *next* buddha, Maitreya.

A somewhat different solution, however, may be found in later popular traditions in which there is a softening of this hard-line position, a softening that was not without its biographical repercussions. This solution was to posit yet more previous births of Gautama prior to the first listed in Table 1.2, that is *over* twenty incalculable ages ago. In these lives, as we shall see, embarkation on the path can take place without a buddha necessarily being present. Prior to the period of the "great cause," we are told, there was a time called the "the epoch of the first arousing of thought" (*paṭhamacittuppāda-kāla*). During this time, the future Gautama had four previous lives in which he made a resolve for buddhahood in the *absence* of a buddha and seemingly inspired by other factors. In other words, he made the kind of resolve that it would be possible to make today, in our buddhaless age. At the same time, as we shall see, he further opened up the bodhisattva path by making one of these resolutions, for the first time, as a woman.

In the first of these stories, the future Gautama is born as a poor man who supports his mother by collecting firewood. Wishing to do better for himself, he embarks on a sea voyage together with his mother to the "land of gold," where he hopes to make a fortune. In the middle of the ocean, however, they are shipwrecked, and the bodhisattva, at great peril to himself, begins swimming to shore with his mother on his back. Looking down from heaven, the god Brahmā sees his heroism and determination and reflects that this is a man who might be capable of aspiring to buddhahood, despite the fact that he recognizes that there is presently no buddha in the world to inspire him to make such a resolution. Accordingly, Brahmā stimulates him (we are not told how) to make a mental resolve for buddhahood, there in the midst of the ocean, and this is said to be valid in embarking the bodhisattva on the path that will ultimately lead to his becoming Gautama. In the Sinhalese version of the same story, it is not Brahmā but the bodhisattva's mother who inspires him to make his resolve, but in both cases, the message is clear: a buddha need not be present for one to embark on the path to final enlightenment; other beings can bring about that aspiration.

The same lesson may be found in the next two of these stories. In the first, the bodhisattva is inspired to renew his vow for buddhahood when, as a result of a series of adventures he comes to realize the power of lust (when he sees a maddened elephant); in the second, it is the truth of suffering that he realizes, when he sees a starving tigress and her hungry cubs. In both cases, he is inspired by these realizations to make a mental resolve for buddhahood. In the second instance, he also sacrifices himself by offering his body as food to the tigress. This, as we shall see, is a *jātaka* that was very popular in the Sanskrit tradition so that its inclusion here may also be related to a desire by the Pali tradition to incorporate it into its heritage. In neither of these stories, however, does a buddha appear on the scene; instead the revelations about the nature of reality are thought to arise due to perfectly ordinary circumstances, i.e., encounters with animals. Clearly, these tales are meant to appeal to persons living in a buddhaless age and to reassure them that it is possible, in such a situation, to embark on the path to buddhahood, since Gautama himself did it long ago.

The last story of this genre addresses a slightly different situation and problem, the orthodox restriction that stipulates that only male humans can walk the path to buddhahood. In this tale, the bodhisattva is born as a female – a princess – the step-sister of a past buddha named Purāṇa ("Former")-Dīpaṃkara. He has a disciple named Pacchima ("Future")-Dīpaṃkara, because he is destined, in the distant future, to become the Buddha Dīpaṃkara. Significantly, the princess does not make her resolve for buddhahood in the presence of her step-brother, the Buddha Former-Dīpaṃkara. Instead, she makes an offering to his disciple, the monk Future-Dīpaṃkara, and makes her mental resolve in his presence. Correspondingly, the Buddha Former-Dīpaṃkara makes no direct confirmatory prediction of the princess's future attainment. Instead, he instructs his disciple, Future-Dīpaṃkara, to convey to her his prediction when she will have been reborn as a man, and when he will have become a buddha. In other words, what we have here is a precursor scenario – a previous-life encounter between Sumedha and Dīpaṃkara, in which the former is a woman and the latter is still just a monk. No actual prediction of buddhahood has been spoken to a woman by a buddha (so orthodoxy has not been violated), but a future prediction has been guaranteed, and in the process, some possibilities at least have been opened up for women on the bodhisattva path.

From all of this, we can draw several preliminary conclusions about Gautama's path to buddhahood: it is very long, lasting over myriads of lifetimes; it generally involves repeated encounters with past buddhas, who both inspire and confirm a renewal of the bodhisattva's resolve for buddhahood; but it is possible to get started on the path without meeting a buddha. Indeed, the further one goes back in time, the more Gautama's previous lives come to resemble the lives and situations of present-day Buddhists, male and female, living in buddhaless times. All told, then, as the narrative of Gautama's *jātakas* expanded to include more and more stories, it portrayed the path to buddhahood as ever longer but, paradoxically, as also increasingly open to ordinary beings. This and the multiplicity of buddhas featured in these stories rather impressively resulted in a dual message, one emphasizing the greatness of the Buddha and what he accomplished, the other the possibility of his path and its openness to all.

## THE PRACTICE OF PERFECTIONS

Somewhat the same dual message may be found in a different and perhaps more familiar type of *jātaka*-story than the ones we have considered so far, those whose "biographical thrust" is to illustrate the various perfections (*pāramitās*) that were practiced by the future Gautama in his past lives. Mention has already been made of the ten perfections as something that Sumedha anticipated having to fulfill. The same theme is developed in the "Introduction" to the Pali *Jātaka Commentary*, where specific suggestions are made as to how some of the 547 *jātaka* tales that follow in the rest of the text can be classified as illustrating one or the other of those perfections. But it becomes an explicit organizational principle in the Pali canonical text known as the *The Basket of Conduct (Cariyāpiṭaka)*. In that text, the ten *pāramitās* are the perfections of giving, of morality, of renunciation, of wisdom, of effort, of patience, of truth-telling, of resoluteness, of loving-kindness, and of equanimity. In the *Basket of Conduct*, the first chapter, consisting of ten *jātakas*, is devoted entirely to stories illustrating the bodhisattva's practice of the perfection of giving; the second chapter is given over to ten more tales about the perfection of morality; and, though the neatness of this organization then breaks down, the fifteen remaining stories are all classified according to the perfections of renunciation, resoluteness, truth-telling, loving-kindness, and equanimity. The final verses of the text then mention the three other perfections – wisdom, effort, and patience – and it is thought that the work might have originally contained or been intended to contain more previous lifestories or at least some illustrative of these as well.

Much the same organizational scheme is hinted at in the Sanskrit *Garland of Birth-Stories (Jātakamālā)* by the poet Āryaśūra, which contains thirty-four stories. One tradition, in fact, though not unproblematic, reports that Āryaśūra originally intended to compose a work containing ten chapters of ten stories dealing with each of the ten perfections, but that he was unable to complete it.

Among these tales meant to illustrate various perfections may be found some of the best known and most popular of all *jātakas*. The *Garland of Birth-Stories*, for instance, features in its first chapter, as an illustration of the perfection of giving, the tale already alluded to of the bodhisattva giving his own body to be eaten by a starving tigress so that she could feed her cubs. Once, we are told, the bodhisattva was born as a learned brahmin. Renouncing the world, he became a hermit, and attracted many disciples. One day, while he was out walking with his disciple, Ajita, he came across a tigress who was so hungry that she was contemplating eating her cubs, to whom she had just given birth. Pitying the beast and her offspring, the bodhisattva told Ajita to go quickly and find some food for her. As soon as his disciple was gone, however, he reflected that it was silly to go and look for meat which might or might not be found, when other meat – his own body – was available on the spot. He therefore killed himself by throwing himself off the cliff, his body landing at the feet of the tigress. She promptly devoured his corpse, and thus fortified could save herself and her cubs.

This story became famous throughout the Sanskrit Buddhist world, in part because it showed the future Gautama's eagerness to achieve buddhahood, in contrast to Maitreya, the next Buddha after Gautama who is here identified with the less eager disciple, Ajita. But, along with three other tales, it was also thought to form a set of *jātakas* illustrating the highest form of the perfection of giving – the willingness to give up one's life or limbs as part of the quest for buddhahood. The sites where these four acts of sacrifice supposedly took place were marked, in Northern India, by a set of "four great *stūpas*" visited regularly by pilgrims. In addition to the tale of the tigress, these stories included the *jātaka* of King Śibi who sacrificed his flesh to ransom a dove from a hawk; the tale of another man, sometimes also identified as Śibi, who readily gave his eyes to a blind man who asked for them; and the story of King Candraprabha who cut off his head as a gift to a brahmin. It was not necessary for the bodhisattva to be human, however, to make such a total gift. Another famous *jātaka* along these lines was the tale of the bodhisattva's birth as a hare who, for the sake of a passing brahmin who had received no other food offering, threw himself into a fire, thereby giving up his body to be eaten.

In addition to the perfection of giving, other stories were intended to illustrate other perfections. An example of the practice of patience (*kṣanti*) may be found in the tale of the bodhisattva's birth as an ascetic named Kṣāntivādin, who was subjected to torture by a wrongly wrathful king, but who nonetheless endured all his suffering without so much as a single thought of ill-will towards his tormenter. Another example of this sort of endurance may be found in the story of the bodhisattva's life as the leader of a troop of monkeys, when he helped his simian followers escape from a tree when they were being hunted down by humans, by letting them run over his body which he extended as a bridge from the treetop to a cliff. An example of the perfection of truth-telling may be found in the story of the bodhisattva's life as Prince Sutasoma who fulfills his promises to various persons, despite obvious dangers to himself; for him, keeping his word is more important than keeping his life. An example of the perfection of wisdom is the *Mahā-Ummagga Jātaka* – a veritable saga featuring the adventures of Mahosadha, the very smart son of a king who resolves problem after problem.

The most popular of all these *jātakas* illustrating the perfections, however, is undoubtedly the story of Prince Viśvantara (Pali: Vessantara) which is commonly thought to have been the penultimate of the Buddha's previous lives, just prior to his rebirth in Tuṣita Heaven. The tale – a sort of mini-epic – may be summarized as follows. From a very young age, Prince Viśvantara, whose father was a king, was inclined to generosity. Even as a boy, in the palace, he used to declare that he would give anything he could to anyone who asked him for it. One day, sometime later, when he was out riding on his white elephant – an animal that was thought to bring good fortune to the state – he met some men from a country suffering from a terrible drought. Thinking the elephant would bring rain to their land, they asked Viśvantara for it, and he, without hesitation, gave it to them.

The people of his own country, however, were angry at him for having given away the state elephant, and they sent him away into exile to a place called Mount Vanka. Before going, he asked for permission to make another donation, and, permission accorded, he proceeded to give away all the palace's possessions – horses, cattle, male and female slaves, money. He then left the city in his chariot, together with his wife and their two children. Along the way, they met someone who asked them for his horses and chariot. Without hesitation, Viśvantara gave them away, and he and his family proceeded on foot. The road to Mount Vanka was long, but because of his great merit, the gods helped shorten it for them; indeed, even nature co-operated, the fruit trees bending down their branches to the travellers so that they could eat more easily. Eventually, they arrived at their place of exile, and the family dwellt together there, in a hermitage on the mountain, in a small hut made of leaves. One day, when his wife was out gathering food, a wanderer came to Viśvantara and asked him for his children as slaves. Filled with joy at being able to be of service, the bodhisattva gave away his boy and his girl, recommending to the passer-by that he might want to go to their grandfather, the king, and ask for a ransom, since the children, being young and weak, might not make very good slaves. When his wife came back to the hermitage to find the children gone, she was terribly distraught, but eventually accepted their loss. Then, however, another wanderer came and asked Viśvantara for his wife, and, once again, he happily gave her away, to dwell on, alone in the forest.

This tale, at least in certain parts of Southeast Asia, is as famous and well-known as even the final lifestory of the Buddha as Gautama. Part of its popularity lies, of course, in its poignancy, which tellings of the tale do not hesitate to underline. But its appeal may also lie in its emphasis on what, for laypersons, came to be the most important of the perfections: the practice of giving, of generosity. In this story, renunciation is, in fact, achieved by generosity: by giving away all of his possessions, his position in society, even his children and his wife, Viśvantara, while still a layperson, manages to achieve a situation not unlike that of a Buddhist monk, who also renounces family and fortune. Here, with Viśvantara, the biographical themes of abandonment, of leaving behind, which, as we shall see, emerge in the story of Gautama's "great departure," are portrayed as acts of self-sacrifice and generosity. "Giving up" becomes "giving."

Buddhists, of course, were not blind to some of the ethical difficulties potentially inherent in this. In *The Questions of King Milinda*, Milinda points out that Viśvantara's generosity, though perhaps worthy of admiration, brought grief and suffering to his children and his wife. The monk Nāgasena, whom he is questioning, admits as much but then suggests that the end justifies the means; it is not that Viśvantara felt no love and sympathy for his children and his wife, it says, but that he loved buddhahood more. By perfecting practices such as giving, the bodhisattva could become a buddha, and by becoming a buddha, he could help everyone.

Because these perfections foreshadow the qualities of his buddhahood, *jātakas* such as that of Viśvantara and the others we have looked at in this section may be thought to magnify especially the greatness of the future Gautama's accomplishment by featuring the extraordinariness of the deeds of self-sacrifice that he performed over the aeons. At the same time, however, it should be noted that the deeds in these stories, like those in some of the lives mentioned above, do not require the presence of a buddha for their performance. They do not even require the presence of any Buddhist monk or even the existence of anything called "Buddhism." The bodhisattva who does them is typically a layperson, who interacts with other ordinary beings. His actions require a tremendous amount of faith and determination, but no special training and no special circumstances.

The practice of giving and of other perfections illustrated in these *jātakas*, has, however, an additional significance when looked at in terms of the Buddha's lifestory. Simply put, by accomplishing these deeds, the bodhisattva is thought to be building the body he will have as the Buddha. More specifically, this physical body is described in terms of the thirty-two marks of the great man (*mahāpuruṣa*) which characterize all buddhas and other great beings such as *cakravartin* kings. I shall return to these thirty-two marks in Chapter 2, below. For now, it is important to realize that buddhahood is not just a mental enlightenment experience, a realization of the Dharma, a doctrinal truth. It is also a karmic achievement that is accomplished and expressed somatically. Buddhahood must be realized in the body just as surely as it must be realized in the mind. What embodies the Buddha are the perfections he practiced in his past lives. Thus the Pali text devoted to describing the "great man's" thirty-two physiognomic marks – the marks of the wheel on the Buddha's hands and feet, the protuberance (*uṣṇiṣa*) on the top of his head, the circle of hair (*ūrṇā*) between his eyebrows, his long tongue, etc. – tries to explain how various marks result from various perfections. The same thing is worked out in greater detail in a number of Mahāyāna texts which show how specific past actions of the Buddha resulted in each of the thirty-two major and eighty minor specific physical features of his body.

## GAUTAMA'S IMPERFECTIONS

Karma is a two-sided coin, however, and while the *jātakas* generally feature the positive side of the bodhisattva's accomplishments, they occasionally mention the negative. The future Gautama is not always portrayed as a paragon of morality, a practicer of the perfections. He too was human, and sometimes, he is shown as succumbing to desire and longing. Thus in the *Saṃkappa-jātaka*, for instance, the bodhisattva, then a great ascetic with supernatural powers, loses his ability to fly through the air and is literally brought back "down to earth" when, on his begging round, he is overcome by lust; flying along he happens to peer into the second-floor bedroom window of the palace, where he sees the queen stretched out, alone and in bed, and, overcome by desire, he loses his concentration and flutters to the ground.

More generally, in this vein, mention should be made of the negative acts done by the bodhisattva in past lives that resulted in certain negative karmic fruits reaped by him in his final life as Gautama. These stories aim to explain certain biographical incidents: why, for instance, the Buddha still has to undergo certain sufferings in his last life as Gautama, such as being assaulted by his evil cousin Devadatta or having to suffer sickness at certain points. At the same time, however, they serve as reminders that the bodhisattva, too, had his negativities. The imperfections suffered by the Buddha in his final life as Gautama – digestive problems, headaches, slight injuries, etc. – are but the tail-end karmic results of rather despicable deeds – murder, false accusations – done by the bodhisattva in past lives, deeds for which he had already reaped the karmic rewards, by having been reborn in the hells for numerous lifetimes, but which he had not yet completely exhausted.

The Buddhist tradition, in fact, knows a whole text devoted to such deeds, extant in Sanskrit and Pali. In the midst of a major assembly of his disciples at Lake Anavatapta, the Buddha recounts the bad karma of almost a dozen of his past lives, and explains the effects of that karma.

For example, in one life, he killed his brother so as to become sole heir of the family fortune. This resulted not only in his being reborn in hell for thousands of years but also in his being wounded (in his big toe) in his last life as Gautama by his jealous cousin Devadatta during the latter's attempt to murder him. This and the remainder of these deeds are summarized in Table 1.3.

*Table 1.3 The Buddha's negative karma*

| Previous life as | Deed committed | Result of the deed |
|---|---|---|
| A householder | Murders his own brother so as to inherit the family fortune | Suffers many years in hell and, in his last life as Gautama, is injured by his cousin Devadatta |
| A merchant | Attempts to sink the boat of a fellow merchant out of spite, and, upon being found out, kills him with a javelin | Suffers many years in hell and, in his last life as Gautama, gets a splinter in his foot |
| A brahmin youth | Spills the food out of the almsbowl of a *pratyekabuddha* | Suffers many years in hell and, in his last life as Gautama, fails to get any food on his almsround at Śālagrāma |
| A Buddhist monk | Out of jealousy, instigates a servant girl to spread false rumors about his brother, an *arhat* | Suffers many years in hell and, in his last life as Gautama, is falsely accused by a nun named Sundarikā |
| A brahmin | Out of jealousy, calumniates an ascetic | Suffers many years in hell and, in his last life as Gautama, is defamed by a young brahmin woman named Cañcā. |
| A young man from Benares | Kills a courtesan who jilted him and accuses a *pratyekabuddha* of the crime | Suffers many years in hell and, in his last life as Gautama, is falsely accused by a young brahmin woman |
| A brahmin from Bandhumati | Bad-mouths the past buddha Vipaśyin and encourages others to give him rotted grain to eat | For thousands of lifetimes, had to eat rotted grain, and did so again in his last life as Gautama |
| A brahmin youth | Raises doubts about the enlightenment of the past buddha Kāśyapa | In his last life as Gautama, had to practice the wrong path of asceticism for six years |
| A doctor | Irked at not being payed, gives the wrong medicine to a sick man | Suffers many years in hell and, in his last life as Gautama, suffers from dysentery just prior to his *parinirvāṇa* |
| A fisherman | Takes pleasure in the suffering of two large fish he caught | Suffers from headaches during many lifetimes, including his last life as Gautama |
| A wrestling champion | Breaks the back of a rival wrestler | Suffers many years in hell, and, in his last life as Gautama, has a backache |

A number of points would seem to be implicit in such stories. First of all, there is the simple lesson that bad deeds inevitably engender bad karmic results, even for someone such as the Buddha. Secondly, however, such stories allow the tradition to mention negative things about their founder in ways that are relatively safe. No evil actions are committed by the Buddha in his last life; instead all his negativities (and this is a tradition that recognizes that even buddhas have their taints – if only to inspire those of us who are yet more tainted) are assigned to previous lives, and only their lingering final karmic effects are connected to this life.

I have argued in this chapter that the *jātakas* play several important roles in the telling of the biography of the Buddha. They provide almost endless opportunities for the amplification of his lifestory, by showing its karmic connections and incorporating into it other tales and traditions; they help clarify both the arduousness and the openness of the bodhisattva path; they extol the figure of the Buddha by magnifying his deeds; and yet they remind us of his humanity by recalling that he too had his shortcomings. Taken together, however, they also serve a narrative function: they prefigure and set up the story of the Buddha's final life as Gautama, to which we must now turn.

# 2 ANCESTRY, BIRTH, AND YOUTH

It is difficult to know where to start an account of the Buddha's final life as Gautama. On the one hand, as a result of his previous existences, he is reborn in Tuṣita Heaven which acts as a sort of staging ground for his final "descent" into this world. On the other hand, he is the son of his parents, King Śuddhodana and Queen Māyā of Kapilavastu, and this gives him a whole genealogical lineage in addition to his karmic one. Śuddhodana and Māyā are both scions of the Śākya clan, and through them, the Buddha can trace his ancestry back to Mahāsammata, the first king who ruled at the beginning of this cycle of time, when the world was just being formed. This genealogy thus inaugurates the theme of the royal connections of the Buddha and provides him with a different sort of pedigree than that found in the *jātakas*. Indeed, if the *jātakas* may be said to trace the bodhisattva's preparations for buddhahood, the accounts of his family ancestry may be viewed as preparing him for kingship. At the same time, this genealogy makes for a focus on the Śākya tribe to which the Buddha belonged. This is important because it will help define the context in which the Buddha was brought up as a young man. In this chapter, then, I want first to trace briefly the Buddha's ancestry, his Śākya lineage. Then I will look at traditions concerning his birth, prognostications about his future, his early life in the palace, and his growing dissatisfaction with that life.

## THE ŚĀKYA LINEAGE

There are a number of different accounts of the Buddha's ancestry, and they vary somewhat. The version that I shall present here is that found in the *Discipline (Vinaya) of the Mūlasarvāstivādins* and it is one of the more developed of these narratives. The text starts with an account of the "Golden Age" at the beginning of the present world cycle. This is an ideal, paradisiacal time of natural, effortless existence. Ethereal, self-luminiscent beings live in bliss and know no discrimination between polar opposites such as male and female, good and evil, rich and poor, ruler and subject. Toil and trouble are unknown, and the earth itself is edible, being made of a soft, sweet-tasting substance that has the texture of butter. Gradually, however, because of karma remaining from a previous world cycle, this Golden Age is lost. During a long period of decline, a "hardening" of the world (in both the literal and metaphorical sense) takes place. The edible earth turns to dirt, and labor, greed, grasping, sex, theft, violence, and murder all come on to the scene. Finally, sheer anarchy threatens and, in order to stave it off, the beings get together to select from among their ranks a king to rule over them and maintain order. This is Mahāsammata, the Great Elect, the first king.

Mahāsammata's role is inherited by his son, Roca, and, after three more generations, the lineage passes on to King Māndhātar. Said to have been born from a blister on the head of his father (and so he was also called Mūrdhaja ["Headborn"]), Māndhātar was an ideal king, a "wheel-turning" sovereign (*cakravartin*) who possessed the thirty-two marks of a great man and ruled over all four continents of the universe in the four cardinal directions. In the Buddhist tradition, such full-fledged *cakravartins* (those who rule over all four continents) are ideal righteous kings who symbolically conquer the world by circumambulating it in a clockwise direction, like the sun, following a great golden wheel of Dharma to the East, South, West, and North before returning to the center. Everywhere they go, their very charisma and presence are enough to guarantee their sovereignty and authority over the realm. *Cakravartins* ruling over three, two, or a single continent are equally wise but are somewhat lesser in stature and increasingly have to resort to the threat of force to assure their sovereignty.

Māndhātar's son and successor, Cāru, was born from a blister on his father's right breast, and ruled like him over four continents. Cāru's son, Upacāru, was born, however, from a blister on his father's left breast and ruled over only three continents; and *his* son, Cārumant, was born from a blister on his father's right foot, and ruled over only two continents, while Cārumant's son, Upacārumant, was born from a blister on his father's left foot, and ruled over only one. We seem to have repeated here, then, in terms of *cakravartins* and places of "birth," the theme of gradual decline from an ideal to a less-than-perfect age. Indeed, after many more generations, crime, sex, and lying set in again, and a son of the king of that time, a hermit who happens to be named Gautama, is falsely accused of the murder of a prostitute. He is to be executed by being impaled on a stake, and the end of the royal line seems near. As he is dying, however, two drops of semen mingled with blood fall from his body and from them, miraculously, twins are born.

At this point, the text engages in some fancy etymologizing in order to explain a number of names and epithets all of which will later be applied to the Buddha. Because the twins were born at daybreak, hatched by the warmth of the sun, they are said (like the Buddha after them) to be of the "Solar Clan" (*Sūrya-gotra*); because their father was called Gautama, they are also given that name; because they came forth from the juice (*rasa*) of his own body (*angin*), they are called "Āngīrasa;" because after their birth, they took refuge in a sugarcane thicket (*ikṣu-vāṭu*), they are called "Ikṣvāku." It is the latter name that is, in fact, adopted by the youngest of the twins who becomes king and starts a new dynasty known as the Ikṣvākus.

One hundred generations pass, and the genealogy then pauses at the reign of Ikṣvāku Virūḍhaka, and with him we come to the founding of the Śākya tribe. Virūḍhaka has four sons by one wife, and then another son by a second, younger wife. The four sons are forced into exile by the machinations of their stepmother who wants the throne for her own child. In exile, they become a very involuted clan; concerned with endogamy and with the purity of their lineage they marry members of their own family, variously described as their own sisters or half-sisters. Eventually, it is said, they do consent to intermarry with a neighboring tribe, the Koliyas (in one tradition, the Buddha's mother's family is said to be of Koliya origin), but only because the Koliyas were descendant from a Śākya princess. In any case, in exile, they settle permanently near the hermitage of an ascetic called Kapila where they found a city which they name Kapilavastu after him. Nearby, they establish another town named Devadṛśa. Because they thus show themselves to be capable (*śak*) in adverse circumstances, they come to be known as the Śākyas.

Fifty-five thousand generations later, Kapilavastu is still their capital, and their king, Siṃhahanu, resides there while a relative of his, Suprabuddha, reigns in Devadṛśa. Siṃhahanu has four sons, one of whom is Śuddhodana, the Buddha's father. (The others are named

Śuklodana, Droṇodana, and Amṛtodana.) He also has four daughters, all of whom seem to have been named to match their brothers, Śuddhā, Śuklā, Droṇā, and Amṛtikā. Meanwhile, in Devadṛśa, Suprabuddha has several children as well, one of whom is Mahāmāyā, the Buddha's mother.

## THE BUDDHA'S BIRTH

In relatively early canonical sources, we are not told much about the Buddha's actual birth. From Tuṣita Heaven, he is simply said to descend and enter the side of his mother, Queen Māyā. He dwells in her womb for exactly ten lunar months, during which time he remains calm, alert, perfectly formed in body, and unsullied by any pollution. In some sources, Māyā is said to be able to see and contemplate him inside of her. At the end of this period, she gives birth while standing up holding on to the branch of a tree. The birth is painless. The Buddha is not born vaginally but emerges from his mother's side. This lack of passage through the birth canal is often said to reflect a concern for purity, but it may also be connected to a pan-Indian tradition that asserts that the trauma of vaginal birth is what wipes out the memory of previous lives. In this context, since the Buddha is aware of his previous existences, he obviously could not have been born vaginally.

Later biographical traditions were to draw out and expand upon this whole scenario, starting with the Buddha's conception. For instance, the Mahāyānist text, the *Living out of the Game (Lalitavistara)*, which does not actually get to the Buddha's birth until its seventh chapter, dwells at first, and at great length, on his activities in Tuṣita Heaven, on his preparations for his final birth, his contemplation of the right time, place, family, and mother for that birth, and on his final teachings to his fellow gods in heaven, followed by his descent into his mother's womb in the form of a great six-tusked white elephant. Some traditions present this elephant merely as something dreamt by his mother. In either case, it is clearly an auspicious symbol of sovereignty (the great white elephant was one of the emblems of the *cakravartin* king), as well as a reference to one of the *jātaka* tales which features the bodhisattva's self-sacrifice as a great six-tusked elephant.

The *Living out of the Game (Lalitavistara)* also describes at length the bodhisattva's intra-uterine life, portraying him as sitting on a divan that is soft as Benares silk and is set within a perfumed chamber, inside a bejewelled palace-like pavilion implanted in his mother's belly. Inside this amniotic chamber, the Buddha is said already to possess the thirty-two marks of the great man, and to receive various divinities who come to visit him and to hear him preach the Dharma. This whole placental palace, the text is careful to point out, in no way harms or brings discomfort to Queen Māyā, and, at the time of the Buddha's birth, it also emerges and is transported up to Brahmā's heaven where it is worshipped as a relic. It is clear, here, that this text has moved very far away from the notion of an ordinary human birth.

The biographical tradition was to locate the event of the Buddha's birth in the village (or park) of Lumbinī, a site that was visited as early as the third century B.C.E. by the emperor Aśoka, and is located just over the North Indian border in what is now Southern Nepal. The Pali commentaries explain that Queen Māyā wanted to have her child in her parents' house in Devadṛśa, but failed to make it all the way home in time and so gave birth at Lumbinī at the halfway point of her journey. A Sanskrit text develops this story further, maintaining that Lumbinī was actually the name of Māyā's mother; the park in question was named for her after having been made by Māyā's father, Suprabuddha, at a point half-way between the towns of Devadṛśa and Kapilavastu.

André Bareau, who likes to demythologize, is inclined to dismiss these explanations. Pointing out that there is no firm mention of Lumbinī (the place) in the earliest canonical accounts of the Buddha's birth, he supposes Gautama to have actually been born in his father's hometown of Kapilavastu, about ten miles away. He suggests that the relocation of the birth to Lumbinī came from a desire to associate the Buddha's mother, Māyā, with the figure of a local fertility goddess who was worshipped there. Indeed, it has often been argued that the posture Queen Māyā is said to take while giving birth associates her with the figures of tree goddesses who were connected to notions of fertility and childbirth and venerated locally, and are similarly portrayed as hanging on to branches. In one account, such a goddess is, in fact, said to reside in the very tree under which the Buddha was born and to have witnessed his birth. "Throughout the three-fold world," she reports, "there shone a supernatural light, dazzling like gold and delighting the eye. The earth and its mountains, ringed by the ocean, shook like a ship being tossed at sea" (Strong, 1983, pp. 129–30, 246).

These ecological/environmental reverberations of the Buddha's birth are significant, and the theme is much developed in some biographies.

In the Pali "Introduction" (*Nidāna-kathā*) to the *Jātaka Commentary*, for instance, the earthquake and the great radiance are just the first of thirty-two portents that are said to manifest themselves at the time of the Buddha's birth (and also of his conception). These include such things as the blind regaining their sight, the deaf being able to hear, the fires of hell being extinguished, fear among animals disappearing, musical instruments sounding on their own, the ocean turning into sweet water, and masses of flowers blossoming everywhere. At the same time, it is said that seven other beings or things are born at the very same moment as the Buddha. The identity of these "co-natals" varies from one text to another, but one source gives them as follows: his future wife Yaśodharā, his future groom Chandaka, his future companion Udāyin, his future royal elephant (alternatively, his future disciple Ānanda), his future great horse Kaṇṭhaka, the Bodhi tree, and four treasure-urns. This tradition is often said to reflect an attempt to parallel the lists of the seven "gems" that are born at the same time as a great *cakravartin* king: the wheel of sovereignty, the elephant, the horse, the woman, the wish-granting gem, the treasurer, and the minister. Be that as it may, the point here is that the Buddha's birth is an event that is marked by the birth of beings who will play important roles in his life and by the response of the whole world around him – natural, animal, vegetable, human, and divine.

On emerging from his mother's side, the Buddha is received by the gods – sometimes specified as the four guardians of the four directions – who keep him from falling on the ground and help bathe him in two streams of hot and cold water that miraculously come down from the sky. He then takes seven steps to the North and, contemplating the four cardinal directions, he makes the following proclamation (in the Pali "Discourse on the Great Legend" [*Mahāpadānasutta*]): "I am chief in the world, supreme in the world, eldest in the world. This is my last birth, there will be [henceforth for me] no more re-becoming" (Walshe, 1987, p. 205). The corresponding sūtra in a Chinese text gives a somewhat more Mahāyānist flavor to this proclamation: "In heaven and on earth, I alone am worthy of veneration; I will free all beings from birth, old age, sickness and death" (Waldschmidt, 1953–56, p. 90 n.1). Either way, this episode has been connected to pre-Buddhist Vedic cosmogonic traditions as well as Indian rituals of royal consecration; in taking these steps the infant Buddha is accompanied by a fly whisk and an umbrella of sovereignty, and later biographical traditions had him actually walk in all four directions, thus repeating the universal monarch's conquest of the world.

## PROGNOSTICATIONS: THE SIGNS OF THE "GREAT MAN"

These royal connections are further emphasized in the next scene in which the Buddha's father has his son examined by various diviners. Inspecting his body, they find on it the thirty-two physiognomic signs of a great man, signs which indicate for him one of two possible careers: if he stays at home and inherits the throne, he will become a universal monarch, a *cakravartin* king; if he leaves home and becomes a wandering mendicant, he will become a supremely awakened one, a buddha (see Table 2.1).

Several of these physical signs – in particular the "bump" on the Buddha's head which is said to be like a turban (*uṣṇīṣa*), the tuft of hair between his eyebrows (his *ūrṇā*), his webbed or net-like hands and feet, his long and slender tongue (said to be able to reach to the top of his head), and his concealed sexual organ – have elicited much wonder and commentary among scholars. Their possible connection to iconography has already been noted in the Introduction above. Suffice it to say that, in the present context, the marks serve to emphasize the parallelism between the career of a Buddha and the career of kingship, sometimes in rather specific ways. Thus, just as a *cakravartin*, with his level feet, will encounter no obstacles or opposition as he conquers the world, so too a buddha will find none who can oppose him as he spreads the Dharma (neither lust, hatred, nor delusion; neither brahmin, recluse, *deva*, nor Māra). Just as a *cakravartin*, with his thousand-spoked wheel, will be surrounded by a great retinue of bodyguards, ministers, courtiers, and others, so too a buddha will be surrounded by a great community (*saṃgha*) of monks and nuns, laymen and laywomen. Just as a *cakravartin*, with his long fingers and toes and projecting heels, will be longlived, so too will a buddha be. Just as a *cakravartin*, with his sheath-encased penis, will have a thousand sons, so too a buddha will have a thousand disciples. Just as a *cakravartin*, with his banyan-like body, will acquire great material fortune, gold, silver, and gems, so too a buddha will have great spiritual wealth, faith, morality, and wisdom. Just as a *cakravartin*, with his long tongue, will command respect when he speaks, so too will people listen to a buddha when he preaches.

To some extent, however, all this ambiguity is artificial. There is no doubt in anyone's mind about the ultimate destiny of the bodhisattva; authors and audience alike already *know* that he will become the

*Table 2.1 The 32 Signs of the Great Man* (Mahāpuruṣa)

1. He has feet with level tread
2. The soles of his feet are marked with thousand-spoked wheel-signs
3. He has projecting heels
4. He has long toes and fingers
5. He has soft and tender hands and feet
6. He has hands and feet that are net-like
7. He has projecting well-rounded ankles
8. He has legs like an antelope's
9. His hands come down to his knees when he stands up straight
10. His penis is enclosed in a sheath
11. His skin is the color of gold
12. His skin is soft and smooth
13. He has but one body hair to each follicle
14. His body hairs grow straight up, are black, and curl to the right
15. His body is perfectly straight
16. His body has seven convex surfaces, i.e., the backs of his arms, legs, shoulders, and his chest
17. His bust is like a lion's
18. He has no hollows between his shoulder-blades
19. His body is perfectly proportioned like a banyan-tree
20. His bust is well-rounded
21. He has an excellent sense of taste
22. He has a jaw like a lion's
23. He has forty teeth
24. His teeth are even
25. There are no gaps between his teeth
26. His canine teeth are very white
27. His tongue is long and slender
28. He has a voice like Brahmā's
29. He has blue eyes
30. He has eyelashes like those of a cow
31. He has a tuft of hair (*ūrṇā*) between his eyebrows
32. The top of his head has a turban-shaped protuberance (*uṣṇīṣa*)

Buddha. Thus, in many biographies, the two-pronged predictions by the diviners as a group are offset by the single-path prediction by the one of them who knows better, the one who is certain about the destiny of the infant Gautama. In one Pali tradition, this is the brahmin Kauṇḍinya, who, upon inspecting the body of the young child, holds up one finger – to indicate a single course of life – in contrast to his fellow seers who hold up two. In other texts, this role is given to the sage Asita, who realizes that because the thirty-two marks are particularly distinct, and because the Buddha also possesses eighty more subtle secondary marks, he will become a Buddha. Knowing this, Asita at first rejoices, and then grieves because he realizes that he himself will die before the child actually attains buddhahood.

There are other signs of the infant bodhisattva's future greatness. Shortly after his birth, he is taken to the Śākya temple to be presented to the clan's tutelary goddess, Abhayā. But when they try to present his head to the goddess for her blessing, it is his feet that he puts forward, and the goddess, acknowledging his superiority, pays homage to him. In the "Introduction" to the Pali *Jātaka Commentary*, much the same thing happens with reference not to a goddess but to the sage Kāḷadevala. In both cases, the argument is made that were the persons in question to receive the homage of the Buddha, their heads would split into pieces, unable to stand such a travesty of etiquette. In other texts, it is the statues of all the divinities in the Śākya temple (including those of the principal Hindu gods) which get down from their pedestals and lie prostrate at the foot of the bodhisattva. Witnessing this miracle, the bodhisattva's father, Śuddhodana, also bows down and pays homage to his son, giving him the name "Devātideva" ("god-above-gods"). This is the first of three prostrations that the biographical tradition portrayed Śuddhodana as making to his son, the second occuring when he witnessed the miracle of the shade of the rose-apple tree (see below), and the third on the Buddha's return home to Kapilavastu after his enlightenment. It is clear here that we have a reversal of regular hierarchical relationships. The bodhisattva is not only "above the gods" but he is also above his father and the rest of humanity.

## UPBRINGING IN THE PALACE

Despite the subtext of certainty about Gautama's eventual destiny of becoming the Buddha, the maintenance of the potential ambiguity about his career serves an important narrative function in the next portion of his biography, for it helps define his life in the palace and the measures his father takes to ensure that he stays at home, inherits the throne, and becomes a great universal king, a *cakravartin*. There can be no doubt that life for the young Gautama is pleasant and that he benefits from all the privileges of his royal position. To be sure, there is the tragedy of his mother's death, supposed to have happened seven days after his birth, despite occasional indications to the contrary. Generally speaking, the biographies claim that this death of the mother is part of the blueprint for all buddhas and is intended to avoid attachments and later grief, although at least one source maintains that it is due to Māyā's being unable to bear the joy caused by the bodhisattva's birth and future promise. But this loss of a parent is soon mitigated by the attention and luxury lavished on the bodhisattva. As an infant, he is said to have multiple nurses to feed him, wash him, hold him, and play with him. As a youth, he continues to enjoy pleasure and privilege. "Monks," he tells his disciples later in life, "I was delicately, most delicately brought up," and he goes on to describe the luxuries of his life as a prince, the three palaces his father built for him (one for the winter, one for the summer, and one for the rainy season), the lotus-pools for different types of blossoms, the marvelous meals that were served, the costly garments he wore, the entertainments he enjoyed, the women who surrounded him.

Not only was his world perfect, but he himself was the perfect prince within it. Thus, in some biographies, his accomplishments in the classroom as well as his training in the arts of the warrior appropriate to his lineage are dwelt upon as being particularly glorious and superlative. In the *Living out of the Game (Lalitavistara)*, for instance, when the still young bodhisattva arrives at school for the first day of classes (accompanied by ten thousand schoolboy companions and a bevy of eight thousand beautiful girls), he asks his teacher (who, like the gods and like his father, has fallen prostrate at his feet), "Which of the sixty-four scripts will you teach me?" And he then proceeds to list all of them. The teacher is astounded at this display of erudition and declares that the bodhisattva has knowledge of scripts that he has not even heard of. Understandably, the lesson that follows is quickly taken over by the bodhisattva who uses the occasion to impart a teaching in Buddhist doctrine to his fellow students, as well as his teacher: "A is for '*anityaḥ sarvasaṃkāra*' – the impermanence of all the aggregates," "B is for '*bandhanamokṣa*' – the deliverance from bondage," "C is for '*caturāryasatya*' – the Four Noble Truths," and so on (Bays, 1983 1, 189–93, modified).

No less phenomenal are his achievements in the warrior's arts, except that they are set in the context of his betrothal and marriage. His father, eager to root his son in the palace and the ways of the world, launches a search for the perfect bride for him. The bodhisattva, reflecting that all previous buddhas did marry, consents to this, and even indicates his preference for Gopā, the daughter of his maternal uncle, Daṇḍapāṇi.

Daṇḍapāṇi, however, is proud and replies that in his family, daughters are only given to young men who excel in manly strength and the warrior's arts, and that the bodhisattva, having grown up pampered in the palace, has yet to prove himself. He proposes a martial arts competition amongst all the young Śākya men: he will give the hand of his daughter to the victor. There ensues a series of contests and confrontations in which the bodhisattva bests all comers (mostly his cousins and other relations, all of them Śākyas). The first demonstration of his amazing strength comes on the way out to the testing ground. The bodhisattva's evil-minded cousin, Devadatta, wanting to prevent the others from taking part in the competition, kills an elephant with a single blow of his hand and leaves it blocking the city gate. The bodhisattva's half-brother, Nanda, then clears it out of the way, managing to drag it some distance by its tail. When the bodhisattva arrives on the scene, however, he quickly shows his superiority: afraid that the carcass will start to stink, he uses no more than the toe of his foot to flick the elephant over the seven walls of the city. It lands just outside of town, and forms a great depression in the ground that was called "the pit of the falling elephant" when the Chinese pilgrim Xuanzang visited it centuries later.

This theme of rivalry between brothers and cousins is continued in the subsequent tests. Without effort, the bodhisattva easily defeats thirty-two Śākyans, including Devadatta, at wrestling. In an archery contest, he alone can bend the great bow of their grandfather, and his shot not only passes through all the targets reached by the others but perforates his own and buries itself in the earth with such residual force that a spring wells up at the spot. The end result of all this is that he wins Gopā's hand in marriage.

Not all the biographies were to develop these scenes quite as much as the *Living out of the Game (Lalitavistara)*. Nor was Gopā always featured as the bodhisattva's wife. In the Pali tradition, that position is occupied by Yaśodharā, generally simply known as "the Mother of

Rāhula" (his son), though the story of their betrothal is much attenuated. In other sources, the bodhisattva is said to acquire three wives in rather rapid succession, each one in different circumstances: Yaśodharā, Gopikā, and Mṛgajā. To these, other texts add thousands of concubines. All of these sources share an emphasis on the valor and splendor of the bodhisattva, and on the ease and enjoyable nature of his life in the palace, all of which, of course, serves the function of stressing how great was the turning away that prompted him to give it all up.

## TURNING AWAY FROM KINGSHIP: THE BEGINNINGS OF DISCONTENT

The biographical tradition as a whole is agreed that, at some point, the bodhisattva grew tired of his life in the palace. In some canonical texts, he is simply said to come to realize that the whole world does not enjoy such ease, but is exposed to suffering; becoming concerned and reflective, he muses on these matters, and resolves to give up his hedonistic pursuits. In more developed traditions, this existential realization is connected to one and/or the other of two experiences: the bodhisattva's "first meditation" at the ploughing festival, and his encounters with the so-called "four signs" – the old man, the sick man, the dead man, and the wandering mendicant – while on an excursion in the park. There are many versions – more or less developed – of both episodes, but, the gist of them is quickly told.

The young bodhisattva's "first meditation" occurs when he goes out to watch his father and the royal court participate in the festival marking the first ploughing of the fields. Sitting under a rose-apple (*jambu*) tree, the bodhisattva enters quickly into the first level of meditative trance. When the women and his father come to look for him in the late afternoon, they see that the shadows of all of the other trees have moved while the tree under which the bodhisattva is sitting still affords him shade. Witnessing this, his father, Śuddhodana, bows down before him in homage a second time. The reason for the bodhisattva's meditation is often said to stem from his observations at the festival. Seeing the laboring oxen, the sweating men, and the insects and worms which are turned up by the ploughs and quickly devoured by the birds, he realizes that what is supposed to be pleasant (the celebration of the festival) is actually filled with suffering. Indeed, some texts developed this theme even further. Thus, in a Chinese biography, a whole chain of suffering is narrated: the worms uncovered by the plough are snapped up by a frog which is then swallowed by a snake, which is eaten by a peacock, which is killed by a hawk which, in turn, is devoured by an eagle. More precisely, however, it should be noted that all this suffering is brought on not just by men ploughing but by the *king* ploughing at a festival which is a royal ritual meant to reassert his sovereignty. The bodhisattva then is making the specific realization that what entails suffering is the reestablishment of kingship.

Like the bodhisattva's experience at the ploughing festival, the encounter with the "four signs" is also transformative. What is supposed to be a pleasurable experience – an excursion into the park, along a path cleared by the bodhisattva's father of all distressing sights – turns into a realization of suffering. Either all on one day, or on successive excursions, the bodhisattva, out for a ride in his chariot, encounters an old man, a sick man, and a corpse. In some texts, these figures are sent down by the gods so as to thwart Śuddhodana's wishes to shelter his son, and spur the bodhisattva on to his quest for buddhahood. In others, they just appear. In either case, we are led to believe that this is the first time the bodhisattva-prince has actually seen such things. "Good charioteer," he asks his companion, "what kind of man is this with white hair, supporting himself on a staff, his eyes veiled by his brows, his limbs drooped and bent? Is this some transformation in him, or his original state, or mere chance?" (Johnston, 1936, p. 37, slightly altered). And the bodhisattva is very moved to learn that this is "an old man" and that all persons, himself included, will one day become like this. Much the same scenario and realization are repeated at the sight of the sick man and the dead man, and all of this distresses the bodhisattva very much. He has come to realize the inevitability and universality of three things – old age, suffering, and death – which would later be incorporated into capsule definitions of the first Noble Truth of "suffering" (*duḥkha*). The fourth sign (which does not figure in all versions of the story) – the sight of a wandering holy man, a mendicant who seems at ease with himself and the world – serves then to give him hope and to inspire him to believe that there is a way out of suffering, or at least a way towards understanding its nature.

In one of the versions of this episode, the bodhisattva encounters the four signs on successive days after leaving the city each time through a different gate. Venturing out through the eastern gate, he meets the old man, through the southern gate, the sick man, through the western gate, the corpse, and through the northern gate, the wandering mendicant. André Bareau has seen in this a recall of the sun-wise circumambulation of the *cakravartin*, and a veiled reference to the Buddha's connections to kingship. One could just as easily, however, see this as indicating the flipside of the experience: the realization that suffering is found in all directions, that, like the rule of the *cakravartin*, it is universal.

In sum, then, we can see that these accounts of the Buddha's birth and youth serve to establish a number of different things. Among these are his connections to kingship, the glory of his person and his achievements, the life of ease and splendor that he led in the palace, and the germs of dissatisfaction that were to result in his departure on his quest for buddhahood. André Bareau, in the conclusion of his study of many of these same traditions, sums them up with two words: exaltation and exemplification. On the one hand, the bodhisattva is presented as heir of a great lineage, king of kings, god of gods, superior to all humans and all relatives. This exaltation, Bareau states, is the only reason for the invention of the biographical episodes featuring his prodigious conception, his unbelievable intra-uterine life, his extraordinary birth and first moments, his amazing achievements in scholarship and the martial arts. On the other hand, the legends of his first meditation, of his encounter with the four signs which raise questions in his mind about his happy, hedonistic youth in the palace, serve to make him into an example, a paradigm to inspire others who, living less in the lap of luxury perhaps, are nonetheless contemplating a life of renunciation.

# 3 QUEST AND ENLIGHTENMENT

In an important "autobiographical" sūtra called the "Discourse on the Noble Quest" (*Ariyapariyasena-sutta*), the Buddha distinguishes between "noble" (*ariya*) and "ignoble" (*anariya*) enterprises. The latter consist of pursuing all those things that are subject to old age, sickness, and death or destruction: family life, possessions, wealth, luxuries. The former is characterized by the search for enlightenment, for *nirvāṇa*, and the Blessed One then recounts how he, one day, embarked on such a quest. When he was still a bodhisattva, not yet fully enlightened, he left home, cut his hair, and shaved his beard, put on a mendicant's robe, and went in search of different teachers. First he studied with a master named Ārāḍa Kālāma, but he was soon dissatisfied with his teaching; he quickly mastered all that he could teach – said to be the realization of the meditative stage of no-thingness – but he concluded that this was not ultimately conducive to tranquillity and *nirvāṇa*. So he sought out another teacher, Udraka Rāmaputra, and under him he reached a higher stage of meditative awareness, the plane of neither-perception-nor-non-perception. Yet he was not satisfied with this either, for still it did not lead to tranquillity and *nirvāṇa*. So he left Udraka and, wandering on alone through the land of Magadha, he eventually arrived in Uruvilvā where he found a delightful grove near a river. Thinking it a good place for meditation, he sat down under a tree and there renewed his striving until he attained *nirvāṇa*. And there arose in him the knowledge and realization that he had put an end to rebirth and had attained certain liberation.

This, in a nutshell, sums up the Buddha's career from his *abhiniṣkramaṇa* – his departure from worldly life – to his *abhisaṃbodhana* – his

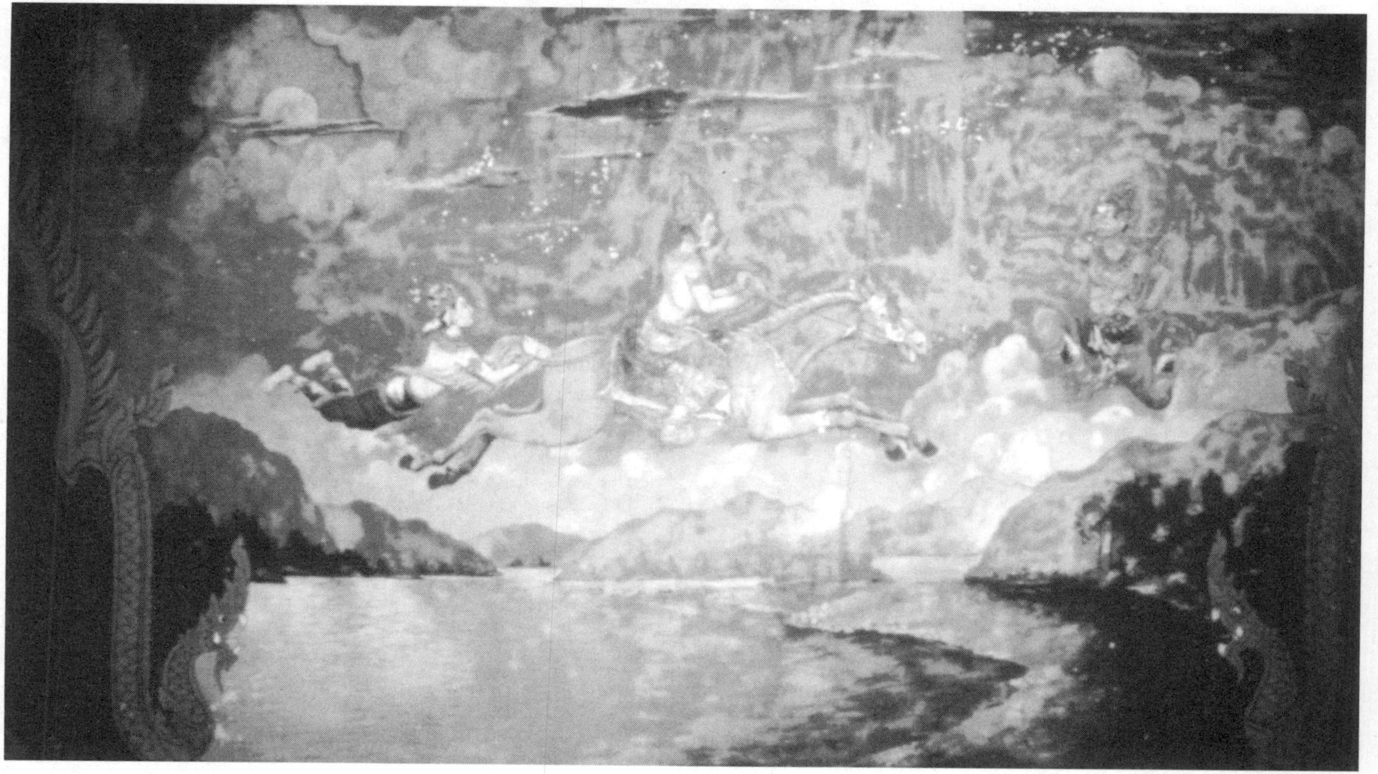

*The bodhisattva's Great Departure, Wat Doi Suthep, Chiangmai, Thailand.*

attainment of perfect enlightenment. On this bare framework, other *sūtras* and later biographical traditions were to hang and embellish new episodes. In this chapter, I will focus on the following: the incitements to leave home, the great departure from Kapilavastu, the making of a monk, the practice of austerities, the abandonment of austerities, the offering of milk-rice, the defeat of Māra, and the attainment of enlightenment, buddhahood achieved.

## INCITEMENTS TO LEAVE HOME

We have already seen that, even in the midst of his life in the palace, germs of awareness and questioning began to take root in the bodhisattva's mind. At the ploughing festival, he observed the suffering of creatures and humans, and achieved a first level of meditative trance under the rose-apple tree; during his excursions into the park he encountered the four signs, the first three of which made him realize the universality and inevitability of old age, sickness, and death, while the last one – the wandering ascetic – gave him a not-quite formulated feeling, a hope that, in order to solve the problems of suffering he had seen, he could drop out and lead an alternative life as a homeless mendicant free from attachments.

In order for this nascent awareness to ring true psychologically, and, indeed, for the whole story of the Buddha's quest to make good narrative sense, we must assume that he has, at least temporarily, forgotten (or that he pretends to forget) who he is: a being whose buddhahood is certain. The gods in heaven, however, have not forgotten. According to the "Introduction" (*Nidāna-kathā*) to the *Jātaka Commentary*, they are the first to realize how close the bodhisattva has come to his actual departure from home. Knowing that he will wander forth, that very night, they come down to earth to adorn him; they take on the form of the bodhisattva's servants who are attending him after his bath in the park, and they dress him magnificently in divine garments and jewels. Clearly this episode is connected to the Buddhist ritual practice of dressing up candidates for ordination in all their finery as they prepare to leave their homes for the monastery, and we shall see below further evidence of the close symbiotic relationship between the legend of the bodhisattva's great departure and the ritual of monastic ordination.

In the narrative context at hand, however, the adorning of the bodhisattva moves directly into the next episode. Arrayed in all his splendor, the bodhisattva enters the city of Kapilavastu, riding in his chariot. It is there that a beautiful Śākya maiden, Kisāgotamī, sees him, looking down from her balcony above the street. She is quite taken by his magnificent appearance, and utters a famous verse: "Blissful is the mother, and blissful is the father of one such as this, and blissful is the woman with a husband like him." The word translated here as "blissful" is *nibbuta*, which can also mean "gone to *nirvāṇa*". This *double entendre* is significant; although Kisāgotamī intends its meaning in the first sense, the bodhisattva takes it in the second, and as such the word is enough to awaken in him the determination to leave his home and set out on his quest. As another version of the story puts it: "When he heard the sound of the word Nirvana, he listened with rapt attention ... [and] meditated on it, having nothing more to fear" (Jones, 1949–56, 2, p. 153). In gratitude to Kisāgotamī for inspiring him, albeit involuntarily, to seek for *nirvāṇa*, he removes a costly string of pearls from his neck and gives it to her "as a teacher's fee,"an action that merely furthers the ambiguity of the situation since she interprets it as a token of his sudden love for her.

With the thought of *nirvāṇa* on his mind, the bodhisattva then enters his palace and lies down on his couch of state. The girls of his harem immediately appear in order to entertain him with dance, song, and music, but, preoccupied, he takes no delight in them. In fact, according to the *Living out of the Game (Lalitavistara)*, their words actually further incite him to leave home because, though the women play very seductive tunes and sing suggestive songs, the gods so arrange it that the bodhisattva hears something completely different: a litany of verses (that in the text goes on for over twenty pages) praising detachment, reminding him of the vow for buddhahood he took under the previous buddha Dīpaṃkara, recalling the many past lives in which he himself had already sacrificed riches, wives, sons, and his very own limbs and life, and encouraging him to rise up, seize the moment, and leave home.

Other accounts are less fanciful. In some, the bodhisattva, tired and bored, simply falls asleep, and when he does, the women naturally stop their dancing and music. Eventually, they too fall asleep (or are made to fall asleep by the gods), and, when the bodhisattva wakes up, he finds them slumbering and snoring, lying in great disarray, arms and legs akimbo, their beauty and attractiveness gone. Virtually all the biographies describe this scene in some detail but none so graphically and extensively as the *Acts of the Buddha (Buddhacarita)*. Some of the women, it says,

> lay in immodest attitudes, snoring, stretching their limbs, all distorted, and tossing their arms about. Others looked ugly, lying unconscious like corpses, with their ornaments and garlands cast aside, the fastening knots of their dresses undone, and eyes moveless with the whites showing. Another lay as if sprawling in intoxication, with her mouth gaping wide, so that the saliva oozed forth, and with her limbs spread out so as to show what should have been hid.

Still others, in various states of undress, were rubbing up against their musical instruments as though they were lovers, while one with "her clothes fallen from her hips and her necklaces scattered ... lay like an image of a woman broken by an elephant" (Johnston, 1936, pp. 72–73, slightly modified).

All of this fills the bodhisattva with a kind of nausea. His palace now appears to him as "a charnel ground full of corpses scattered here and there." He realizes that this is "the real nature of woman in the world of the living" (Jayawickrama, 1990, p. 82), and he comes to understand the inherent impurity and impermanence of the body. This realization is important; it is the first thing that is taught to candidates for Buddhist ordination who are asked to meditate on the impermanence and loathsomeness of the various parts of the body. It also foresees the so-called "cemetery meditations" in which decaying corpses are contemplated by monks seeking the same understanding. The harem, the bodhisattva realizes, is a trap, in which men pursue the Unreal. Indeed, in one text, he launches into a set of thirty-two similes on the sleeping women, whom he calls "these ignorant ones." They are said to be "like idiots clutching pretty vases full of vomit," "like excited dogs in the midst of bones," "like fish caught in a net," "like moths throwing themselves into burning flames" (Bays, 1983, pp. 312–13). The net result of all of this is an intense and urgent desire on his part to leave.

## THE GREAT DEPARTURE

The bodhisattva's father Śuddhodana, however, has seen the mood of his son, and has been worried about it for some time, so that he has even had premonitory dreams about his imminent departure. Moreover, ever since his son's birth, when the soothsayers foretold that he would be a *cakravartin* king, but only if he did not leave home to become a wandering ascetic, he has taken care to watch his son carefully. In addition to encircling him with entrancingly beautiful women, he has made sure that he is well guarded. As one text puts it:

> iron doors were put in each city gate. Very loud bells were attached to the doors, so that whenever they were opened, they could be heard up to a distance of a league around . . . Armed men and riders were posted outside on the walls, and they patrolled everywhere, keeping watch all around. Five hundred men were likewise stationed at the door to the bodhisattva's harem and ordered to sound the alarm in King Śuddhodana's quarters were that door to be opened. (Strong, 1995, p. 10)

The bodhisattva is worried that these forces may prevent his ever leaving, but, on the night of his great departure, his fears are allayed by the gods, who favor his going forth and put the entire city into a deep sleep.

In this context, the Buddha summons his groom, Chandaka (whom he has some trouble awakening), and orders him to bring his horse, Kaṇṭhaka. Depending on the text, Chandaka's reaction to this varies. In some sources, he is only too willing to comply and assist the bodhisattva in his plans. In others, however, he resists, for he is, after all, in the king's employ. Thinking it bizarre that the prince is calling for a horse in the middle of the night, he suggests that he wait until morning, and recommends that, in the meantime, he relax and enjoy himself in his harem. When the bodhisattva insists that he wants his horse immediately, Chandaka figures out that he is planning to leave home, so he raises the alarm, crying out in a loud voice so as to waken King Śuddhodana and all the people of Kapilavastu. Kaṇṭhaka, the horse, likewise starts to neigh loudly. Both of these alarm-givers, however, are unable to rouse the guards who remain in a deep slumber.

Given this context of urgency, it is interesting to note that, prior to his departure, the bodhisattva still feels the need to take leave of his father Śuddhodana and of his wife Yaśodharā, who is often portrayed as asleep with their newborn son, Rāhula.

Different texts situate the parting with his father at different points in the story, sometimes prior to the sleeping-women-in-the-harem scene, sometimes afterwards. In the *Living out of the Game (Lalitavistara)*, the bodhisattva leaves his chambers in the early part of the night and goes to Śuddhodana's quarters to tell him of his intention to depart, thinking it would be wrong and ungrateful for him to leave without getting his father's permission and blessing. Śuddhodana urges him to change his mind. The bodhisattva says he will do so if his father can guarantee him a life without old age, sickness, misfortune, death, or rebirth. Śuddhodana cannot do that, of course, and tells his son to be content with what he has, which is quite a bit. This, of course, is unacceptable to the bodhisattva, and in the end, Śuddhodana capitulates and concludes their visit by giving his son his blessing: "May you do great good in the world. May you rejoice in liberating beings, and may all you intend come to pass" (Bays, 1983, p. 303).

In another version of the story, the bodhisattva stops to see his father on his way out of the city, again thinking that the latter would be upset if he, as prince, did not come to take his leave at this final moment. But Śuddhodana is sleeping soundly, and rather than wake him, the bodhisattva circumambulates his bed and says: "Father, I am leaving not out of lack of respect, not out of lack of reverence, but for no other reason than that I wish to liberate the world ... from the fear of the suffering that comes with old age and death" (Strong, 1995, p. 12).

Alfred Foucher speculates with good reason that these scenes are motivated by a desire to comply with Indian notions of filial duty. More specifically, however, this scenario also needs to be seen in the context of Buddhist ordination rituals. According to Buddhist monastic code, no candidate for ordination can be accepted into the community without the permission of his parents, and proof of parental leave is one of the things that is asked for in the course of the ordination ceremony. In so far as the bodhisattva's great departure represents his own initiation into monkhood, some story-tellers, apparently, felt it necessary to portray him as getting that permission.

The episode of his midnight farewell visit to his sleeping wife, Yaśodharā, is a bit more complex, for here we encounter two basic versions of the great departure scenario that differ significantly from each other in terms of their attitudes towards the family. On the one hand, we have a tradition found in Pali texts and related sources. In this, the farewell is made to both Yaśodharā and their sleeping son, Rāhula, who is just seven days old. While Chandaka is going to get his horse, the bodhisattva has a sudden desire to look at his son one last time. So he goes to his bed-chamber:

> At this time a lamp fed with scented oil was burning inside the room. Rāhula's mother [Yaśodharā] was sleeping in her bed strewn with ... jasmine, and she was resting her hand on her son. Stepping upon the threshold and standing there the bodhisattva looked at him and thought, "If I remove the queen's hand and take my son into my arms she will wake

> up, and that will prevent my journey" [so he goes on his way without doing that]. (Jayawickrama, 1990, p. 83)

This is rather touching and not quite in line, emotionally, with the bodhisattva's earlier declaration at the time of his son's birth that "an impediment [*rāhula* – whence his name] has come into being, a bond has arisen" (Jayawickrama, 1990, p. 81). Nonetheless, it still shows a certain coldness and determination to resist the attachments of wife and child and abandon the householder's state.

Rather different is an alternative tradition that is found in the *Discipline [Vinaya] of the Mūlasarvāstivādins* and corroborative sources. In this version of the story, Rāhula has, in fact, not yet been born by the time of the bodhisattva's great departure. Instead, that night marks the moment of his conception for, far from not waking his wife on his way out of town, the bodhisattva decides to make love to her. The *Vinaya* is explicit about this: "Lest others say that the prince Śākyamuni was 'not a man' and that he wandered forth without 'paying attention' to . . . his wives [the bodhisattva entered his bedchamber], and thinking 'let me now "pay attention" to Yaśodharā,' he did so, and Yaśodharā became pregnant" (Strong, 1997, p. 115).

Obviously, psychologically, this presents a rather different picture of the bodhisattva at this crucial moment. Instead of turning away in disgust from sexuality and abandoning the family life, the bodhisattva here, in his last act as a prince, affirms the householder's state and fulfills his sexual duty by engendering a son. It is also possible that we have here, once again, an episode that reflects connections with Buddhist ordination. Indeed, one of the prerequisites for ordination to the monkhood is that candidates cannot be "lacking in maleness." Still today, one of the questions asked of the ordinand at the time of his joining the *saṃgha* is "are you a male?" and, in ancient India at least, steps were taken by a candidate's preceptor, at the time of dressing him in his new robes, to verify whether or not he was a "eunuch" or had some other sort of physical sexual disqualification. In this light, it may be that this biographical episode, set just prior to the bodhisattva's wandering forth, serves not only to engender his son Rāhula but also to prove his "maleness," one of the qualifications for the monkhood.

In any case, having made love, both Gautama and Yaśodharā fall asleep and each one dreams several dreams. The bodhisattva is said to dream that he was lying on his back with the whole of the earth as his bed, Mount Meru as his pillow, and his arms and feet in the surrounding cosmic ocean; an upright reed grew up out of his navel and reached as far as the sky; big black and white birds stood at his feet; other birds of different colors (*varna*) came from the four directions, and, standing before him, became one color; finally he dreamt he walked back and forth unsullied over a mountain of feces. These five dreams – subconsciously interesting, perhaps, for a "great man" (*mahāpuruṣa*) who has just impregnated his wife – are said to be presages of the bodhisattva's imminent attainment of buddhahood. They also have connections to non-Buddhist mythology, recalling for instance, the image of Viṣṇu sleeping on the cosmic waters.

Yaśodharā's dreams, on the other hand, appear to be much less auspicious and are fairly clearly expressions of her underlying unconscious anxiety that she is about to lose her husband. Her dreams number eight: "that her maternal lineage was cut off, that her magnificent couch collapsed, that her bracelets were broken, that her teeth fell out, that the braid of her hair was undone, that happiness departed from her house, that the moon was eclipsed by Rāhu, and that the sun rose in the East but then set there again" (Strong, 1997, p. 115). Waking up, she tells the bodhisattva of these dreams but he, seeking to comfort her, explains them away:

> You say your maternal lineage was broken, but is it not established? You say your couch collapsed, but look, it is standing. You say your bracelets were broken, but you see they are not. You say your teeth fell out, but you yourself know they haven't. You say the braid of your hair was undone, but it is itself, look. You say "happiness has left my house," but for a woman a husband is happiness, and I am right here. You say the moon was eclipsed by Rāhu, but is that not the moon over there? You say the sun rose in the East and then set again, but it is now midnight, the sun has not yet risen, how then can it set? (Strong, 1997, p. 115–16)

Yaśodharā listens to her husband's explanations but then, still anxious, she extracts a promise from him: "Lord," she requests, "wherever you go, take me with you." And the bodhisattva reassures her by saying: "So be it. Wherever I go, I will take you" (Strong, 1997, p. 116).

By morning, however, the bodhisattva is gone and Yaśodharā has been left behind. The text explains that his promise to her had been made, thinking that he would take her along with him not physically on his great departure, but spiritually to *nirvāṇa*. This little bit of prevarication actually points to a deeper sense in the text that the bodhisattva is not alone in his quest for enlightenment. Indeed, as the rest of the *Vinaya* story makes clear, there is a direct parallelism between the bodhisattva's quest and Yaśodharā's quest, and the symbol of that parallelism is their son Rāhula.

At the risk of jumping ahead in our narrative, it may be useful to trace some of this parallelism here, for, in this tradition, Rāhula, engendered by the bodhisattva on the night of his great departure, is not born until the day of his father's enlightenment at Bodhgaya, six years later. In the interval, during the whole time of the bodhisattva's quest, the Śākyas in Kapilavastu keep themselves informed about his doings, because the bodhisattva's father Śuddhodana, and his maternal grandfather, Suprabuddha, send out spies to report back daily on his activities. Moreover, the five ascetics who share in the bodhisattva's endeavors and later become his first five disciples are portrayed not simply as fellow questers, but as attendants who were sent by Śuddhodana and Suprabuddha to look after him. Yaśodharā thus learns what her departed husband is doing, and, in close sympathy with him, replicates those activities. For instance, when it is reported that the bodhisattva is fasting, eating meals of "one sesame seed, one grain of rice, one jujube, one pulse pod, one kidney bean, one mungo bean," Yaśodharā too fasts, and she too begins to eat "one sesame seed, one grain of rice, one jujube, one pulse pod, one kidney bean, one mungo bean" (Strong, 1997, p. 118). When it is reported that the bodhisattva is now sleeping on a bed of grass, she gets rid of her couch and does likewise. As a result of these austerities, Yaśodharā, like the bodhisattva, becomes very emaciated, the foetus inside her stops growing, and her pregnancy goes unnoticed. When, however, the bodhisattva abandons extreme asceticism and resumes eating, consuming the meal of milk-rice offered him by Sujātā (see below), Yaśodharā also resumes eating, and her pregnancy, developing once more, becomes apparent. And when the bodhisattva, having given up his austerities and regained a wholesome body, is forsaken by his five ascetic companions (sent by the Śākya clan), Yaśodharā, now clearly with child, is also forsaken by the Śākyas back in Kapilavastu who suspect her of infidelity. Finally, when the bodhisattva attains enlightenment under the bodhi tree and becomes a Buddha, Yaśodharā becomes a mother; she gives birth to Rāhula at that very same moment, having kept him in her womb for six full years. And his name is explained not as meaning "an impediment" (*rāhula*) but as being related to the auspicious eclipse of the moon by the divinity Rāhu at the time of his birth.

But we have moved ahead of ourselves. Returning now to Chandaka who is waiting with the horse Kanṭhaka, we need to finish the account of the great departure. The bodhisattva mounts his horse and Chandaka, who is to come along, holds on to his tail. The locked and barred city gate either opens of itself when the bodhisattva wills it to, or is opened by the gate's sympathetic attendant deity, or Kanṭhaka is able to leap over it by flying into the air.

Several stories are then told about what happens to them as they flee. First of all, once they have cleared the city walls, they stop and the bodhisattva, in one text invoked by the goddess of the city, turns and looks back at Kapilavastu, and makes a vow that he will never return there until he has achieved enlightenment. In another tale, while they are still in mid-air, Māra, the Evil One, who is always trying to thwart the Buddha's career, attempts to block their way. He tries, unsuccessfully, to convince the bodhisattva to return to Kapilavastu arguing that, in seven more days, the wheel of a *cakravartin* will appear for him and he will become ruler of all four continents. In another tale, it is the bodhisattva's cousin, Mahānāman, who is on patrol outside the city, who confronts him, telling him of all the sorrow that his departure will cause to his family and begging him to go back. These confrontations are not without their ritual connections. To this day, in Southeast Asia, relatives of a candidate for ordination sometimes take on the role of Māra and his forces, and mimic opposition, standing in the doorway pretending to block his going forth, arguing that he really does not want to become a monk.

In another story, as the bodhisattva and Chandaka are fleeing, it apparently begins to rain. Chandaka, surprised at this, asks the cause, and it turns out that this is not rain that is falling, but the tears of the many deities who dwell in the harem of the palace and are mourning his leaving. Other divinities, however (Brahmā and Indra and their hosts are often featured) are clearly happy about the bodhisattva's great departure; they assist him in his journey and cheer him on by raining down on him showers and showers of blossoms (so many, in fact, that in one text, the horse Kanṭhaka is said to have difficulty cutting through the tangle of flowers and garlands that come up to his flanks). Here again, there may be ritual connections: today, at the time of a candidate's leaving home for the monastery, a ceremony is held in which various divinities – Brahmā, Indra, Śiva, Viṣṇu – are all invoked to come and protect the candidate and assist him in his endeavors. Alternatively, friends of the candidate may take on the role of these gods.

In any case, by morning, the bodhisattva and Chandaka find themselves on the bank of the river Anomiya, variously said to be located six, twelve, or thirty leagues from Kapilavastu. They have made good their escape, and now it is time for them to part, and for the bodhisattva to proceed on alone in his quest.

## THE MAKING OF A MONK

The bodhisattva's first acts after his Great Departure are to take off his princely jewels, to cut his hair with his own sword, and then to exchange his princely clothes for the robes of a monk. In some cases, these are provided to him by the gods, in others, he trades garments with a passing hunter who is actually the god Indra in disguise. All of these acts are, again, important parts of Buddhist ordination ceremonies in which candidates for ordination are divested of their ornaments, have their heads tonsured, and exchange their lay clothes for monastic robes. It is clear that, even though there is as yet no community (*saṃgha*) for the bodhisattva to join (he will have to found it), and no ritual prescriptions for him to follow (he will have to establish them), he is here portrayed as making himself into a Buddhist monk, a *bhikṣu*. As if the robes and tonsure were not specific enough, in one text, the god Brahmā also provides him at this time with the further requisites of a monk: a bowl, a razor, a needle, a belt, and a water-strainer.

After cutting his hair and taking off his ornaments and princely clothes, he must, however, also dispose of these things. The hair and the princely clothes are quickly taken by the gods up to heaven where they are enshrined as relics for the divinities to worship. The ornaments and other regalia are given to Chandaka who is now sent back to Kapilavastu with the horse. Chandaka is not eager to leave; in one text, it is clear that he considers it to be his duty to take care of the bodhisattva and protect him from wild beasts and brigands; in another, he expresses the wish that he too could renounce the world. It may be also that he is worried about the reception he will get when he returns to Kapilavastu after having helped the bodhisattva escape. Nor does the horse Kanṭhaka want to leave. In one tradition, in fact, he dies, broken-hearted, on the spot, and is immediately reborn as a god in heaven. In another, he goes back with Chandaka but then dies of grief a week later.

The dismissal of Chandaka and Kanṭhaka is important because they represent the bodhisattva's last tie binding him to his home. At the same time, as Foucher has shown, his refusal of their help corresponds to a more general dismissal of the help of the gods. Up until this point, various deities and divinities (at least in some biographies) have been heavily involved in most of the actions of the bodhisattva, intervening on his behalf and aiding him frequently. Though they continue to be present throughout his life, from here on, at least until his enlightenment, he will be much more on his own. As he was later to say to his disciples, he will have to "work out his own salvation with diligence," and do it in the midst of a "forest" that, in India, was seen as a terrifying place, filled not only with wild animals but dangerous spirits. Thus later, when the gods offer, in the midst of his fasting, to sustain him with divine nutrients fed through the pores of his skin, he turns them down, and when Indra offers to wash and sew a new robe for him, he again refuses, and does it himself. This "dismissal of the gods" will entail an important shift in tone from this point on in the biographical narrative. As Foucher put it: "Henceforth the mythomaniacs will be reined in by the theologians, and the legend will take a turn that is more scholastic than fantastic" (1987, p. 120).

The gods, however, are not the only ones whose help will be dispensed with. Shortly after dismissing Chandaka and Kanṭhaka, royal help is also rejected, in the form of the bodhisattva's refusal of King Bimbisāra's offer of half of his kingdom. This curious episode takes place when the bodhisattva arrives in Rājagṛha, the capital of Magadha. King Bimbisāra, seeing him from a distance, is tremendously impressed by his demeanor and invites him to receive untold wealth and power. But the bodhisattva is not to be tempted. Having abandoned his family and possible career as a *cakravartin*, he is not interested. Having dismissed the gods, he now dismisses the king, though he promises to come back once he has attained enlightenment.

It takes him a bit longer, however, to dismiss the spiritual help that he obtains from his first two teachers. As indicated at the start of this chapter, having wandered forth, the bodhisattva searches for a teacher, a common pattern among questers of the time. He apprentices himself first to Ārāḍa Kālāma and then to Udraka Rāmaputra. He quickly masters all that they can teach him, but, concluding that it does not conduce to enlightenment, to *nirvāṇa*, he leaves them and quests on alone. Ārāḍa is said by some to have been a teacher of Sāṃkhya dualism and Udraka a master of yoga, but what the bodhisattva learns from them is not doctrine but a meditation technique that enables him to achieve, mentally, the trance of no-thingness (under Ārāḍa) and then the trance of neither-perception-nor-non-perception (under Udraka). In Buddhist meditational schemes, these are said to be the seventh and eighth of the eight trance states (*dhyāna*), preliminary to the realization of cessation. At the same time, they may be thought of as advanced realizations in the realm of formlessness. In such states of mind, the meditator has quite removed him or herself not only from the sensory world but from the ordinary mental one as well. Buddhist enlightenment, however, involves not only abstracting oneself from the world but also perceiving it as it is. The realization of cessation that comes as a result of the formless trances is akin to *nirvāṇa*, but, as we shall see, the Buddha actually attains enlightenment not from the realm of formlessness (which comprises trances 5–8), but from the lower fourth level of trance, still in the realm of forms. This is a meditative state characterized by complete equanimity and mindfulness, in which the world has not been blotted out. Once again, we can see the middle-way mentality of Buddhism at work; the "world" should be transcended but it must not be left behind. In this light, it becomes clear why the bodhisattva concludes that what he has learned from Ārāḍa and Udraka is not conducive to enlightenment; it is not only that they have taken him "not far enough" (i.e., that there is another stage beyond trance states seven and eight, the realization of cessation), it is also that they have, in a sense, taken him "too far" (i.e., to trance states seven and eight, when he will attain enlightenment from trance state four).

## THE PRACTICE OF AUSTERITIES

One of the assumptions of Buddhism is that, in order to walk a "middle path," one has first to explore the extremes. There is a sense in which Ārāḍa and Udraka represent one such extreme, even though they are not usually presented as such. It is ironic but understandable, therefore, that, on quitting them, the bodhisattva embarks on another: the way of extreme austerities. These are quite graphically described in an "autobiographical" *sūtra* in which the Buddha recounts to a Jain monk named Saccaka the practices he undertook at the beginning of his quest. They are of two types: extreme breath-control, and extreme fasting.

The form of concentrated breath-retention that the bodhisattva undertakes consists of clenching the teeth and pressing the tongue to the palate so as to block off the respiratory passage. At first, holding his breath with his mouth and nose closed, results only in a very loud noise of air escaping through his ears. This causes him pain and does not lead to a state of calm. He therefore blocks his ears (we are not told how) and the result is that the inner breath hits the top of his skull, which causes loud sounds in his head, followed by intense headaches. Mastering these, he continues the practice but only to feel intense winds cutting through his stomach, followed by a fierce heat throughout his body. At this point, some divinities, observing him, believe that he is dead. Others claim he is not dead but an *arhat*. He is neither, of course, but the point seems to be that he has taken this practice of breath-retention as far as it will go, and it has not satisfied him.

The second austere practice he recounts is that of fasting. He tells Saccaka how he systematically cut down on his food consumption so that he was eating only a few drops of soup a day.

> Because I ate so little, all my limbs became like the joints of withered creepers; because I ate so little, my buttocks became like a bullock's hoof; because I ate so little, my protruding backbone became like a string of balls; because I ate so little, my gaunt ribs became like the crazy rafters of a tumble-down shed; because I ate so little, the pupils of my eyes appeared lying low and deep; because I ate so little, my scalp became shriveled and shrunk as a bitter white gourd. . . . If I thought "I will touch the skin of my belly" it was my backbone that I took hold of. If I thought: "I will touch my backbone," it was the skin of my belly that I took hold of. . . . If I thought: "I will obey the calls of nature," I fell down on my face then and there, because I ate so little. If, soothing my body, I stroked my limbs with my hand, the hairs, rotted at the roots, fell away. (Horner, 1954–59, 1, p. 300, slightly altered)

All of this, understandably, leads only to extreme pain: to feelings that are acute, sharp, severe. It does not lead to enlightenment. In the midst of this pain, however, the Buddha suddenly recalls the meditative experience he had as a child, sitting under the rose-apple tree, and he realizes that attainment can occur without such extreme asceticism. He resolves accordingly to resume eating, in moderate amounts, to adopt a diet that would not be indulgent, but would be adequate to sustain the body.

The "futility" of the way of extreme asceticism is not just realized mentally, it is also signalled somatically. In the "Introduction" to the *Jātaka Commentary*, as a result of his fasting, the bodhisattva's body loses not only its golden hue but also its thirty-two marks of the great man. It thus becomes clear, physiologically, that he is on the wrong track. Elsewhere, it is said that the bodhisattva collapses in a faint, and, just as in the case of his breath-control experiment, some deities think that he is dead. They make this known to the people of Kapilavastu, and there is great lamenting. Not everyone believes them, however; the Buddha's father, Śuddhodana, certain that his son would not pass away before becoming either a Buddha or a *cakravartin*, refuses to accept the news that he is dead.

Even more poignant is the tale found in the *Living out of the Game*. There, the false rumor about the bodhisattva's premature death reaches the Buddha's mother, Queen Māyā, who has been reborn as a deity in heaven. Stricken with grief, she comes down from heaven in the middle of the night, and, seeing her son lying there like a corpse, she begins to mourn, to weep and tear her hair and beat her breasts. She especially bemoans the fact that now the prophecies will not come true:

> When you were born in the garden called Lumbinī, O my son, like a lion you took seven steps forward all by yourself, and after gazing in the four directions, you pronounced these beautiful words: "This is my last birth". Now these words will go unfulfilled. When Asita declared: "He will be a Buddha in the world," his prophecy proved false. . . . Nor have you tasted the splendor which delights the heart of Cakravartin kings. O my son, without obtaining supreme Enlightenment, you have gone to your death in the forest! What a great affliction this is for me! To whom can I now turn for help? Who will give the breath of life back to my son? (Bays, 1983, p. 385)

Her lamentations are enough to rouse the bodhisattva from his stupor, but he does not recognize her, since she no longer has the body of his mother. When she identifies herself to him, however, he revives completely and utters a new determination to pursue his path to enlightenment. It is at that point that he decides to resume eating. Māyā, comforted, honors him with flower offerings and returns to her abode in heaven.

Self-starvation was, in ancient India, a practice commonly associated with the Jains, and indeed, the founder of the Jains, Mahāvira, a contemporary and rival of the Buddha, was famous for his austerities. It should be noted that Saccaka, to whom the Buddha addresses his discourse on his ascetic practices, was a Jain. It is thus quite possible that, in these descriptions of the bodhisattva's mortifications, we have an attempt by Buddhists to show the ultimate futility of the Jain enterprise.

It may also be that these various passages are aimed not only at Jains but at elements within the Buddhist community who were inclined towards such practices. At the same time, there is clearly a certain amount of oneupmanship in these stories, with the text going out of its way to make it clear that the Buddha practiced austerities more intensely and more thoroughly than anyone else, that he was, in André Bareau's (1963, p. 50) words, "a recordman of asceticism."

It is likely, however, that there is also something else at work here. The realization of the corpse-like nature of the body – "seeing the body-as-bones" – is even in Buddhism an important experiential step on the way to full enlightenment, for, like a cemetery meditation, it can be a means for seeing reality as it is. In his harem on the night of his great departure, the bodhisattva views the bodies of the sleeping women, and sees them as impure, impermanent, dead. In his practice of extreme asceticism, he realizes this about his own body, become skeletal through his mortifications. In this way, the two extremes come together, the two wrong paths of hedonism and asceticism that the Buddha rejects in favor of a Middle Way are paired as providing similar lessons: both need to be experienced and seen through in an ongoing quest.

The bodhisattva's realization, through his austerities, of the corpse-like nature of his body is reinforced in some texts by a curious episode. In the midst of his mortifications, he suddenly worries that the robes he has been wearing for six years have now become worn out. "How fine it would be," he thinks, "if I were to find something with which to cover myself" (Bays, 1983, p. 405). What he finds is a discarded shroud of a woman who has just died. He takes it, washes it (rejecting the god Indra's offer to wash it for him), and sews it into a "new" monk's robe. This, of course, is intended to explain the origin of the Buddhist monastic robe par excellence – the *paṃśukula* or "rag-heap" robe – but the insertion of the episode at this point in the narrative, at the end of his austerities, serves to reinforce the sense that the Buddha has come to realize his own corpse-like nature.

It also furthers the connections between the great departure and the ritual of ordination. In Buddhist ordination ceremonies, the candidate for monkhood, just prior to putting on his robes (ritually his "rag-heap robes," regardless of their actual origin) recites the fivefold formula of meditation on the perishable nature of the human body, the *tacapañcaka*. This consists of contemplating the first five of the thirty-two loathsome parts of the body: hair of the head, body hair, nails, teeth, skin. In this way, the ordinand, like the fasting Buddha of the biographies, ritually practices in an encapsulated form a cemetery meditation on himself, and its net effect is supposed to be to engender in him a vision of reality as it is.

## THE ABANDONMENT OF AUSTERITIES

The biographical tradition is generally agreed that it was the recollection of his meditation as a child under the rose-apple tree that prompted the bodhisattva to give up his extreme austerities. The *Book of the Discipline [Vinaya] of the Mūlasarvāstivādins* describes this decision succinctly:

> I remembered when, as a boy, I sat down in the shade of the rose-apple tree while attending a festival at the palace of my father Śuddhodana. At that time, I attained a trance state that was free from sensual desires, free from sinful and demeritorious things, thoughtful, reflective, arising from discrimination, and blissful. [And I thought]: "That must be the way, that must be the path that will lead to knowledge, seeing, and unsurpassed total enlightenment." (Strong, 1995, p. 16)

He realized, however, that that way could not be won while his body was weak, emaciated, and on edge with fasting, so "he began to take substantial food, porridge and gruel, and he rubbed his limbs with ghee and oil, and he took a warm bath . . . and gradually he regained his bodily strength, his vigor and energy" (Strong, 1995, p. 16). This is not succumbing to temptation or self-gratification, but the first definition of the Middle Way, a path between indulgence and self-denial, that will transform him from being a bodhisattva into being a fully enlightened buddha.

Another tradition was to present this realization of the Middle Way as the result of an intervention by the god Indra. While the bodhisattva is fasting, Indra comes down from heaven disguised as a three-string-lute player. When he plucks the first string, the bodhisattva observes that the sound is too shrill and the string so tight that it is on the verge of breaking. When he plucks the second string, he can hardly hear the sound at all for the string is too loose. Finally, he plucks the third string, presumably the middle one, and the sound is perfect, for the string is neither too tight (i.e., like extreme asceticism) nor too loose (i.e. like hedonism).

In artistic depictions of this scene, the bodhisattva is sometimes shown learning this lesson not only in the presence of Indra but of his five companions – the five ascetics who eventually become his first five disciples – and who, it should be remembered, are with him throughout the time of his austerities, said to be a period of six years. The presence of these five companions is usually eclipsed from the biographical narratives which focus on the bodhisattva's inner strivings, but one text, at least, gives them the role of attendant disciples: they sweep his cell, bring him his one grain of sesame or one grain of rice per day, and spend their time saying "Now he will become a Buddha! Now he will become a Buddha!" (Jayawickrama, 1990, p. 89.) In vain, they think he will achieve this status as a result of his super-asceticism. They are sorely disappointed, therefore, when the bodhisattva abandons his severe austerities and resumes eating solid food. When his body regains its golden hue and the thirty-two marks of the Great Man, they conclude that "he now leads a life of indulgence and has swerved from his exertions" (Jayawickrama, 1990, p. 90), and they abandon him, going off to take up residence in the Deer Park near Benares, where, in fact, they will eventually become the audience for the Buddha's First Sermon.

## THE OFFERING OF MILK-RICE

Shortly thereafter, there occurs an important episode featuring the offering of a meal of milk-rice by a local woman who is called Sujātā, or, in another tradition, by two local women who are named Nandā and Nandabalā, the daughters of a village headman. Again, the *Vinaya of the Mūlasarvāstivādins* describes the scene succinctly:

> Nandā and Nandabalā had heard that the bodhisattva was the prince of the Śākyas, who had been born in the foothills of the Himālayas ... not far from the hermitage of the sage Kapila, and that brahmin soothsayers had predicted he would become a *cakravartin* king. ... So they prepared for him, in a crystal bowl, some sweetened milk-rice condensed sixteen times. ...
>
> Then the bodhisattva consumed the milk-rice, and, after washing the bowl, he threw it into the Nairañjanā River. There the *nāgas* took hold of it. But the gods are aware of what happens down below, and Indra, king of the gods, took on the form of a *garuḍa* bird, stirred up the waters of the river, terrified the *nāgas*, took away the bowl, and instituted a Festival of the Bowl among the gods in his heaven.
>
> Then the bodhisattva asked Nandā and Nandabalā: "What did you seek by virtue of your gift?"
>
> They replied: "Blessed One, as a result of the merit of our gift and of our resolution, we would like to have you, the Prince of the Śākyas, as our

> husband, ... you who, the soothsayers predicted, would become a *cakravartin* king."
> The bodhisattva replied: "This is not possible; I am one who has wandered forth and have no desire for sensual pleasures."
> They said: "Blessed One, if that is the case, let the meritorious fruit of this act of giving be your highest enlightenment." (Strong, 1995, pp. 16–17)

Other biographical traditions were to develop some of the details of this episode at length. In the *Great Story (Mahāvastu)*, for instance, Sujātā is presented as having been the bodhisattva's mother in five hundred previous existences. She presents her offering to him so that he may attain buddhahood, and he responds by predicting her future enlightenment in a subsequent life. The "Introduction" to the *Jātaka Commentary*, on the other hand, describes Sujātā as a girl who has promised the deity of a banyan tree that she will give him a votive offering if she gives birth to a son. When her wish comes to pass and her son is born, she sends her maid to the tree to prepare the place for the offering. Finding the bodhisattva under the tree, the maid thinks that he is the tree-deity who has manifested himself in person to receive the meal.

In the *Living out of the Game*, the bodhisattva takes a bath in the river prior to his consumption of the milk-rice, and this becomes the occasion for various beings to collect relics of the future Buddha: the gods scoop up some of the river water in which the bodhisattva bathes and take it away to enshrine it in *stūpas* in their heavenly abodes; Sujātā gathers some of the Buddha's hairs (come off in the bath) and takes them back to her village; after his bath, a *nāga* princess prepares a throne for the bodhisattva to sit on, which she then she takes away after he has finished eating. Finally, the above-mentioned story of the relic of the discarded bowl, fought over by the *nāgas* and gods and eventually ending up enshrined in heaven, is also told.

In other texts, this bowl is made to act as a sort of omen of the bodhisattva's imminent enlightenment. In throwing the bowl into the river, he declares: "If I succeed in becoming a Buddha this day let this bowl go upstream; if not, let it go down with the current" (Jayawickrama, 1990, p. 93). The bowl, of course, miraculously floats upstream and then sinks down to the bottom of the river where it comes to rest on the bowls of the three previous buddhas of this aeon, who had all consumed their offerings of milk-rice at exactly the same spot. Hearing the sound of the bowl striking those of the bodhisattva's predecessors, the *nāga* king, Kāla, who has dwelt in the river for the whole of the aeon, realizes that it is time for another buddha to be enlightened.

Sujātā's (or Nandā and Nandabalā's) offering of milk-rice is important because it marks the start of the actual enlightenment process. It is a special meal that is said to be nutritious enough to sustain the bodhisattva for the next forty-nine days. Thus it and another special meal – the rice offering made to the Buddha seven weeks after his enlightenment by the merchants Trapuṣa and Bhallika – serve as a dietary frame for the enlightenment narrative. In the Pali tradition, the bodhisattva divides the milk-rice offering into forty-nine rice balls (*piṇḍa*) before eating it, an act that is significant because the word *piṇḍa* refers not only to offerings that are made to Buddhist monks on their begging rounds but also, in the pan-Indian tradition, to the lumps of rice that are given to the spirits of the dead. The number forty-nine reinforces this notion: forty-nine days (seven weeks) is often said to be the length of time between death and rebirth. Having just experienced himself as a corpse and had his demise announced as a result of his austerities, the metaphor, it would seem, is here continued: the Buddha-to-be is given food fit for the dead. With the offering of milk-rice, he may be thus thought to be entering a sort of liminal period, which will last for seven weeks, during which he will neither eat, nor defecate, nor bathe. During this rite of passage, he will make himself into a Buddha. It is noteworthy that in parts of Northern Thailand, Sujātā's offering is reenacted at the ritual consecration of Buddha images which also serves to make them into buddhas. Forty-nine bowls of milk-rice are ritually prepared, offered to the image and then to the monks, and consumed by those participating in the ceremony. Truly, this is Buddha-making food.

Thus nourished, the bodhisattva approaches the bodhi tree which, in all traditions, is the site of his enlightenment. The *Living out of the Game (Lalitavistara)* devotes an entire chapter to describing his procession to the bodhi tree, and its cosmic reverberations. On the way, he meets the *nāga* king Kālika and his wife who honor him, and foretell his imminent enlightenment. Near the tree, he encounters the grass-cutter Svastika, who provides eight bundles of *kuśa* grass for him to sit on in this the culmination of his quest for enlightenment. In the Pali tradition, he must find the exact spot where he should sit down. He first goes to the southern side of the bodhi tree, but when he stops there, the great earth begins to quake in protest. So he goes on around the tree to its western side, but the same thing occurs. It happens again on the northern side. Finally, when he reaches the eastern side of the tree, he perceives no earth quaking: this is the stable spot at which all buddhas before him have attained enlightenment, and here he lays down his grass seat. This search for the right spot is presented slightly differently in the *Living out of the Game*. While the bodhisattva is approaching the bodhi tree, the deities adorn and enhance no fewer than eighty thousand bodhi trees, setting up magnificent thrones at the base of each of them, hoping to entice the bodhisattva to sit and attain enlightenment under *their* tree. Out of compassion for them, the bodhisattva creates a miraculous display called the *lalitavyūha* (the "playful arrangement") in which he causes his body to appear seated under each and every tree simultaneously. Then, returning to reality for the sake of regular beings, he approaches the "real" bodhi tree and lays his seat down there. In both traditions, as he sits down, he makes a famous vow: "My body may shrivel up, my skin, my bones, my flesh may dissolve, but [I] will not move from this very seat until I have obtained enlightenment" (Bays, 1983, p. 439; cp. Jayawickrama, 1990, p. 94).

## THE DEFEAT OF MĀRA

It is at this point that his final trial and temptation occur. Māra, the Wicked One, who has been watching the bodhisattva ever since his great departure, makes a final attempt to prevent his enlightenment. Māra is often thought of as a demonic figure, the Buddhist equivalent of Satan, but this is somewhat misleading. He is actually a high-ranking god, one of the chief divinities of the realm of desire, and so a lord of death and rebirth. He is by nature opposed to any attempt by anyone to escape from his realm, hence his antagonism towards the Buddha. We have already seen how he tried to block the bodhisattva's wandering forth. In a *sūtra* that prefigures his assault on the Buddha under the bodhi tree, he is further portrayed as trying to get the bodhisattva to give up his ascetic strivings and to return home to Kapilavastu to do good works and make merit as a *cakravartin* king.

Māra has good cause to worry about the bodhisattva escaping from his realm. Not only has he followed his career from the start; in one text, he is said to have had thirty-two bad dreams in which he saw his own dwelling, family, and self defeated and destroyed in various ways as a result of the wandering forth. His opposition to the bodhisattva on the seat of enlightenment takes on three basic forms: armed attack, assertion of superior merit, and attempt at seduction.

The armed assault is most graphically described, perhaps, in the *Great Story (Mahāvastu)*: Māra dons his armor, mounts his thousand-horse chariot, and rallies his troops

> of frightful and monstrous beasts which made a rumbling clamour. Some of these beasts had the faces of horses, others of buffaloes, others of asses, others of goats, ... rams, ... deer, ... lions, ... tigers, ... panthers, ... bears, ... dogs, ... hogs, ... cats, ... ravens, ... cocks, ... vultures, ... eagles. Some were headless trunks, others were one-headed, others many-headed, others two-headed. Some were eyeless, others one-eyed. Some were without hands, others without feet. Some were without arms, others had ten arms. Some carried knives, others swords, others hatchets, ... spears, ... pikes, ... tridents, ... ploughshares, ... discuses, ... clubs, ... hammers, ... axes, ... scimitars. ... Some breathed fire from their mouths, others snakes. Some brandished in the air wheels with blades on their rims. Some rushed on foot against the bodhisattva carrying an elephant, others carrying a buffalo, others a horse, ... an ass, ... a headless trunk, ... skulls, ... mountain-tops, ... whole trees including the roots. (Jones, 1949–56, 2, pp. 364–65)

But none of these monsters frightens the bodhisattva in the least. In the "Introduction" to the *Jātaka Commentary*, this assault takes the form of nine storms – of wind, rain, rocks, weapons, embers, ashes, sand, mud, and darkness – which Māra launches against the bodhisattva, but each is thwarted in turn: the gale-force winds fail to ripple even the hem of his robe; the downpour of rain fails to wet him; the rocks are turned into garlands, the weapons into flowers, the embers, ashes, and sand into sandalwood powder and different kinds of blossoms, the mud into scented ointment, and the darkness is quickly dissolved by the Buddha who shines like the sun.

Māra next tries to claim that, by right, the seat of enlightenment should be his rather than the bodhisattva's, due to his superior merit. The claim is not completely ridiculous; to reach the divine position that he holds Māra must indeed have spent many lifetimes doing meritorious activities. The bodhisattva points out, however, that he has not practiced the ten perfections during countless aeons, and he asks Māra who will testify to his good deeds. Māra counters by pointing to his army and saying "All these are my witnesses" and indeed, his followers do acclaim him. Māra then asks the bodhisattva, who is alone, who will be *his* witness? In response, the bodhisattva reaches out with his right hand and touches the ground, and calls on the earth to testify to his merit, and the earth resounds and echoes with a roar of affirmation, such that Māra's hosts flee in panic. This gesture of touching the ground became formalized iconographically as the "earth-touching *mudrā*" and came to be one of the most popular ways of depicting the Buddha, recalling this crucial moment of victory over Māra.

In other versions of this scene, the earth is actually personified as a great goddess, Sthāvarā. Emerging with the upper half of her body out of the ground, and accompanied by a whole throng of goddesses, she bows with joined hands to the bodhisattva and says: "Just so, Great Being. It is indeed as you have declared! We appear to attest to it" (Bays, 1983, p. 482). In Southeast Asia and elsewhere, this episode came to be connected to the further tradition of the earth-goddess wringing out her hair when she appears, thereby creating a flood that routs the forces of Māra. The explanation behind this must stem from a ritual tradition; throughout South and Southeast Asia, it is common for persons who make merit or wish to transfer it to others to mark the occasion by ritually pouring out some water on to the ground. The theory here is that, over the aeons, all of the water (whether actual or not does not matter) that the bodhisattva poured out on to the ground (i.e., on to the Earth-Mother's head) while doing great deeds of merit was retained in the goddess's hair. Thus the water that she wrings out of her hair is quite accurately a measure of the merit made by the bodhisattva, and, as popular depictions of the scene attest, it is enough to drown Māra's army.

Māra's third attempt to halt the bodhisattva in his progress towards buddhahood is to get his daughters to seduce him. Sometimes, as we shall see, his daughters, who are allegorically identified with Pleasure, Restlessness, and Desire, appear *after* the Buddha's enlightenment and try to distract him then. In the *Living out of the Game (Lalitavistara)* and related traditions, however, Māra calls on his many daughters, all of them goddesses, to go to the seat of enlightenment and to try to seduce the bodhisattva there and then. They do so by manifesting the "thirty-two kinds of feminine wiles" which are described in the text. Conscious of the fact that different kinds of women may appeal to different kinds of men, they take on the forms of young girls, young women with young children, more mature middle-aged women, and older women. They also sing to the bodhisattva a song about springtime and its pleasures, inviting him pretty explicitly to come and enjoy himself with them. But this is all nautch for nought; the bodhisattva remains unmoved, and untempted, and rejects their advances in no uncertain terms. When they return to their father, Māra, they acknowledge their failure. Their places are taken by eight goddesses of the bodhi tree who sing sixteen verses in praise of the bodhisattva, and then by a host of deities who appear and mock Māra and predict his defeat. Māra attempts to rally his forces one last time, but, in fact, he has failed utterly.

## ENLIGHTENMENT

The bodhisattva's enlightenment – that which finally makes him a "buddha" – an "awakened one" – takes place during the night following his defeat of Māra. It is generally described as consisting in the acquisition of three "knowledges" (*vidyā*), one in each of the three watches of the night, though some texts give a list of six. The realization of buddhahood is thus not so much a single experience as a set of interrelated experiences, the result of many years and lifetimes of striving. Moreover, it is not something that is achieved in one's ordinary frame of mind; sitting under the bodhi tree, the bodhisattva starts by entering into the first level of meditative trance, the very same as he had achieved as a boy under the rose-apple tree. He then proceeds to enter the second, third, and fourth levels of meditative trance, achieving a state of concentration "which has neither anguish nor joy and is entirely purified by equanimity and mindfulness" (Horner, 1954–59, 1, p. 302).

We have already seen that the fourth level of trance is important as the stage from which the bodhisattva attains enlightenment. Significantly, it is characterized by a mental state that still perceives the realm of forms and is not completely abstracted from this world. Traditionally, it is said to be from the fourth level of trance that a meditator attains the six "superknowledges" (*abhijñā*). Five of these are said to be mundane, i.e., directed towards this world: the knowledge of certain magical powers such as levitation and the creation of illusory forms, the attainment of the "divine ear" enabling one to hear all sounds everywhere, the ability to read minds, the ability to recall one's former lives, and the attainment of the "divine eye" enabling one to see all beings dying and being reborn according to their deeds. The sixth is said to be supermundane, i.e., directed beyond this world: the knowledge of the elimination of all mental impurities (*āśravas*). This list is important because the three knowledges (*vidyā*) that define the Buddha's enlightenment experience are, in fact, the fourth, fifth, and sixth superknowledges (*abhijñā*).

Thus, in the first watch of the night, with his mind composed, the bodhisattva directs his thoughts towards his own former existences, remembering one birth, two births, three, four, five, ten, twenty, a hundred, a thousand, hundreds of thousands of births. He reviews aeons and aeons of lifetimes during which he recalls:

> I was such and such a person, my name was this, my race was this, my lineage was this, my caste was this, the food I ate was such and such, this the span of life, this the length of time that I remained there; this the happiness and unhappiness which I experienced (Bays, 1983, p. 518).

This recalling of his own karmic history – ending with his final birth in Lumbinī – is important. It is not only one of the superknowledges resulting from the fourth level of trance, but it also gives a temporal dimension to the Buddha's realization. It shows that there was never, until now, a time for him in which death and rebirth did not exist. It is a direct review of the path he took, of the names (*nāma*) and forms (*rūpa*) he had and of the law of karma that governed those names and forms. For this reason I call it "karmalogical knowledge." This review helps both reinforce and undermine the notion of self. It reinforces it in that it shows the process of enlightenment to be the result of ongoing and continuous striving by one karmic "individual." It undermines it in that it shows that individual to have had no single self, to have been many different beings reborn in many situations with many identities.

In the second watch of the night, the bodhisattva directs his still-composed mind towards the passing and arising of other beings. With his so-called "divine eye" (another superknowledge resulting from the fourth level of trance), he surveys the whole cosmos and looks upon beings who are good, beings who are bad, beings who are in between. He sees some who are dying and who, as a result of their meritorious actions, and as a result of their right views, are then reborn in one of the heavens; he sees others who are dying and who, as a result of their demeritorious actions, and as a result of their wrong views, are then reborn in one of the hells. He sees beings reborn as hungry ghosts, as animals, as humans. This vision of other beings in the different realms of rebirth gives a spatial dimension to the Buddha's realization. It shows that there is no place of refuge, no state of existence in this cosmos, where one can escape death and rebirth, and for this reason, I call it "cosmological knowledge." It also shows that the law of karma applies universally, and it helps make the point that the Buddha's realization is not a selfish one; it is compassionately oriented towards comprehension of the situation of others.

In the third watch of the night, the bodhisattva directs his still-composed mind to a direct understanding of reality as-it-is. This is "dharmalogical knowledge" in which the Truth is realized doctrinally, analytically. Accordingly, depending on which specific doctrinal terms are used, different accounts of this third-watch experience describe it differently. In some texts, in accordance with the definition of "super-knowledges" given above, what is emphasized is the realization of the destruction of the *āśravas*, a term that is sometimes translated as "intoxicants" or "cankers" or "evil inclinations" or "impurities" or "outflows". *Āśravas* are all the negative influences that attach a person to this world, and are seen as flowing out towards this world. Specifically, they come to be defined as sensual desire (*kāma*), clinging to existence (*bhāva*), speculative views (*dṛṣṭi*) and ignorance (*avidyā*).

Often the knowledge of the destruction of the *āśravas* is paired in the description of the Buddha's third-watch experience with a realization of the Four Noble Truths: the truth of suffering (*duḥkha*), of the origin of suffering, of the cessation of suffering, and of the path to the cessation of suffering. The Four Noble Truths were to become one of the fundamental doctrinal statements of the Buddhist tradition. They were the subject matter of the Buddha's first sermon at the Deer Park in Sarnath and I shall examine them more thoroughly when we come to that sermon. Suffice it to say here that although the truth of suffering is never identified as an *āśrava* (it is, rather a consequence of the *āśravas*), the analytical scheme of the Four Noble Truths nevertheless gets applied to the *āśravas*. Thus, the Buddha is said, in this third watch of the night, to realize not only the four Noble Truths about suffering, but also the "truth of the *āśravas*, the origin of the *āśravas*, the cessation of the *āśravas*, and the way to the cessation of the *āśravas*" (Bareau, 1963, pp. 86–87).

Other texts, however, define this dharmalogical realization in terms of the doctrine of interdependent origination (*pratītya-samutpāda*). This Buddhist theory of causation posits a series of two-way links that tie together not only suffering, desire, and ignorance, but also the very world as we know it, with its physical forms (including our bodies), sense perceptions, feelings, consciousnesses, and the processes of rebirth itself.

The basic causal principle at work here is described as follows: "When this is, that comes to be; from the arising of this that arises. [And conversely], when this is not that does not come to be; from the non-arising of this, that does not arise" (Strong, 1995, pp. 99). Applying this, the Buddha comes to realize that what he calls "this great heap of suffering" (i.e., old age, death, sorrow, lamentation, suffering, depression, and dismay) is due to rebirth, which in turn is due to coming-to-be, which is due to clinging-to-existence, which is due to desire, which is due to feelings, which are due to contact, which is due to the six senses, which are due to individuality (name and form), which is due to consciousness, which is due to karmic constituents, which are due to ignorance. The elimination of ignorance, therefore, will result in the elimination of all the other links of the chain and ultimately of suffering.

However it is described, the Buddha's doctrinal realization marks the end of his enlightenment experience, and this is generally signalled in the biographies by an ecstatic proclamation. In the *Vinaya of the Mūlasarvāstivādins*, having realized the Four Noble Truths, he declares: "Destroyed is rebirth for me; consumed is my striving; done is what had to be done; I will not be born into another existence!" (Strong, 1995, p. 17, slightly altered.) In the *Great Story (Mahāvastu),* he makes a "doubt-dispelling utterance" to the deities who want to know whether he in fact has reached nirvāṇa: "Having cut off craving, I have rid myself of defilement. The dried-up *āśravas* do not flow. The road of craving has been cut off, and is no longer there. This then is the end of suffering" (Jones, 1949–56, 2, p. 368, slightly altered). In the *Living out of the Game*, he says much the same thing, except that the divinities demand a more graphic sign of his enlightenment, and the Buddha obliges them by levitating into the air "to the height of seven palm trees" (Bays, 1983, p. 524). In the "Introduction" to the *Jātaka Commentary*, he makes this utterance said to be customary with all buddhas:

> Through the round of many births I roamed without reward, without rest, seeking the house-builder. Painful is birth again & again. House-builder, you're seen! You will not build a house again. All your rafters broken, the ridge pole destroyed, gone to the Unformed, the mind has come to the end of craving (Thanissaro, 1998, pp. 43–44; see also Jayawickrama, 1990, p. 100).

# 4 TEACHINGS AND COMMUNITY

With Gautama's enlightenment, the aeons and aeons he spent as a bodhisattva have come to a close; he is henceforth a buddha – "the Buddha" as far we are concerned – and as such he will make known his doctrine (his Dharma) to the world, and establish a community (*saṃgha*) of followers. But the experience of *nirvāṇa* is momentous; it takes a while for him to readjust. In what follows, therefore, I shall first look at the weeks immediately following the Buddha's enlightenment which feature, among other things, his decision to preach the Dharma. I shall then consider his first sermon at Benares, and his second sermon there along with other early teachings. I shall then look at further conversions he makes in Benares and in Magadha, where he continues to build his community. Finally, I want also to examine his return to his hometown of Kapilavastu where he converts many of his own family members.

## THE WEEKS FOLLOWING ENLIGHTENMENT

Immediately after his enlightenment, the Buddha spent some weeks in the vicinity of the bodhi tree in Bodhgaya. The biographies generally agree that these weeks were important but they differ in their descriptions of what events marked them. Basically, two accounts may be found: an orderly one that lists seven post-enlightenment weeks and systematically recalls the events which took place during each one of them, and which connect them to particular sites of pilgrimage in Bodhgaya; and a narrative account that is more casual in its definition of the weeks and where they were spent but that seeks to tell a story coherently connecting a number of post-enlightenment experiences.

We may use as our guide to the first, the account found in the "Introduction" (*Nidāna-kathā*) to the *Jātaka Commentary*. In this text, we are told that the Buddha, after making his ecstatic utterance of enlightenment, reflects that the place where he is seated is a unique place, and so he resolves not to rise from it quite yet, and spends the next seven days there under the bodhi tree, experiencing the bliss of emancipation (or, alternatively, formulating the law of interdependent origination, in those sources in which he has not yet worked it out). Divinities, seeing him remain there, come to think that perhaps his enlightenment is not complete, perhaps there is still more to come. So as to dispel their doubts, the Buddha, at the end of this first week, flies up into the air and performs a miracle display. He then goes to a place slightly removed from the bodhi tree, called the "shrine of the steadfast gaze," where he stands for a second week staring with unblinking eyes at the seat of enlightenment, thinking that that was where he attained omniscience. The third week he spends practicing walking meditation, going back and forth along a path that comes to be known as the "shrine of the jewelled meditation walkway." The fourth week is spent thinking out the seven books of the Abhidharma in a hut called the "shrine of the house of gems." Then he goes to a place called the "banyan tree of the goatherd," and there, further enjoying the bliss of emancipation for another week, he also has another encounter with Māra's daughters who, wishing to cheer up their despondent father, think they can seduce the now fully enlightened Buddha. In the sixth week, the weather turns cold and it begins to rain. The Buddha stays at a place called Mucilinda, where he is sheltered by a great *nāga*, the serpent king Mucilinda, who winds his coils around him seven times and shelters him from the downpour with his hood. From Mucilinda, the Buddha then goes to the Rājāyatana tree where he sits for the final, seventh week, experiencing the bliss of meditating on the path and its fruits.

Towards the end of this seventh week, while he is still seated under the Rājāyatana tree, two merchants, Trapuṣa and Bhallika, pass by with a caravan of carts. Encouraged by a local divinity who had been their mother in a former existence, they stop their carts in order to make an offering of food (a sweetened rice dish) to the Buddha under the tree. The Blessed One, at this point, has eaten nothing since the milk-rice given him by Sujāta, forty-nine days earlier. Moreover, he does not even have a bowl in which to receive Trapuṣa and Bhallika's offering, having discarded in the river the bowl Sujāta gave him. The four divine guardians of the four quarters, however, are quick to spot his predicament, and, always ready to help out, they come down from heaven, each one bringing a bowl. The Buddha, not wishing to upset any one of them, accepts all four bowls and fuses them together into a single receptacle. In this, he then accepts and consumes the merchants' offering, and, in gratitude to them, he thanks them with a few words of Dharma. As a result, they become his first lay disciples, taking "double refuge" in him and in the Dharma (there being, as yet, no *saṃgha*). Finally, in recognition of their need for something to venerate after his departure, the Buddha gives them eight hairs from his head, which they take away and enshrine as relics in their home country.

All of this then culminates in a very important event. After taking leave of Trapuṣa and Bhallika (and so, technically, after the end of the seventh week), the Buddha returns to the banyan of the goat herder and there he reflects that the doctrine (the Dharma) that he has discovered is "deep, difficult to see, and difficult to understand," and that people in this world are given to passion and pleasure and are generally ignorant, so that they will not be able to understand such things as interdependent origination and the need to destroy desire and the elimination of *āśravas*. He wonders, therefore, whether he should even attempt to communicate his enlightenment experience to others, whether or not a career as a teacher will be, for him, nothing more than an exercise in futility.

This, obviously, is a rather crucial decision. There were, in the Buddhist tradition, beings known as *pratyekabuddhas* ("Buddhas for themselves alone") who attained buddhahood much like Gautama but then refrained from teaching the Dharma to others, but lived on in solitary enjoyment of the bliss of emancipation. The option not to preach thus was a real one. Fortunately, at this point in the story, the god Brahmā, worried that all will be lost if Gautama does not communicate the Dharma to others, decides to take action. Coming down from heaven, he implores the Blessed One to agree to teach, pointing out that there are, indeed, some beings who will be able to understand and attain enlightenment, and arguing that, otherwise, the land of Magadha (and by extension, the whole world) will be left in the benighted condition it has been in.

The *Discourse on the Fourfold Assembly* (*Catuṣpariṣat-sūtra*) and the related *Discipline* (*Vinaya*) *of the Mūlasarvāstivādins* present an account of post-enlightenment events that puts things in a rather different order and in a more narrative framework. It is also possible to detect seven events in their sequence but they are not thought to take a whole week each. Initially, the Buddha does spend a week at the foot of the bodhi tree, enjoying the bliss of emancipation. There he is visited by two deities from Brahmā's heaven who are concerned that no one has given him any alms, but who, rather than give him food themselves, shower praises upon him. At the end of the seven days, the two merchants Trapuṣa and Bhallika arrive and take care of the alms problem by offering the Buddha a meal of milk and much honey. The meal, however, upsets the Buddha's stomach (it gives him gas). Knowing that he is thus suffering, Māra then approaches him and urges him to pass immediately into complete extinction. The Buddha refuses. The god Indra then arrives on the scene and gives the Buddha a medicinal myrobalan fruit to ease his stomach pain. The cure is effective. The Buddha then goes to the abode of the *nāga* Mucilinda who protects him from the rain for seven days. He then returns to the bodhi tree where he reflects on the doctrine of interdependent origination for seven days. Then he reflects that the Dharma he has found is profound and that no one will be able to understand him, at which point Brahmā himself comes to implore him to teach.

Comparing these two accounts, we can see very clearly how the first has been affected by the pilgrimage tradition. Each week is associated with a particular spot, so that the first column in Table 4.1 actually features places as much as it does events. We know also from the accounts of Chinese pilgrims that many of these places were important sites of veneration in the immediate vicinity of the bodhi tree at Bodhgaya. Thus, Xuanzang mentions, in addition to the bodhi tree, the place where the Buddha performed walking meditation for a week, the place where he gazed steadfastly at the seat of enlightenment for a week, and the jewel house. Faxian adds to this the story of the *nāga* Mucilinda and the goatherd's banyan tree. It is easy to imagine how serious-minded pilgrims, intent on recalling the Buddha's experience, might spend a week venerating each spot. Moreover, as mentioned before, the careful counting, in this tradition, of the number of days (7 × 7), during which the Buddha is sustained by Sujātā's milk-rice, may be connected to notions of the liminal period between death and life, or, more appropriately here, between absence and presence. In this context, the Buddha's decision to preach, at the end of this period, can be seen as a

*Table 4.1 Two versions of the post-enlightenment weeks*

| "Introduction" (*Nidāna-kathā*) to the *Jātaka Commentary* | Discourse on the Fourfold Assembly (*Catuṣpariṣat-sūtra*) |
|---|---|
| *Week 1*: under bodhi tree. Gods are worried he has not moved. Affirmation of enlightenment to the gods | Under the bodhi tree. Visit of two gods, who worry he has not eaten. Affirmation of enlightenment |
| *Week 2*: at shrine of the steadfast gaze, looking at the seat of enlightenment | Meal offered by Trapuṣa and Bhallika |
| *Week 3*: walking back and forth at the shrine of the jewelled meditation walkway | Suffers from flatulence; Māra urges him to enter final extinction |
| *Week 4*: at the shrine of the house of gems built by Indra, reflecting on the Abhidharma | Receives medicinal myrobalan from Indra |
| *Week 5*: at the banyan tree of the goatherd. Māra's daughters attempt to seduce him | Sheltered by the *nāga* Mucilinda |
| *Week 6*: at Mucilinda's tree, sheltered by the *nāga* Mucilinda | Under the bodhi tree. Reflects on interdependent origination |
| *Week 7*: under the Rājayātana tree: receives offering from Trapuṣa and Bhallika. After the week is over, Brahmā implores him to preach | Brahmā implores him to preach |

decision to "re-enter" this world, to be present within it, for a while longer, at any rate. The second account, in the second column, on the other hand, seems more or less oblivious to the pilgrimage tradition. It mentions only by name one place, the bodhi tree. It clearly is very concerned about the question of food offerings, but the counting of the number of days (7 × 7) breaks down. Some events last a week, others, just a moment. The two accounts both lead up, however, to the same conclusion: the Buddha's decision, prompted by Brahmā, to preach the doctrine.

## THE FIRST SERMON: THE MIDDLE WAY AND THE FOUR NOBLE TRUTHS

Having made up his mind to remain in the world and teach, the Buddha must, however, decide to whom he should give his first sermon. His first thought is to go back and tell his new-found doctrine to his former teachers, Ārāḍa and Udraka, but he realizes that both of them have recently passed away. So he resolves instead to teach his former five companions with whom he had practiced austerities (before they abandoned him when he opted to start eating again). They, it will be recalled, had repaired to the Deer Park at Sarnath near Benares, and, with that in mind, the Buddha sets out to find them.

On his way, he meets a wandering ascetic, the *ājīvika* Upaka who is impressed by his demeanor and asks him who his master is. The Buddha replies that he has no master, that, on his own, he has become an *arhat*, a Victor (*Jina*), and that he is on his way to Benares to "beat the drum of deathlessness in a world that is blind." Upaka is non-commital. Rather than become a disciple of the Buddha, he merely says "it is possible," and goes on his way. The Buddha next comes to the Ganges river which he must cross. The ferryman asks him to pay the toll for crossing, but the Buddha has no money, has no regard for money, and has given up the use of money. The ferryman is not about to let him ride for free, so the Buddha passes over the river by flying through the air. These two stories, which are most developed in the *Great Story (Mahāvastu)*, are not thematically unrelated to each other. They both reassert the greatness of the Buddha's achievement, but also share in common the message that not everyone will recognize that greatness, that the Buddha's task of spreading the Dharma to others is not necessarily going to be an easy one. Questers such as the *ājīvika* Upaka may not be impressed by his claims, and laypersons, such as the ferryman, may not be overwhelmed by his charisma.

Things change a bit, however, when, finally, the Buddha arrives in Benares. His five former companions are still upset with him for having given up the way of asceticism, and seeing him arrive from a distance, they resolve to snub him. But seeing him up close, they are willy-nilly attracted to him, and they welcome him, calling him by his name and saying "friend." The Buddha immediately reprimands them, telling them that he is a fully enlightened *tathāgata arhat*, a self-awakened sage who has attained *nirvāṇa* and who teaches the Dharma; he should not casually be addressed by his name and called "friend." He then sits down and preaches a sermon which in most biographies is called the "Setting in Motion of the Wheel of the Dharma" ("*Dharmacakrapravartana-sūtra*"). This is famous as the first discourse of the Buddha, and in it he clarifies both the Middle Way and the doctrine of the Four Noble Truths. The version found in the *Great Story (Mahāvastu)* begins as follows:

> Once, when the Blessed One was dwelling in Benares, at the Deer Park in Ṛṣivadana, he spoke to the "Fortunate Five," the group of elders who were his first disciples.
>
> "Monks," he said, "for one who has wandered forth, there are two extremes. What two? On the one hand, there is attachment to sensual pleasures; this is vulgar, common, ignoble, purposeless, and not conducive to a chaste and studious life, to disgust with the world, to aversion from passion, to cessation, monkhood, enlightenment or *nirvāṇa*. On the other hand, there is addiction to exhausting the self through asceticism; this is suffering, ignoble, and purposeless. Monks, for one who has wandered forth, these are the two extremes. Staying with the Tathāgatha's Noble Doctrine and Discipline, away from both of these extremes, is the middle course, fully realized [by the Buddha] bringing about insight, and conducive to tranquillity, disgust with the world, aversion from passion, cessation, monkhood, enlightenment, and *nirvāṇa*." (Strong, 1995, pp. 32–33)

This Middle Way, he further explains, consists of eight limbs. Two are related to wisdom: right views and right discrimination; three are related to correct ethical conduct: right speech, right action, and right livelihood; and three are related to meditation: right effort, right mindfulness, and right concentration.

The Buddha then turns to focus on the Four Noble Truths. These can, in brief, be described as follows: that life in all realms of rebirth is ultimately unsatisfactory, suffering (*duḥkha*). This is true by definition. As the Buddha puts it in his sermon: "Birth is suffering, old age is suffering, sickness is suffering, death is suffering. Involvement with what is unpleasant is suffering. Separation from what is pleasant is suffering. Also, not getting what one wants and strives for is suffering." Indeed, the very constituents that make up the personality (the *skandhas*, on which, see below) are suffering. Secondly, there is a reason for this suffering, an origin (*samudaya*) which is bound up with desire, a thirst that leads us to cling to possessions, to persons, to life itself. This thirst, as the Buddha points out, can occasionally be satisfied, but it cannot ultimately be assuaged. Thirdly, nonetheless, there is a thing such as freedom from or the cessation (*nirodha*) of this unsatisfactory state, this suffering, which will come with the rooting out of its causes, the elimination of that ongoing thirst. The Buddha describes this as being "without passion, [a state of] cessation, forsaking, abandoning, renunciation." Finally, the Buddha concludes, the way to do this is to practice the Noble Eightfold Path (*mārga*), described above.

At the conclusion of this sermon, it is said that the eldest of the five disciples of the Buddha, Kauṇḍinya, perceived the truth of the Buddha's words, and the Buddha immediately ordained him as a monk by uttering the simple formula, "Come, monk, the Dharma is well proclaimed. Follow the chaste course to the complete termination of suffering" (Robinson and Johnson, 1997, p. 33). Eventually, the four other members of the group of five also came to understand and to be ordained as monks. The first sermon thus led directly to the first formation of the Buddhist community, the *saṃgha*.

## THE SECOND SERMON AT BENARES: NON-SELF AND IMPERMANENCE

The "Discourse on the Setting in Motion of the Wheel of the Dharma" was not the only sermon preached by the Buddha to the group of five. Various sources hint at various other teachings, but among these the most famous is the second sermon of the Buddha in which he relates his teaching on suffering to two other cornerstones of Buddhist doctrine: his teaching on non-self (*anātman*) and his teaching on impermanence (*anitya*). The version found in the *Great Story (Mahāvastu)* begins as follows: "And [the Buddha] addressed the venerable good group of five saying, 'Monks, body [*rūpa*] is not the self ... If, monks, the body were the self, it would not be liable to affliction and suffering ...'" (Jones, 1949–56, 3, pp. 328–29, slightly altered). It is clear that by "self" (*ātman*), the Buddha has in mind here something very particular – something unchangeable, permanent, ineffable, and fundamentally different from this world, something, in other words, very much like the notion of the Absolute Self in the Upaniṣads. Some people may find it useful to think of it as a "Soul" rather than a "self." If the body were such a Soul, it should not be liable to sickness, old age, and death. But since it does suffer those things, it must be not-soul (*anātman*). The same analysis is then applied to the other *skandhas* (aggregates), the constituents that make up an individual personality: feeling (*vedanā*), perception (*saṃjñā*), the karmic constituents (*saṃskāras*), and consciousness (*vijñāna*). All these are declared likewise to be "not-self" (*anātman*). (Jones, 1949–56, 3, pp. 331ff.)

Part and parcel of this view is the understanding that the body as well as the other aggregates (*skandhas*) are also impermanent (*anitya*), unstable, subject to change. And it is this doctrine of impermanence that the Buddha puts forth next in his sermon to the group of five. With this, then, they come to realize what the tradition was later to call the "three marks" of existence: namely that all composite things are characterized by suffering (*duḥkha*), by impermanence (*anitya*) and by not-self (*anātman*). Having come to realize (and not just understand) this through the Buddha's teaching, the five monks attain enlightenment and are freed, like the Buddha before them, from the intoxicating influences (*āśravas*) that bind them to the world. At that point, we are told, there are six enlightened beings in the world (the five plus the Buddha).

## OTHER TEACHINGS TO THE GROUP OF FIVE

Finally, according to some texts, the Buddha preaches yet another sermon in Benares. In this, he presents for the first time his analysis of sensory reality as being made up of: material forms that can be cognized by the eye; sounds that can be cognized by the ear; smells that can be cognized by the nose; tastes that can be cognized by the tongue; and tangibles that can be cognized by the body. All that is missing from this list of what came to be known as the twelve spheres of reality (*āyatanas*), is the addition of mental factors that can be cognized by the mind. In the present sermon, the Buddha is more concerned with warning his disciples that the various sense-spheres can be a trap in which they can be caught just as certainly as a deer is entangled by the snares of a hunter. If, however, they discipline their minds so as to see the sense-spheres for what they are and not be enslaved or infatuated by them, then they will be like a deer who lies down in the forest on top of a hunter's trap but is not caught by it. Such a deer can live in the forest, walking, standing, sitting down, and going to sleep confidently. The deer metaphor seems particularly apt here, in view of the setting of the sermon in the Deer Park at Benares, but the Buddha extends it to compare the hunter and his traps to Māra and his wiles. He then ends the sermon by instructing his five disciples in the techniques of disciplining the mind through meditational trances.

None of these sermons is very lengthy, but, taken together they establish a basis of Buddhist doctrine that was to be elaborated on by the Buddha and by the subsequent tradition. The first of the Four Noble Truths – the fact of suffering – was to be connected to the assumed doctrines of karma and *saṃsāra*, the endless round of rebirths in which we are all trapped by our actions, good or bad. The second Noble Truth

– the origin of suffering – was to be amplified by the elaboration of doctrines of causality, including that of Interdependent Origination which, we have seen, may have formed part of the Buddha's original experience at Bodhgaya. The third Noble Truth – the cessation of suffering – was to feed ongoing speculation about the nature (or non-nature) of *nirvāṇa*, the Buddhist soteriological goal. The fourth Noble Truth – the path to the cessation of suffering – was to give rise to well-developed doctrines of what constituted moral action, of what characterized knowledge and wisdom, of what made up the practice of meditation. The doctrines of impermanence and non-self, presented in the second sermon, were to set the themes for Buddhist metaphysics and theories of being and give rise, eventually, to sophisticated doctrines of emptiness. Finally, the kind of analysis found in the sermon just presented, as well as in the doctrine of the five aggregates (*skandhas*), was to flower into the extensive and elaborate analytical approaches to reality known as the *Abhidharma*.

## FURTHER CONVERSIONS IN BENARES: YAŚA AND HIS FAMILY

The group of five disciples formed the initial core of a Buddhist community (*saṃgha*) that was not to be long in growing. Indeed, the next sections of the Pali *Book of the Discipline (Vinaya-piṭaka)* as well as the *Discourse on the Fourfold Assembly (Catuṣpariṣat-sūtra)* are devoted to recounting the circumstances under which the Buddha made new conversions, and to keeping a sort of running score on the size of the community.

The first to be counted is Yaśa, the son of a local guild-master. One night, after being entertained by the women of his harem, he woke up to find them stretched out, dishevelled, limbs akimbo, making noises in their sleep. Thinking his own apartments had been turned into a cemetery, he could not stand it anymore and fled the city. This, of course, is exactly the same story as that of the bodhisattva's great departure, and it is widely thought to have provided the model for it. Like the bodhisattva, Yaśa soon comes to a river. Here, however, the stories diverge, because at the river, Yaśa happens to meet the Buddha. "I am oppressed, O ascetic, I am afflicted," he laments, and the Buddha, seeking to calm him says, "Come here, young man, there will be no more oppression for you and no affliction" (Kloppenborg, 1973, p. 32).

He then takes Yaśa to the place where he was staying, on the other side of the river, and there he instructs him with a sermon on generosity (*dāna*), good conduct (*śila*), and the joys of rebirth in heaven. In other words, he covers the standard list of topics that came to characterize what were later called the "preliminary discourses" appropriate for teaching to laypersons. Then, perceiving that Yaśa is ripe for further instruction, he proceeds by teaching him the Dharma itself, with a sermon on the Four Noble Truths, which Yaśa comes to understand.

In the meantime, Yaśa's parents have realized that he is missing and his father sets out in search of him. He worries that his son has been kidnapped to be held for ransom, and worries even more when he finds his sandals by the side of the river. Finally, he tracks him to the Buddha's place, but the Buddha, wishing to keep Yaśa with him a bit more, initially hides him from his father by making him invisible. In response to the father's inquiries, he preaches a sermon to him, and the father, impressed by the teaching, becomes the first lay disciple to take triple refuge in the Buddha, the Dharma, and the *saṃgha*. In the meantime, Yaśa, who has been listening to the Buddha while invisible, attains full enlightenment (*arhat*ship). The Buddha then renders him visible again. Yaśa's father wants to take his son home with him. "Come boy," he says, "your mother weeps, her body tired and exhausted." But it is determined that it would be inappropriate for Yaśa, now an enlightened *arhat*, to return to the householder's life. The Buddha therefore ordains him, saying "Come, monk," and he remains with the Blessed One. They agree, however, to visit his family the next day. At this point, there are seven monks – all of them enlightened – in the *saṃgha*: Yaśa, the group of five, and the Buddha. The following morning, the Buddha, taking Yaśa with him as an attendant disciple, arrives in the guild-master's home. There he has a meal and then preaches a sermon to Yaśa's mother and to his former wife, both of whom convert and become the Buddha's first laywomen disciples.

Later tradition was to identify Yaśa's mother as Sujātā, the woman who made the offering of milk-rice to the bodhisattva before his enlightenment, and Yaśa himself as the son she had wished for from the god of the banyan tree. In any case, in the present context, he is presented as being from a very prominent family, and as having many friends. Four of them, young men from the families of great merchants, are intrigued to learn that he has become a monk. They go and visit him, and are further intrigued when, while there, they listen to the Buddha preach a sermon. They ask to be ordained and soon thereafter attain enlightenment. Now there are eleven monks in the *saṃgha*. Then fifty other friends of Yaśa, all from prominent families, hear that he has wandered forth, and, in a repeat of the same scenario, they too become ordained and enlightened, and the *saṃgha* now numbers sixty-one monks, all of them *arhats*.

At this point, the Buddha decides that with the ongoing growth of the community, it will become difficult for him alone to preach and ordain further disciples. Accordingly, he tells his monks that, since they are enlightened just as he is enlightened, there is no reason why they should not teach on their own. They may also ordain new monks but not with the "Come, O monk" formula but by having them take refuge more ritually, and shave their hair and beards and put on yellow robes. Then, in a famous injunction, he urges them to go and preach: "O monks, wander! We will go forward for the benefit of many people ... out of compassion for the world, for the good, welfare and happiness of gods and men. May no two of you go the same way!" (Kloppenborg, 1973, p. 43.) All this will contribute to the further spread of the doctrine.

## THE RETURN TO MAGADHA: THE THIRTY FRIENDS, URUVILVĀ KĀŚYAPA, KING BIMBISĀRA, AND ŚĀRIPUTRA AND MAUDGALYĀYANA

The Buddha himself decides to go back from Benares to Uruvilvā in Magadha, where he had practiced austerities and attained enlightenment. On the way, he happens across a group of thirty friends, all young men of good standing, who have been amusing themselves with their wives in a woodland. One of the young men, being single, had brought along a courtesan as his companion, and while they were variously disporting themselves, this woman stole some of their belongings and ran away. The friends give chase and, coming across the Buddha sitting under a tree, they ask him whether or not he has seen a woman. The ensuing dialog is revelatory of both the Buddha's character and his proselytizing:

> "What do you think ... young men? [he asks.] Which is better for you, that you should seek for a woman or that you should seek for the self?"
> "Truly this were better for us, Lord, that we should seek for the self."
> "Well then, young men, sit down and I will teach you the Dharma." (Horner, 1938–52, 4, p. 32, slightly altered)

As a group they then listen to him, come to see the light, and request ordination. As a result thirty new monks are made. Nothing is said about the courtesan who escapes or about their wives who are left in the woods.

So far, the conversions effected by the Buddha have all been, more or less, relatively free from supernatural or miraculous events. Psychologically, they seem "down to earth," and much in tune with the Buddha's own experience. The Buddha appears as a somewhat demanding, charismatic teacher who has a new impressive teaching, and who convinces young men from prominent families – the bored sons of merchants and guild-masters – to give up their hedonistic lives and wander forth as his disciples. The Buddha's audience and techniques change somewhat, however, when he reaches the town of Uruvilvā, where he converts a matted-haired ascetic known as Uruvilvā Kāśyapa, and his five hundred followers. Uruvilvā Kāśyapa is not young (he is said to be 120 years old), and he is not frivolous, since he is "honored, esteemed, revered, respected and celebrated as an *arhat* by the people of Magadha" (Kloppenborg, 1973, p. 50). He is, moreover, convinced of his superiority to the Buddha. Accordingly, the story of his conversion (and of the conversion of his two brothers who live further downstream from him) is "a great contrast to the picture of [the] Buddha's character and methods that prevails in the canonical stories, and closely resembles the tales of astonishing miracles and magic worked by *arhats* in later compilations" (Thomas, 1927, p. 91). In all, it is said to take the Buddha three and a half thousand miracles in order to win over Kāśyapa: he uses his supernatural powers of engendering smoke and fire in order to defeat a ferocious *nāga* who resides in one of the ascetic's cells; he bests him in a contest of flying through the air; he ensures that the ascetics cannot kindle their sacrificial fires and then kindles them all himself simultaneously, etc. All of this impresses Uruvilvā Kāśyapa but it does not convince him of the Buddha's superiority, and he persists in believing that he alone is enlightened. Finally, the Buddha opts for a direct approach: he tells Kāśyapa bluntly that he is not enlightened, that he never has been enlightened and never will be if he insists on pursuing the path he is on. This, at last, shakes the ascetic to his very foundations, and, converting to Buddhism along with his five hundred disciples, he requests ordination. They all cut off their matted locks and throw them in the river along with their ritual implements for performing fire sacrifices.

The hair, floating downstream, is seen by Uruvilvā Kāśyapa's brothers, Nadī Kāśyapa and Gayā Kāśyapa, who come to inquire what has happened and are promptly converted by the Buddha as well. The Buddha preaches to them a sermon appropriate to men who have been focussed on their sacrificial fires: "Everything," he says,

> is burning. ... The eye is burning ... the ear, the nose, the tongue, the body, and the mind are burning. ... With what are they burning? With the fire of passion, with the fire of hatred, with the fire of delusion. They are burning because of birth, old age, disease, death. ... They are burning because of suffering. (Horner, 1938–52, 4, pp. 32–43, slightly altered; see also Kloppenborg, 1973, p. 74)

At the conclusion of the sermon, all of the former "fire worshippers" are enlightened.

The conversion of Uruvilvā Kāśyapa and his brothers represented something of a "coup" for the Buddha, and, shortly thereafter, together with the Kāśyapas, he is invited to visit the court of Bimbisāra, the king of Magadha. People are still confused and want to know whether Uruvilvā Kāśyapa has indeed become the Buddha's disciple or whether the Buddha has become a follower of Uruvilvā Kāśyapa. The record is set straight by Uruvilvā Kāśyapa himself who explains to Bimbisāra why he abandoned his ascetic practices and his fire-worship and who makes it clear in no uncertain terms that the Buddha is his master. The Buddha then uses the occasion to preach a sermon to Bimbisāra who ends up taking refuge and becoming a lay disciple. He punctuates his conversion by offering to the Buddha a dwelling-place in his own pleasure park, the Veṇuvana or "bamboo-grove" situated neither too far from nor too near to the city. This becomes the first permanent monastic park (*ārāma*) of the Buddha.

While the Buddha is staying at the Veṇuvana, the last significant event in this cycle of conversions in the Magadha region takes place. This is the conversion of two wandering ascetics, who become the two chief disciples of the Blessed One, Śāriputra and Maudgalyāyana. They are said to be followers of the great heretical sceptic, Sañjayin. Significantly, they are introduced to the Dharma not by the Buddha himself, but by one of his disciples, Aśvajit. One day, in Rājagṛha, Śāriputra happens to meet Aśvajit on the street and asks him who his teacher is and what doctrine he professes. Aśvajit replies that "the wanderer Gautama of the Śākya clan" is his teacher, and that his doctrine, though hard to explain at length, can be summed up in a single verse: "The Tathāgata has explained the cause of those elements of reality that arise from a cause, and he . . . has also spoken of their cessation." This verse – which became famous as an epitome of the whole Dharma – strikes a chord with Śāriputra, who immediately grasps its full significance. He then goes and finds his friend Maudgalyāyana, and the latter, seeing Śāriputra coming, immediately notices something different about his demeanor.

> "Your senses are serene," he says, "your face is at peace, and the complexion of your skin is utterly pure. Did you reach the deathless state?"
>
> "I reached it," Śāriputra replies.
>
> "Then teach me the Dharma" requests Maudgalyāyana, and Śāriputra repeats to him the above verse, and he too comes to see the light. (Strong, 1995, pp. 51–52, slightly altered)

Together, they then go to the Veṇuvana monastery where they find the Buddha and are ordained by him.

## THE RETURN TO KAPILAVASTU: THE CONVERSION OF THE ŚĀKYAS

It is not possible to follow, chronologically, all of the conversions and sermons of the Buddha during this period of his life, but mention should be made here of one further significant series of conversions which occurs when he goes back to his hometown of Kapilavastu. There, he meets again with his father, Śuddhodana, his stepmother, Mahāprajāpatī, his wife, Yaśodharā, his son, Rāhula, his half-brother, Nanda, his cousins, Ānanda, Aniruddha, and Devadatta, his uncles, and other relatives and their servants (such as Upāli). All of them eventually join the Buddhist order, but the stories of their re-encounters and reunions with their returned relative, the Buddha, are among the most touching tales in the whole biography, and were much developed by the tradition.

The biographies are generally agreed that it is while the Buddha was staying at the Veṇuvana in Rājagṛha that his father, hearing of his fame from a distance, wishes to see him again. Accordingly, he sends one of his ministers (accompanied by a thousand men) to invite him, but, upon arriving in Rājagṛha, they listen to a sermon being preached by the Buddha and, forgetting their mission, they all decide to become ordained as monks. Nine more times Śuddhodana sends out ministers to invite his son home, but always with the same result (Jayawickrama, 1990, p. 115). Finally, he turns to Udāyin who had been a childhood friend of the Buddha's. Udāyin too is unable to resist the Buddha and becomes ordained as a monk, but he does not forget his mission. The following autumn, he sings the praises of travelling in the cool season, and he convinces the Buddha it is time for him to visit his family.

While the Buddha travels home, slowly, along the same path that brought him originally to Bodhgaya, the Śākyas prepare to receive him in a monastic park (the Nigrodha-ārāma) they have prepared for him outside of Kapilavastu. But the Śākyas are a proud people, and when they welcome him there, none of them wants to bow down in front of someone they still think of as a junior member of their tribe. This is potentially a problem, since failure to bow down in front of the Buddha is said to result in having one's head split into pieces. Accordingly, out of compassion for his relatives, the Buddha levitates himself up into the air, thus accomplishing their prostration for them. He then performs various other miracles and, seeing these, his father, Śuddhodana, bows down to his son for the third time in his life, the other occasions having been immediately after his birth and in the temple of the Śākya clan. The Buddha then preaches to the assembled Śākyas the *Viśvantara jātaka*, an appropriate sermon for one who needs to explain why he abandoned his family (see Chapter 1).

The accounts of what happens next vary from one tradition to another, but they generally revolve around interactions with particular individuals. We shall limit ourselves in what follows to episodes involving the Buddha's father, Śuddhodana, his stepmother, Mahāprajāpatī, various other male Śākya relatives, and the Buddha's wife, Yaśodharā and their son, Rāhula.

The seeds of Śuddhodana's conversion have already been planted, but the story of his gradual coming to understand his son's teaching and his own eventual enlightenment usually unfolds around the question of food. Śuddhodana is very upset to see his son going from house to house on his begging round, thinking that such a thing is a disgrace for a Śākya, a descendant of Mahāsammata. The Buddha tells him that this royal lineage may be his (Śuddhodana's), but he himself comes from a lineage of Buddhas, all of whom begged their food in this manner. Gradually, in this way, the Buddha wins over his father. Śuddhodana never seems actually to become a monk, but, in one tradition at least, he wishes to give up the throne to his brother Śuklodana. The latter too, however, has seen the light and so he refuses. So do Śuddhodana's two remaining brothers, Droṇodana and Amṛtodana, for the same reasons. The throne, therefore, is passed on to Śuklodana's son, Śākyarāja Bhadrika. In other traditions, Śuddhodana remains as king, looking out for the interests of the *saṃgha* on the one hand, and the needs of his kingdom on the other. Towards the end of his life, he attains the different stages of enlightenment, including *arhat*ship.

Śuddhodana regularly invites the Buddha to have his meals in the palace, and on one such occasion, the Buddha meets his stepmother, Mahāprajāpatī. She invites him in turn to her own place, where he preaches to her and to all the women of the court a preliminary discourse followed by an exposition of the Dharma. Hearing his sermon, she attains the first level of insight into the doctrine. The logic of the story is such that, normally, one would expect her to become ordained as a nun at this point, but that is not possible since, despite the existence of monks, laymen, and laywomen, the order of nuns (*bhikṣuṇīs*) has not yet been established by the Buddha. Nonetheless, Mahāprajāpatī is the one who eventually does manage to have it instituted, and, given the importance of that accomplishment, it may be appropriate to recount the episode here. It happens a few years later, on a subsequent visit of the Buddha to Kapilavastu, when he has come to resolve a dispute over water rights between the Śākyas and the Koliyas. After his successful intervention, the Buddha preaches the Dharma and five hundred Śakya men decide to become monks. Their abandoned wives rally around Mahāprajāpatī who goes to the Buddha and demands that he create for them an order of nuns. The Buddha refuses. She and her companions respond by shaving their heads, putting on robes and following the Buddha about. Once again they make their request, only to be turned down even more firmly. Finally, Mahāprajāpatī asks the Buddha's disciple Ānanda to speak to the Buddha on her behalf. He does so, and with great difficulty, manages to convince the Blessed One to institute an order of nuns. Although in the process the Buddha hobbles it with additional rules and regulations, the order is established and Mahāprajāpatī becomes its leader.

Less problematic and more immediate is the ordination of various male relatives. Although King Śuddhodana himself remains a layman, at this time, Ānanda, Devadatta, Aniruddha, Bhadrika, Nanda, and, eventually, no fewer than five hundred additional Śākya youths all become monks. According to the *Great Story (Mahāvastu)*, a rule is established by Śuddhodana that in any family with several sons, one of them should join the order, and the others remain at home. In this way, for example, the two brothers, Aniruddha and Mahānāman, cousins of the Buddha and both sons of Amṛtodana, must decide which of them should wander forth. After a comparative discussion about lay and monastic lifestyles, Aniruddha opts for ordination, while his elder brother, Mahānāman, decides against it.

Śuddhodana's "rule" seems to reflect an attempt, on his part, both to support the Buddhist community and yet to keep at least one *lay* man in each of the different households so as not to "lose" a whole generation of Śākyas to the *saṃgha*. On the other hand, there are indications that Śuddhodana wishes also to "stock" the *saṃgha* with *kṣatriyas*, specifically Śākyas. So far, many of the Buddha's prominent converts (the Kāśyapa brothers, Śāriputra, Maudgalyāyana, etc.) have been from the brahmin caste, and it would be inappropriate, Śuddhodana declares, for his son, a *kṣatriya*, to have a following dominated by brahmins. This, however, may reflect less a feeling of Śākya pride as a more general desire to undermine the caste system. Thus, when the Śākyas do decide to become monks, *en masse*, no mention is made of brahmins. Instead, the clan's low-caste barber, Upāli, is ordained first so that he will actually be senior in the *saṃgha* to the rest of Śākyas who are ordained second. This is said to be a way for them to overcome their pride and arrogance.

Śuddhodana's "rule" of one monk per family, however, is not always clearly followed. Thus, for example, Ānanda and Devadatta, sons of the Buddha's uncle Amṛtodana, both become monks at this time. Ānanda, as we shall see, eventually becomes the Buddha's personal attendant and a leader of the *saṃgha*. In Pali sources, he is said to have been born on the same day as the Buddha, but in the *Book of the Discipline of the Mūlasarvāstivādins,* he is portrayed as being the same age as the Buddha's son, Rāhula, something that makes better sense in view of his later roles. He is thus still very young when he becomes a follower of the Buddha. Ordinarily, his brother, Devadatta, should have remained a layman, but that would have put him in line for the Śākya throne. Thus, according to one tradition, he was tricked into ordination in order to prevent this possibility.

Devadatta, as we have seen, is a person who is much maligned in Buddhist legend; he is portrayed as a childhood rival of the young Gautama, and their antagonism is traced back through countless previous lives. He is also shown later as trying to murder the Buddha, an act that results in his instantly plunging into the deepest hell. Yet behind these stories lies a tradition that presents him not only as an ordained monk, but as an important figure in the early *saṃgha*, one who, in fact, challenges the Buddha for leadership of the community. Indeed, at one point, he actually goes to the Buddha, points out that he is tired and is getting old, and suggests that he, Devadatta, be allowed to take over. The Buddha replies in no uncertain terms: he would not hand over the leadership of the community even to Śāriputra and Maudgalyāyana; how then could he give it to a "vile drooler of snot" such as Devadatta? There are indications, however, that Devadatta is not simply interested in power and prestige. Beneath and behind the insults, it is possible to see him as the leader of a faction worried that the monastic order is becoming lax, and eager to maintain a different lifestyle for monks. Thus, as the basis of his movement, he proposes that the Buddha make obligatory certain stringent ascetic practices (including life in the open, in the forest, not accepting invitations to eat at laypeople's houses, wearing only robes made out of rags scavenged on cremation grounds, and strict vegetarianism). This the Buddha refuses to do; for him such ascetic pursuits should only be voluntary.

Finally, mention should be made of the son of Mahāprajāpatī, the Buddha's half-brother Sundara-Nanda, who in some ways is the mirror-opposite of Devadatta. In the *Great Story (Mahāvastu)*, we are told that, because he was the Buddha's half-brother, he was excused from joining the *saṃgha* (according to Śuddhodana's rule), and it is true that this text does not seem to know the story of Nanda the monk. Other traditions, however, were to develop his tale at great length. Having just married the most beautiful woman in the whole Śākya tribe, with whom he is utterly infatuated, Nanda is visited by his half-brother on his begging round. He dutifully fills the Buddha's bowl with food, taking it in his hands to do so. The Buddha, however, then departs without taking back his bowl, leaving Nanda with no choice but to follow along after him, carrying it. Without wishing it, Nanda has been put into the position of being a *paścatśramaṇa* – a junior "monk who follows along" after a senior monk (his teacher), carrying his bowl. In this way, the Buddha leads him all the way back to the monastery, and, before he can object, Nanda finds himself ordained! He cannot, however, forget his beautiful bride. He tries to escape and return to her, but he is thwarted in his attempts. Seeking to teach him a lesson on the relativity and impermanence of physical beauty, the Buddha then takes Nanda up to one of the heavens, and shows him some stunningly beautiful goddesses, next to whom Nanda's wife (or rather his memory of her) pales in comparison. Then, in what the tradition would call "expedient means" in teaching, he promises

Nanda that if he forgets his wife and practices very hard in the monastery, he can have all these beautiful goddesses for himself. Nanda redoubles his efforts at meditation, and quickly attains enlightenment. When he does, of course, he finds that he is no longer interested either in his wife or in the celestial goddesses.

The tale of the conversion of Nanda is sometimes told in conjunction with the tale of the conversion of the Buddha's own son, Rāhula. Indeed, this story, along with that of the Buddha's reunion with his own wife, Yaśodharā, forms, in the biographies, one of the highlights of the Buddha's return to his home town. Virtually all of the texts recount it, although the degree to which they develop it and the poignancy they give to it vary greatly. Most are agreed that Yaśodharā refuses to go and see the Buddha at her father-in-law Śuddhodana's palace. She is invited but she declines, saying, "If there is any virtue in me, my lord will come to me himself" (Jayawickrama, 1990, p. 122). He subsequently does. Their meeting is sometimes mediated by Śuddhodana who explains to the Buddha how much Yaśodharā has suffered due to his absence. At this, the Buddha shows little emotion. Her reactions, however, are varied. In some texts, there are indications that she still hopes to persuade the Buddha to come back to her, and she even attempts to seduce him. In others, there is no sign of this at all. Instead, she falls down in front of the Buddha, holds him by his ankles and bathes his feet with her tears, rolling her head and worshipping him with great emotion. This is allowed because the Buddha has already warned his disciples who are with him not to interfere and to let Yaśodharā greet him however she wants.

In still other traditions, she voices her own feelings at having been abandoned by her husband. One particularly moving development of this is the relatively late Northern Thai rendition of the story known as "Bimbā's Lament." In that text, Bimbā's (i.e., Yaśodharā's) meeting with the Buddha is preceded by a remarkable dialog between her and her servant. "O servant", she says,

> I shall tell you why I am so sorrowful. I am sad because the Lord Buddha ... no longer loves me even though I have done nothing wrong [and] faithfully performed all my wifely duties towards him. I must be a person of little merit. I can accept being abandoned, but the Buddha should have sympathy for his son, Rāhula. He is lovable and innocent. (Swearer, 1995, p. 548)

Then, turning to her little boy, she says:

> O, my beloved Rāhula. You were a misfortune for your father from the very beginning. ... Rāhula, you and I, having been abandoned, are persons of no account. ... Everyone accuses you of being illegitimate; and people look down on me as a widow. My suffering brings only tears. How can I continue to live?

And, having asked the question, she goes on to contemplate suicide: "I am ashamed before everyone. It is better for me to take poison and die or to put a rope around my neck and hang myself from the palace" (Swearer, 1995, p. 548).

At this point, her servant tries to console her, and Bimbā begins to remember fondly some intimate details about the Buddha's habits when he was her husband, how he used, sometimes, to talk in an affectionate and playful manner; how sometimes, when he came home, he would wash his own feet and fold the towels himself. But all this makes her even more upset that the Buddha has not yet come to visit her, although he returned to Kapilavastu three days before. Thus, when he finally does come to see her, she gives vent to her emotions. Looking directly at him, she says:

> "[You ask] why do I cry? I'm angry because my husband has not even greeted me. We were married for only seven years and he abandoned me. I was still young. It was not as though my Lord was leaving me in his old age. I felt very lonely". ... [Then], unfastening her hair, she dusted off his feet and fanned [them] back and forth, moving tenderly like the fronds of a banana tree. ... Sobbing, she spoke to the Enlightened One. ... "O my Lord, I pay my respects to you. I am unlucky and ashamed before you. ... You abandoned me and our child without any compassion. In the old days I never considered myself unlucky. You never gave any indication that you would leave me alone for such a long time. Prince Rāhula was just born, but you left without any concern for me. You made your departure at midnight ... [and] I was left deserted." (Swearer, 1995, pp. 550–1)

In this story, she then makes young Rāhula honor his father. In others, she tells him to ask his father for his "inheritance," i.e., for the wealth that he will need when he, Rāhula, becomes king. But this too backfires on Yaśodharā. The Buddha, reflecting that the wealth that Rāhula asks for is bound up with suffering, decides to give him instead "the sevenfold treasure which I received at the foot of the Bodhi-tree," and to make him an heir to the Dharma. Accordingly, he instructs Śāriputra to ordain young Rāhula as a novice. Having lost a husband, Yaśodharā now also loses a son. But Śuddhodana and the Śākyas are presented as being even more upset because, with the ordination of Rāhula, the heir to the Śākya throne itself is lost and, with him, the whole lineage of Mahā-sammata. Because of this, Śuddhodana extracts a promise from the Buddha that, henceforth, no one is to be ordained without his parents' permission.

In the *Great Story (Mahāvastu)*, this story is told slightly differently. The Śākyas, anticipating trouble, seek to keep Rāhula away from his father and forbid anyone to tell the child of his relationship to the Buddha. One day, however, Rāhula happens to see the Buddha and he feels an unaccountable thrill. He asks his mother whether or not this recluse might have any connection with him, since no one has ever affected him in this way. Not wishing to lie to her son, Yaśodharā admits to him that this man is his father. Rāhula's response is immediate; he takes hold of a corner of the Buddha's robe, clings to it, and declares that he will wander forth and follow the paternal path. Yaśodharā tries to convince him to change his mind, explaining how hard and uncomfortable a monk's life is, and that in wandering forth he will be forsaking his royal duty and the Śākya lineage. But Rāhula will not relent, and, in the face of his determination, Yaśodharā finally accepts the decision of her son and tells him, rather touchingly, to be a good monk, to apply himself with vigilance, to observe the proper way of standing, walking, and sitting down, and always to follow the rules layed down by his father, the Buddha. And, in a final bit of maternal advice, she warns him that if he wishes to attain *nirvāṇa*, he will have to exhibit good self-control, for young gracious and beautiful women will come to pay obeisance to the Buddha, and when they do, he should have no desire for them at all, but treat them as he would his own mother. With her blessing, then, Rāhula is ordained, but not without her sorrow as well; as his head is being shaved, she gathers up his cut hair, and holding it in her lap, she cries.

Yaśodharā, it should be added, eventually joins the *saṃgha* herself (she has to wait until the order of nuns is established), and there achieves some degree of consolation. In fact, she is said to become enlightened. Though exceptional by virtue of her close relationship to the Buddha, in many ways, her experience and motivation for becoming ordained are not unique among the Buddha's female converts. Many of them choose a life in the *saṃgha* when life outside of it becomes intolerable, often for family reasons. The nun Paṭācārā, for example, suffers the loss of her husband, and then the rather ghastly deaths of her two children, and the coincidental passing of her parents. She goes quite mad and, when she finally meets the Buddha, he offers her not only insight into suffering, but also an alternative life within a new family, the Buddhist *saṃgha*. It is no accident that the Buddha, his teaching and his community, are all called "refuges."

Other converts, of course, have other reasons for joining the order: they are impressed by the Buddha's charisma, or convinced by his magical powers, or they are intellectually taken with his doctrine, or wish to follow in the footsteps of a relative or a friend. Individual motives for joining the *saṃgha* are ultimately as diverse as the number of converts. Nor should it be thought that the Buddha is always welcomed. Some persons, parents in particular, are concerned about the appeal of this yellow-robed master and, not unlike their modern counterparts who criticize cults and sects, are worried about his influence on their children. "The wanderer Gautama is coming," warns a brahmin villager in one text. "His band is like a hailstorm that decimates the crops. Those of you who are parents are without a doubt going to be deprived of your sons!" (Strong, 1997, pp. 59–60, slightly altered.)

Nevertheless, the appeal of the Buddha, his doctrine, and his community, was enough to cause many to join his movement during the first few years of his ministry, either as laymen or laywomen, or to take the fuller step of ordination. In time, many of these monks and nuns opted out of a life of wandering and settled down in permanent monastic dwellings. As they did so, the "Discipline" (*Vinaya*) of the Buddhist Order was developed, its rules and regulations for the governing of all aspects of monastic life being credited to the Buddha. In time, also, the Buddha's teachings were developed by the community, becoming more elaborate and refined, and eventually giving rise to a vast literature, at first oral and then written, said to preserve the Dharma. And in time, disagreements over both discipline and doctrine resulted in schisms within the Buddhist community, schisms which were sometimes healed, but sometimes led to the creation of different Buddhist sects.

# 5 DAILY ROUTINES, MIRACLES, AND DISTANT JOURNEYS

Throughout the next forty years and more of his career, the Buddha continues to live in Northern India, visiting and revisiting different communities, preaching the Dharma, converting beings of all sorts, and settling doctrinal and disciplinary questions that arise. I shall not attempt a chronological account of his many activities during this period, but instead will focus on what might be called the gradual "settling down" of the Buddha, i.e., the growth of monasticism in those periods when he was not traveling, and his own opting, after twenty years, for a more or less permanent place of residence in Śrāvastī. In particular I want to look at his establishment at the Jetavana monastery in Śrāvastī, which became his permanent pied-à-terre, so to speak, for much of the latter portion of his life. At the same time, I want to give some sense of how the tradition imagined his daily monastic life there. This is interesting because it tells us something not only about the way Buddhist monks later imagined the Buddha's mode of being in the world, but also it reveals something about their own monastic routines. Then, I would like to consider in some detail a sequence of important biographical events, the first of which, in fact, occurs in Śrāvastī. This is the great miracle display he puts on in order to defeat the heretical masters. This leads directly into a second important biographical event: the rains-retreat he spends in the Trāyastriṃśa Heaven preaching to his mother who has been reborn there. This in turn ends with a third episode, also involving a miracle: his descent from that heaven in the town of Sāṃkāśya. Finally, I will examine some conversions that the Buddha makes on a number of his so-called "apocryphal" journeys to distant lands. The Buddha is sometimes called, in relatively late sources, a "world wanderer," an epithet reflecting the tradition that he made numerous "missionary trips" to establish Buddhism in lands beyond India. More specifically, I want to look at three of these: a tour he makes (in a single night) to the whole Northwestern region of the continent, to parts of what are now Kashmir, Pakistan, and Afghanistan; another journey (one of three) to the island of Sri Lanka, off the southern tip of India; and another to a land called Śroṇāparānta, which has been situated in Southeast Asia in what is today Myanmar (Burma).

## SETTLING DOWN: RULES AND CONTENTIONS

Mention has just been made of the rains-retreat that the Buddha spends in heaven preaching to his mother. It should be explained that it became the Buddhist rule, held in common with other Indian wanderers of the time, to spend three months of the rainy season, each year, in a particular place. During this time, monks were forbidden to travel, the nominal reason being that the roads were impassable and one ran a greater risk of treading on young plants (which angers farmers) and destroying small creatures.

The rains-retreats, however, are also important biographically, since the Pali commentarial tradition eventually developed a list of the various places where the Buddha passed each of his rains-retreats. The result is a kind of partial chronology, a year-by-year framework for his overall ministry. Thus, we are told, he spends his first rains-retreat in Benares, the next three at theVeṇuvana in Rājagṛha, the fifth in Vaiśālī, and so on. The entire list may be studied in Table 5.1.

A number of scholars have argued that the annual periods of the rains were significant in the formation of the monastic community, in bringing about a transition from a wandering to a sedentary life. Though they may have overstated their case, it is nonetheless true that the annual rainy season constituted one of the most important times of the Buddhist year, ritually and spiritually, and socially.

These annual occasions are commonly called "retreats," and, as we shall see, the Buddha sometimes used them to be alone, to withdraw from the world. But the rainy season should not generally be thought of as a time for solitary seclusion. On the one hand, the fact that during this period the monks had to stay put in one place often meant that laypersons residing nearby could have greater (rather than less)

*Table 5.1 Where the Buddha spent the 45 rains-retreats of his career*

| Year after enlightenment | Place of rains-retreat |
|---|---|
| 1 | Benares |
| 2–4 | Veṇuvana in Rājagṛha |
| 5 | Vaiśālī |
| 6 | Mount Makula |
| 7 | Trāyastriṃśa Heaven |
| 8 | Bhesakalāvana in the land of Bhaggā |
| 9 | Kosambi |
| 10 | Pārileyyaka forest |
| 11 | Brahmin village of Nāḷā |
| 12 | Verañjā |
| 13 | Pāliya mountain near Rājagṛha |
| 14 | Jetavana in Śrāvastī |
| 15 | Kapilavastu |
| 16 | Āḷavī |
| 17 | Rājagṛha |
| 18–19 | Pāliya mountain near Rājagṛha |
| 20 | Rājagṛha |
| 21–44 | Śrāvastī, at Jetavana and Pūrvārāma |
| 45 | Beluva near Vaiśālī |

interaction with them. On the other hand, the fact that the monks were generally living *together* in groups for the whole three months, without the opportunity to wander off by themselves if they so wished, meant that they had to develop certain rules aimed at promoting harmony and consensus.

These communal rules, said to have been promulgated by the Buddha as the need for them arose, include both general moral injunctions (e.g., against sexual intercourse, theft, and murder) and "rules and regulations" governing monastic routines and the use of such things as bowls, robes, and rooms. The occasions for the formulation of these rules are recounted in the various books of Discipline (*Vinaya*), and in time over 225 of them came to be codified in a list known as the *Prātimokṣa* (Pali: *Pātimokkha*), to be ritually reaffirmed and recited by the assembled monks every fortnight.

Among the rules of the *Prātimokṣa*, there are no fewer than six seeking to prevent various kinds of actions leading to dissension and discord among the members of a given community. It comes as no surprise, then, to learn that the Buddha is portrayed as having to deal with a number of schismatic crises. One such occasion is the case of the quarrelsome monks of Kauśāmbī (Pali: Kosambī) which is worth recounting here. In the tenth year after the Buddha's enlightenment, a dispute arises in the community at Kauśāmbī over a seemingly trivial matter. A monk, said to be a preacher of the Dharma, leaves some waste water in the bathroom; another monk, said to be a student of the *Vinaya*, tells him that this was an offence and he should confess it. He, however, responds that he was not aware of this rule, and so cannot be held guilty of intentionally violating it. The point is a subtle and rather tricky one; ignorance of the law is generally no excuse in Buddhism, but the unintentional violation of a rule, especially a minor one, incurs no guilt or penalty. In this case, however, the second monk takes formal action against the first and has him put on probation. The "offending" monk, however, continues to argue his case and refuses to accept the legality of his probation. Quickly two factions form around these two individuals, and the whole *saṃgha* is soon at odds over the matter. The Buddha, informed of the situation, recognizes its complexity, and tells the factions that they are both at fault and should mend their differences and unite once again as a single community. They refuse. Twice more he asks them to settle their dispute, but without success. Accordingly, disaffected with the quarrelsome ways of the monks of Kauśāmbī, the Buddha simply leaves town without telling anyone where he is going, and retires to a solitary spot in the Pārileyyaka forest. There he spends the whole rainy season by himself, attended by a wild elephant. This turn of events is interesting for it is possible to detect within it a kind of nostalgia for solitude, for a simpler life, for peace and quiet. As the Buddha puts it in one text: "Formerly, beset by those monks of Kosambī, makers of strife, makers of quarrels, makers of disputes, makers of brawls, makers of legal questions in the Order, I did not live in comfort; but now that I am alone with no other, I am living in comfort removed from those monks" (Horner, 1938–52, 4, pp. 503–04).

This "retreat" of the Buddha, however, is distressing to the laypeople of Kauśāmbī who want to enjoy and benefit from his presence. Blaming the quarrelling monks for his absence, they refuse to invite them to meals any more, or to provide for them on their begging rounds. This ultimately proves to be effective; hungry and ashamed, the quarrelsome monks finally seek out the Buddha, beg him to return, ask for his forgiveness, and reconcile themselves to living together again in harmony. The crisis is over and the Buddha "returns to the world" and continues his preaching career.

## THE JETAVANA MONASTERY

It is clear from the listing of rains-retreats in Table 5.1 that eventually the Buddha comes to spend most of his time in Śrāvastī, the capital of Kosala and one of the great cities of Northern India. This preference for Śrāvastī has led some scholars to think of that city as the Buddha's principal monastic home, especially in the latter part of his life. Indeed, one text makes this quite clear. For twenty years, it states, the Blessed One had no fixed place of residence, but lived wherever he found it suited him. After that, however, for twenty-five years, he settled permanently in Śrāvastī.

One of the reasons for this is not hard to find; Śrāvastī is where the Jetavana monastery is located. The story of its foundation is a famous one. Following his visit to his hometown of Kapilavastu, the Buddha returns to Rājagṛha, and while there he meets and converts Anāthapiṇḍada (Pali: Anāthapiṇḍika), a rich merchant who is in town on business, and who quickly becomes one of the chief male lay supporters of the Blessed One. Anāthapiṇḍada is from Śrāvastī, and he invites the Buddha to visit him in his home city, and there he wishes to prepare for him a magnificent monastery in a park known as the Jetavana. Anāthapiṇḍada is said to purchase the land from Prince Jeta by covering the whole acreage with gold pieces, layed side by side. He then spends another 540 million pieces of gold on the monastic buildings. The dedication festivities last nine months, culminating with the arrival of the Buddha:

> Then the great merchant ... sent his son decked with all ornaments together with five hundred other boys also in festive attire. He, together with his retinue carrying five hundred banners radiant with cloth of five different colours, went ahead of the Blessed One. Behind them followed Mahāsubhaddā and Cūlasubhaddā, the two daughters of the merchant-prince, together with the five hundred maidens carrying water pots filled to the brim. Behind them walked the merchant-prince's wife decked in all her splendour, attended by five hundred women carrying filled bowls. Behind all of them came the great merchant-prince himself, dressed in

> new garments, accompanied by five hundred other merchant princes also dressed in new garments, and he went forward to meet the Blessed One. . . .
>
> The Blessed One, attended by his large retinue of monks, entered the monastery of Jetavana with his unequalled glory and infinite grace . . ., as though with the radiance from his body turning the forest groves into clusters of feathers sprayed with the essence of gold. Thereupon Anāthapiṇḍika asked him, "Lord, how shall I act in connection with this monastery?"
>
> "Now, O householder, dedicate this monastery to the Brotherhood of monks whether present here or to come hither hereafter."
>
> "Yes, my Lord," said the great merchant prince; and taking a golden water pot he poured the water of dedication on the hand of the Lord of Ten Powers and offered it saying, "I give this monastery of Jetavana to the Brotherhood of monks with the Buddha at their head, to those of the four quarters whether present or to come hither hereafter." (Jayawickrama, 1990, p. 126)

The Jetavana, however, was not the only monastic dwelling of the Buddha in Śrāvastī. Somewhat less opulent but still very grand was the Pūrvārāma, built for the Blessed One by his eminent female lay disciple, Viśākhā. There the Buddha spent a total of six rains-retreats. Though this is fewer than the number of rains-retreats he spends at the Jetavana, he seems to have wished to keep something of a balance between his two great lay supporters in Śrāvastī, for we are told that it was his custom always to rest at the Pūrvārāma after eating at Anāthapiṇḍada's house, and to rest at the Jetavana after eating at Viśākhā's house.

The reception of the Jetavana and the Pūrvārāma does not mean, of course, that the Buddha stops his wanderings. But it does reflect the tradition that, after twenty years of travel, he establishes himself in one place that he goes out from and comes back to; from then on, the old ideal of wandering, though never completely lost, had to vie with a new ideal of settlement.

## DAILY ROUTINE

At the center of the Jetavana, Anāthapiṇḍada builds a special residence for the Buddha, the so-called "perfumed chamber" (*gandhakuṭi*). There the Blessed One lives and follows a daily monastic routine which the fifth-century Pali commentator, Buddhaghosa, divides into morning, afternoon, first, second, and third watch of the night activities. These may be summarized as follows.

Each day, the Buddha gets up early in the morning, rinses his mouth, and otherwise cares for his person, and then sits until it is time for his begging round. Then, dressing in his robes and taking his bowl, he goes into town for alms, sometimes by himself, sometimes with other monks. Wherever he walks, the way is even and easy: clouds let fall a sprinkle of water to lay the dust at his feet, gentle winds scatter flower blossoms on his path, bumps in the road level themselves, and depressions fill themselves in. As soon as he gets to the city limits, rays of six colors illuminate the buildings with a golden glow, and melodious sounds are heard. In this way, the people know that the Buddha has come for alms, and they vie with each other to invite him in and serve him a meal. After eating, the Buddha, teaches the Dharma to his hosts, and some of them take refuge, and some the five precepts, and some attain various degrees of insight into the Doctrine and decide to wander forth. The Buddha then returns to the monastery, where he waits for all the monks to finish their meal, before going into his perfumed chamber.

There he sits down on a seat prepared for him by his personal attendant and has his feet washed. He then goes out on to the landing of the staircase leading to his perfumed chamber and exhorts the monks to work hard at their practice, reminding them that the appearance of buddhas in the world is rare. Some ask him for exercises in meditation which he provides, and then they all withdraw to places of practice – some to the forest, some to the foot of trees, some to the hills. The Buddha then re-enters his perfumed chamber and lies down to rest for a while. In the meantime, people from the city assemble in their best clothes, with perfumes, flowers, and other offerings. The Buddha then preaches the Dharma to them, after which, they do obeisance and depart.

In the evening, the Buddha enters the bathhouse, if he so wishes, and bathes in water made ready by his personal attendant. He then sits down in the perfumed chamber on a seat prepared for him and plunges into meditation for a while. Then various monks come, during the first watch of the night, to ask questions about doctrinal topics or meditational exercises.

During the second watch of the night, the monks are replaced by deities: this is their time to visit the Buddha and ask him any questions that they may have. The Blessed One answers them all.

Finally, in the last watch of the night, he first walks back and forth on a meditation walkway; then he rests in his perfumed chamber, lying down on his right side, mindful and conscious; finally, he spends the remainder of the time before dawn surveying the world to discover any individual who might in a past life have made a vow under some previous buddha, thinking to confirm their aspiration and meritorious deed.

This description, with its mixture of the mundane and the miraculous, gives us a fascinating glimpse of the Buddha as a teacher with a full agenda who must tend to the spiritual needs not only of his monks, but also of laypeople and divinities. In many ways, this is a combination that will mark the rest of his career.

## THE GREAT MIRACLE AT ŚRĀVASTĪ

Śrāvastī, however, is important not only for the Jetavana monastery, but also because it is said to be the place where, even before he settled there, the Buddha displays "the miracle of double appearances" (*yamaka-prātihārya*). We have had ample opportunity to see the Buddha exhibiting various sorts of supernatural powers during his life. The miracle at Śrāvastī, however, is listed as one of the ten "indispensible acts" and one of the "thirty obligatory deeds" on the "blueprint" of acts which all buddhas must perform during their lifetimes (see Introduction above). Alternatively, it is mentioned as one of the events that makes Śrāvastī one of the eight great pilgrimage places in Buddhism. Many texts mention the miracle and many works of art depict it. In what follows we shall pay particular attention to two distinct accounts found in the Pali *Commentary on the Dharma Stanzas (Dhammapadaṭṭhakathā)*, and the Sanskrit "Discourse on the Miracle" (*Prātihārya sūtra)*.

The Pali version starts with the story of the Buddha's disciple, Piṇḍola, who gratuitously uses his magical powers of levitation in order to obtain a prize – a sandalwood begging bowl – that has been hung from the top of a high pole. The Buddha reprimands him for this and establishes on the spot a new monastic precept against such displays of supernatural powers. Hearing this, the six heretical teachers (various kinds of non-Buddhists), thinking they now, at last, have a chance to best the Buddha, challenge him to a contest of magical powers, which they urge King Bimbisāra to arbitrate. Much to their surprise and dismay, the Buddha accepts the challenge, explaining that the precept he propounded was meant to apply to his disciples but not to himself, just as it is against the law for people to pick fruit from the royal orchard, but not against the law for the king to do so.

The Buddha declares he will perform his miracle at the foot of a mango tree in Śrāvastī, because that is where all previous buddhas have done it. The heretics, desperate now to avoid the contest, which they know they will lose, uproot all the mango trees in the region. They are thwarted, however, when the time for the contest in Śrāvastī comes, by the Buddha's performance of a preliminary miracle. He eats a ripe mango, received on his begging round from the king's gardener, and then has the seed planted just by the city gate. He washes his hands over the spot, and immediately a mango tree springs up and grows into a huge tree. This is then named after the gardener and called "Gaṇḍa's Mango tree" (*Gaṇḍamba*). The "mango-trick" has long been a commonplace of Indian magic, but here it proves to be too much for the chief heretic, Pūraṇa Kāśyapa, who drowns himself in a river, while the other heretics flee.

In the meantime, the gods have built a pavilion of precious stones for the Buddha at the foot of the mango tree, and the time has now come for him to perform his great miracle. A large crowd of people assemble to watch, not yet knowing what he will do. The Buddha starts by creating a jewelled walkway in mid air, and stands upon it. Then, wishing to spare him the further trouble of having to put on a magical show, a laywoman follower, a layman follower, a seven-year-old female novice, a seven-year-old male novice, a nun, and a monk all, in turn, offer to perform various kinds of miracles in his stead, but the Buddha turns them all down; this is something that buddhas must do themselves. Then, right there in the midst of the crowd, he performs the miracle of double appearances: from the upper part of his body, flames shoot up, while from the lower part a stream of water pours forth; then, he reverses things and flames emerge from the lower part of his body and water from the upper part. Then flames and water simultaneously emerge from the front and back of his body, from his right and left eyes, from his right and left ears, from his right and left nostrils, shoulders, hands, sides, feet, fingers, etc. Both flames and water shoot up as far as Brahmā's heaven and out to the edges of the universe, illuminating the whole cosmos. All the while, the Buddha, walking up and down on the walkway, preaches the Dharma to the multitude. While doing so, he realizes that he himself is the best one present to ask questions as well as to answer them, so he creates a double of himself, who then asks questions to which he responds, or who walks back and forth while he sits, or sits while he walks back and forth. In this way, two hundred million people are brought to a comprehension of the Dharma (Burlingame, 1921, 3, pp. 38–47).

The Sanskrit version of this story agrees for the most part with the Pali, although it shows certain variations and makes a number of additions to it. No mention is made in the Sanskrit text of the preliminary episode of Piṇḍola. Instead, the six heretic masters, jealous of the Buddha's popularity but confident of their own powers, propose a miracle contest to King Bimbisāra. He refuses, telling them they are crazy to want to compete with the Buddha. So they go to Prasenajit, the king of Kosala, and he agrees to see if the Buddha will participate. The Blessed One says that he generally tells his disciples not to do such things, but to focus instead on leading the moral life. However, he realizes that all buddhas are destined to perform the great miracle at Śrāvastī, and so he agrees. There is no mention of the quick growing mango tree in the Sanskrit text. Instead, a number of other preliminary miracles are featured: the king's brother, whose hands and feet have been wrongfully cut off for a crime he did not commit, has his limbs miraculously restored through an act of truth; the Buddha himself flies through the air, puts out a fire using his supernatural powers, and so on. In each case, the heretics argue that it is not clear whether or not these marvels are actually being accomplished by the Buddha; given the size of the crowd, someone else may be responsible for them. Finally, the time for the main event arrives. Various disciples again offer to act in the Buddha's stead, but he turns them all down. The miracle of the double appearances of water and fire is much the same, although to it the Buddha now adds another: sitting on a huge lotus blossom brought to him by two *nāga* kings, the Buddha creates above, in front of and behind him, other lotus thrones on which sit replicas of the Buddha. In this way, he multiplies his own body and does not stop until he has filled the whole sky with buddhas, up to the heavens. Some are seated, some standing, some walking, some lying down, and they exhort the crowd with these words: "Start now! Leave home! Apply yourselves to the Buddha's Teaching! Overthrow the army of Death the way an elephant smashes a reed hut! For whoever goes forth intent on the Doctrine and Discipline will put an end to suffering and abandon this cycle of rebirth" (Burnouf, 1876, p. 164).

After this, King Prasenajit turns to the heretics and tells them it is now their turn to perform a miracle. But they are unable even to stand up. A great wind arises and blows over their pavilion and they flee in all directions. Their leader, Pūraṇa Kāśyapa, commits suicide in much the same way as he does in the Pali text. Finally, the episode concludes, as in the Pali text as well, with the Buddha producing a single magical replica of himself with whom he can converse, and this dialogic mode of teaching results in the conversion of hundreds of thousands of beings.

What are we to make of this episode? A number of interpretations have been proposed. Alfred Foucher long ago noted that, iconographically at least, it was the multiplication of buddhas found in the Sanskrit text (and not the simultaneous issue of water and flames) that was often featured. Following Foucher's lead, Paul Mus has argued that in this multiplication of buddhas throughout space we may find a Buddhist version of a cosmological theme paralleled in the brahmanical tradition of Prajāpati, the Lord of Creatures. "The Great Miracle," he says,

> in function of a cosmology that irradiates from a central point, develops the idea that, seated at the keystone of the spatio-temporal system, the Buddha occupies simultaneously all the directions of space. Space has become as if unreal under him, it is concentrated in one point: this is what one might call the "total" direction. (Mus, 1998, p. 274)

It is not clear, however, that in the texts the multiplication of buddhas (which is not even mentioned in the Pali) is the main point of the miracle of double appearances. Seeking to interpret the event as a whole, Mus, then, ultimately takes a different tack. He notes, in the story, the conjunction of three items: a tree (the mango), a "hut" (the pavilion of precious stones built for the Buddha), and a meditation walkway (in mid air). The same trio may be found at Bodhgaya in the bodhi tree (contemplated by the Buddha with steadfast gaze during the second week after his enlightenment), the jewelled meditation walkway (on which he walked back and forth during the third week), and the house of gems (where he spent the fourth week; see above, Chapter 4). And it may further be detected in accounts of the Buddha's birth (the tree under which he is born, the seven steps that he takes at birth, and the jewelled amniotic pavilion featured in the *Living out of the Game*; see Chapter 2 above). All these sources, Mus claims, point to a common scenario in which "near a tree, the Buddha emerges from a shelter, and walks without touching the ground" (Mus. 1935, 2, p. 413). This in turn is said to reflect a Buddhism that emphasizes an ideology not of great monasteries but of small hermitages, not of city-monks but of forest-dwellers.

There are certain difficulties with this view. It may well work when applied to Bodhgaya and Lumbinī, but it is less appropriate in the case of Śrāvastī which, after all, was a big city. Indeed, one of the thrusts of the whole story of the miracle at Śrāvastī (and of the Buddha's settling at the Jetavana and of his relationship to Anāthapiṇḍada) seems to be an attempt to move Buddhism "out of the woods" and to associate it with a major urban center. There is moreover a passage in the Sanskrit account of the miracle in which the Buddha specifically criticizes going to find refuge "in the mountains, the woods, at hermitages or sacred trees" (Cowell and Neil, 1886, p. 164; Burnouf, 1876, p. 165).

Mus's interpretation also fails adequately to consider two elements featured in the texts themselves: the "double" nature of the magical appearances, and the defeat of the heretics. It is, in fact, not exactly clear what the "double" in the name of the miracle refers to. The texts clearly indicate that, in this episode, it is the "double" appearance of both fire and water. In this light, the thrust of the miracle would be to assert the Buddha's mastery over the elements, his ability to effect a conjunction of opposites, and, at the same time, his meditative powers that enable him to focus on two things at once – water and fire. Other references to the miracle of the double, however, are less clear, and seem to indicate that the "double" refers to the two buddhas – himself and a replica of himself – that he is also said to create in both the Pali and the Sanskrit texts. This too would reflect the Buddha's tremendous meditative powers, his ability to concentrate on two things at once, to project an "other" who acts and talks seemingly independently. With this in mind, perhaps, the "Discourse on the Miracle" specifies that this is a power unique to buddhas. When *arhats* create magical replicas of themselves, they cannot converse with them because they are mere mirror-images who speak only when the *arhat* speaks and move only when the *arhat* moves. The Buddha's miracle at Śrāvastī goes beyond this in creating two buddhas who can do and say different things at the same time. Buddhologically, this is a significant step and may account in part for the popularity of the episode. The basic Buddhist rule was that two buddhas cannot co-exist simultaneously, but must live either in different worlds or in different aeons. This dictum came to present certain ideological problems, however, and was soon contradicted by Mahāyānist texts such as the *Lotus Sūtra* which dramatically portrayed Śākyamuni and Prabhūtaratna, a "past" Buddha from a "distant" world, as coming together in the same place at the same time. The solution of the story of the miracle of Śrāvastī is less bold, perhaps, than the *Lotus Sūtra*'s, but by presenting a scene in which apparently two buddhas are conversing with one another, and then making it clear that one is an original buddha and the other a projected image, it seems to be toying with a solution to the same problem.

Finally, we need to address one more important theme in the accounts of this episode, namely the fact that the miracle has, as its intent, the defeat of the heretical masters. Though the practice is sometimes questioned, the use of magical powers to convert non-believers to Buddhism is a commonplace in Buddhist legends. Here, however, there seems to be no intention of converting the heretics, but only of defeating them, of chasing them away, or worse, of bringing about their death, as in the case of Pūraṇa Kāśyapa. The intent appears to be not only to establish the greatness of the Buddha, but also to make clear the oneness of the Dharma.

There may be ritual reasons for this emphasis. It is important to remember that the miracle at Śrāvastī takes place just prior to the monastic rains-retreat. Indeed, the very next thing the Buddha does, after the miracle, is to go to the Trāyastriṃśa Heaven to spend the rains there, preaching to his mother. The *Book of the Discipline (Vinaya piṭaka)* does not seem to prescribe any particular rite for entering the rains-retreat. To this day, however, in Southeast Asia, monks who are to pass the rains together assemble and hold a brief ceremony during which they recite the "teachings to be remembered." These primarily advocate harmony and co-operation among fellow practitioners, but they end with an advocacy that all present should agree on right doctrinal views. Indeed, the whole purpose of the ceremony is stated at its very beginning when the monks are advised: "Do not let angry quarrels arise among you; share what you have with one another; do not annoy others with wrong behavior or wrong opinions" (Wells, 1960, p. 164). Given the obligation to spend three months together during the rains-retreats, a period of special purity and practice, the elimination of "wrong views" or "heretics" at its beginning may have seemed particularly important.

## THE RAINS-RETREAT IN TRĀYASTRIṂŚA HEAVEN

In the *Commentary on the Dharma Stanzas*, the story of the great miracle at Śrāvastī moves directly into the tale of his spending the rains-retreat in heaven. Even as he is preaching to the crowd, we are told, he reflects, "Where have buddhas of the past kept residence after performing this miracle?" He realizes that "it has been their invariable custom to enter upon residence in the World of the Thirty-three [gods; i.e., the

Trāyastriṃśa Heaven] and to expound the Abhidharma Piṭaka to their mother" (Burlingame, 1921, 3, p. 47, slightly modified). Accordingly, like the Hindu god Viṣṇu, he takes three strides and covers the cosmos: he first plants his right foot on the summit of Mount Yugandhara, then he puts his left foot on the top of Mount Meru, to reach with his last step the Trāyastriṃśa Heaven which is the residence of Indra, king of the gods. His departure is so abrupt and rapid that the crowd left in Śrāvastī thinks he has disappeared. They mourn his absence fearing that they will never see him again, and they have to be reassured by the Buddha's disciples that he has simply gone to heaven for the rainy season.

In heaven, the Buddha is welcomed and honored by the gods and seated on a great throne. The divinities, including his mother, all assemble to hear him recite the *Abhidharma piṭaka*. The seven books of the *Abhidharma* (which differ in Pali and Sanskrit) consist for the most part of lengthy categorizations and cross-categorizations of elements of reality. Though as narrative they may be less than gripping, they are conceptually interesting, epistemologically edifying, and helpful to meditators in their attempts to see clearly ontologically. More importantly, they are considered in some circles to be the height of the Buddha's teaching. It is sometimes said that the Buddha felt that neither the *Vinaya* nor the *Sūtra piṭakas* were sufficient to repay the kindness of his mother; only the *Abhidharma piṭaka* would do. It takes the Buddha a full three months to recite all seven books. His sermon goes on without stopping. Every day, he takes a break to go on his alms round (for which he travels to the Northern continent of Uttarakuru), and then to eat. During this time, however, he creates a double of himself and tells it to keep preaching until he gets back.

It is not only in heaven, however, that such a double is created. According to a well-known tale told to the Chinese pilgrims Faxian and Xuanzang when they visited Śrāvastī, the first Buddha image on earth was created when King Prasenajit, impatient at not seeing the Buddha while he was absent in the Trāyastriṃśa Heaven, had an artist carve a likeness of him out of sandalwood and put it in the place where the Buddha usually sat. When the Blessed One finally returns to earth, the image gets up and greets him, and the Buddha thanks it for taking his place and reminds it that its services will be needed again after he himself passes into final *nirvāṇa*.

This parallelism is significant for it illustrates the homology between a properly fashioned statue and a magically projected image, both of which can act as substitutes for the Buddha in his absence. The same connection between events in heaven and events on earth is reinforced in the Pali version of the story by the fact that the Buddha's disciple, Śāriputra, is said to visit him daily in heaven, during his lunch hour. Far from taking a rest from preaching, the Buddha uses this time to keep Śāriputra abreast of what he is teaching the gods. Śāriputra can then go back down to Śrāvastī and relay the Buddha's sermon to an audience of monks there. In this way, the *Abhidharma* comes to be known not only in heaven but on earth as well.

Given the importance of the Buddha's mother in the explication of the reasons for this whole scenario, it is curious how little attention is actually payed to her. The Buddha (perhaps because he is constantly preaching) is never said to interact with her on anything like a personal basis, and her own emotions are not touched upon. She is mentioned only at the very beginning and at the very end of the episode, and yet, one of the reasons for this whole rains-retreat sermon is that one of the indispensible acts performed by all buddhas is to bring their father and mother to a vision of the truth. The conversion of his father he has already accomplished by virtue of his visit to Kapilavastu, the conversion of his mother he accomplishes here. At the conclusion of his recitation, we are told eight hundred thousands of millions of deities come to understand the Dharma, including Mahā Māyā, who, moreover, attains the level of stream-winner. She is, in other words, his best pupil.

This relationship with his mother is stressed more in ritual re-enactments of this whole episode. Shway Yoe, at the end of the nineteenth century, describes an annual Burmese festival in which devotees recall these events in the Buddha's life by preparing "a platform . . . from twenty to fifty or sixty feet in height . . . over which is raised . . . a tower-like spire with seven diminishing roofs." This symbolizes the Tawadeintha (= Trāyastriṃśa) Heaven. Leading up to it is a ramp that represents the path which the Buddha took up to heaven. About half-way up this slope there may be a small stage which is called Ugandaw Hill, i.e., Mount Yugandhara, the site of the Buddha's first step. In the ritual which re-enacts the Buddha's ascent, he is represented by an image seated "on a little carriage, fitted to run on a tramway" that will take him right up to the top. It is pulled up slowly by means of a rope and windlass, stopping at the Yugandhara way-station, and allowing plenty of time for participants in the festival, many of whom have dressed up as various deities and kings and grandees, to make merit. When the statue reaches the top, it is finally time for the sermon. This is delivered by a monk with a loud voice who crouches behind the image. The crowd, however, is not treated to the *Abhidharma* but to a sermon on filial piety, specifically on the impossibility of fully repaying the debt one owes to one's mother. "I," says the Buddha's stand-in,

> I, the great Sraman, the mightiest of all beings, the teacher of ne'ban [*nirvāṇa*] and the Law [the Dharma]; I, the all-powerful, who by my preaching can lead my mother into the path of salvation and the final deliverance; I, who know all things and have beat down the passions under my feet; even I, with all this can [hardly] repay the debt due to [just] one of the breasts that suckled me. (Shway Yoe, 1882, pp. 329–30)

The message is clear: a mother's love and care know no bounds. Even the Buddha could not fully thank her for her kindness. Yet he tried, and so should we.

## THE DESCENT FROM TRĀYASTRIṂŚA HEAVEN

In the Burmese festival just described, the image of the Buddha is left at the top of the tower overnight and then, the following evening, it is brought back down again, either by the same route, or, in more elaborate cases, by another pathway down the other side of the "mountain."

This represents the descent of the Buddha from heaven to the town of Sāṃkāśya, another one of the indispensible acts of a buddha. The event came to be popularly represented in Buddhist art, and is annually celebrated in many parts of Southeast Asia at the end of the rains-retreat.

The Buddha's audience has been waiting for him in Śrāvastī. The Buddha, however, wants to see his disciple Śāriputra who happens to be in the city of Śāṃkāśya, over three hundred kilometers away towards the West. He therefore chooses to descend there, asking Maudgalyāyana to help the people who are waiting for him in Śravastī to move to the new site. This change in venue is interesting. Śāṃkāśya is located on the upper reaches of the Ganges and is far removed from the other major pilgrimage sites associated with the life of the Buddha. As Alfred Foucher points out, this is not the heartland of Buddhism but of Brahmanism; it is also wheat rather than rice country, a land of dry cultivation rather than paddy.

The actual descent is made by means of three flights of stairs from heaven made by the gods for the occasion. The Buddha comes down on a middle staircase made of precious gems, while to his right and left, Indra and the gods use a staircase made of gold, and Brahmā and his followers a staircase made of silver. These three staircases (or ladders) are the most prominent feature of the story's depiction in art. They were also the focal point of the pilgrimage tradition. Faxian, visiting Sāṃkāśya in the early fifth century, reports that after the Buddha and the gods came down, the three flights of stairs disappeared into the ground, all except the top seven steps which were still visible. He further reports that King Aśoka, hoping to uncover them, dug down into the ground but could not reach their end because he hit water. Faxian's report is intriguing because it shows that what was thought of as a staircase to heaven came to be seen as a ladder to the underworld. Foucher hypothesizes that the staircases are, in fact, to be associated with the artificial irrigation ramps which still today dot the region around Sāṃkāśya and are the most conspicuous feature of the local landscape. These long, high, earthen ramps, set at angles of thirty degrees, were used by teams of oxen to haul up underground water in great skin sacks for irrigation. This is all speculative, of course, but the imagery is suggestive of the period at the end of the rains, when not only do monks come out of seclusion and re-enter the world, but the water also returns underground.

The presence of the gods on this occasion is also important and the whole event is called a "descent of the gods" (*devāvatāra*) and not a descent of the Buddha. Indeed, it is said that, at Sāṃkāśya, the whole cosmos is revealed so that gods can see humans and humans can see gods, and everyone has a clear view from the highest heavens to the deepest hells.

The assembled crowd of laypersons and monastics vie to be first to venerate the Buddha. The Pali tradition specifies that it is Śāriputra who has this honor, and, in fact, uses the scene to enhance Śāriputra's reputation *vis-à-vis* some of the Buddha's other disciples. A number of Sanskrit texts, however, feature the nun Utpalavarṇā. Eager to be the first to welcome the Buddha back to earth, she disguises herself as a great *cakravartin* king so as to be able to push her way through the crowd and occupy a front row position. In some texts, the Buddha reprimands her for this enthusiasm to see him physically and approves instead his disciple Subhūti who did not even come to Sāṃkāśya, but instead kept meditating in a cave, far away in Rājagṛha.

The eagerness to greet the Buddha and honor him with offerings, however, reflects a ritual tradition of making special donations to the monks at the end of the rains-retreat. In the *Book of the Discipline*, two rituals are prescribed for this period: the "termination ceremony" (*pravāraṇā*), which involves only the monks, and the offering of cloth for robes (*kaṭhina*) ceremony which is an occasion for merit-making by laypersons who supply the monks with the wherewithal for new robes. The *pravāraṇā* is intended to ascertain and affirm the purity and unity of the saṃgha and features each monk asking the community as a whole whether anyone knows of any offense he has committed during the whole of the rains-retreat. In the *Commentary on the Dharma Stanzas*, the Buddha celebrates the *pravaraṇā* in heaven just prior to his descent to this world. The reception he is given by Utpālavarṇā and others is not exactly a *kaṭhina* ceremony, but it has its counterpart in a festival of giving and merit-making that, in some parts of Southeast Asia today, overlaps with the *kaṭhina* rite. Kenneth Wells has described the festival as follows:

> Certain temples have traditional ceremonies at the time of *Ok Barnsa* [i.e., the end of the rains-retreat] such as bringing an image of Buddha down from a hill, or lowering an image from the top of a cetiya amid a fanfare of music, or conveying an image to the temple in a decorated cart followed by a procession of monks and worshipers. When food is given to monks walking in this procession it is an act of merit called *Devorohana* or "Coming down from the deva world." This is in memory of the return of Buddha from Indra's heaven. (Wells, 1960, p. 104)

On this day, Wells goes on, a dramatic account of the event is often read, in the evening, by three monks, one of whom takes the part of the Buddha, another, the role of Śāriputra (he also doubles in the role of Mahāmāyā), and a third, the role of Maudgalyāyana. Together, they re-enact the whole Trāyastriṃśa experience, putting questions to the Buddha about the occasion being celebrated as well as about *Abhidharma* matters.

## DISTANT JOURNEYS: THE VISIT TO THE NORTHWEST

We come now, finally, to the "apocryphal" journeys that the Buddha is said to make to distant lands. We have already seen that Sāṃkāśya, where the Buddha came down from heaven, was located far to the west of where he carried out most of his ministry. According to a tradition preserved in the *Discipline [Vinaya] of the Mūlasarvāstivadins* and other sources, however, Sāṃkāśya did not represent the limit of his wanderings. Even further up the Ganges was the town of Hastināpura not far north of present-day Delhi, and from there, the Buddha is said to have taken off on a great tour of what is now North India, Pakistan, and Afghanistan, before returning to the city of Mathurā, south of Delhi. It is, of course, highly improbable that the historical Buddha ever undertook such a journey. As Etienne Lamotte has shown, this whole story was part of a propaganda effort devised by later Buddhists of the region to associate the Blessed One with different places in their vicinity. Nonetheless, the episode is biographically interesting for it reveals at least one aspect of the Buddha's life that we have not yet fully touched upon: his ways of dealing with demonic forces or indigenous divinities.

Lamotte has identified three stages in this journey to the Northwest. The first of these appears to be a perfectly ordinary trip. From Hastināpura, the Buddha goes, together with his disciple Ānanda, on foot to Rohitaka, a town further to the North and West. Similarly, later on, in the "third stage" of this trip, he and Ānanda will go from Rohitaka south to the city of Mathurā. Sandwiched between these two trips, however, is a fantastic voyage which seems to take place all in one night. One evening, in Rohitaka, he leaves his disciple Ānanda behind, and taking along his supernatural body-guard henchman, the *yakṣa* Vajrapāṇi, he flies off through the air, crosses the Indus River, and visits a whole series of places in what is now Afghanistan and Kashmir. The next morning, Ānanda is very surprised when he wakes up to learn that the Buddha has been absent. During this expedition, however, the Blessed One, with Vajrapāṇi's help, converts no fewer than seventy-seven thousand beings. We shall look at two of these: his conversion of the ogress Kuntī; and his conversion of the dragon king (*nāga*) Apalāla.

The story of the ogress (*yakṣinī*) Kuntī, may be summarized as follows: When the Buddha arrives in the Northwestern town of Kuntīnagara, he learns of the fierce ogress named Kuntī who lives there. She is in the habit of devouring all the children born to local brahmin householders. As a group, these brahmins appeal to the Buddha, asking him to do something about her. The Buddha's approach is simply to confront Kuntī and to broker a deal between her and the townspeople: if she agrees to stop eating their children, they will agree to build a Buddhist monastery in her honor. There, she will become the object of a cult so that her hunger can ritually be assuaged. Where previously she ate children, she will now receive worship and offerings, as the indigenous tutelary divinity of the monastery.

Unfortunately, our sources do not give us any details about this cult, but Kuntī is sometimes thought to be a local manifestation of a better known ogress, Hārītī. Both of them were probably goddesses of smallpox, who were seen ambivalently as both harriers and sparers of children. Hārītī too was in the habit of devouring babies, and she too is converted by the Buddha when the people appeal to him. In her case, the Buddha's tactics are a bit different. While Hārītī is out, he goes to her house and kidnaps her youngest son whom she loves very much. He hides the child in his begging bowl. When Hārītī returns, she looks frantically for her baby, searching everywhere in vain. Desperate with grief, she finally turns to the Buddha for help. He uses her anguish to drive home a lesson about the cruelty of her ways, telling her that now she knows how the parents whose children she devours feel. Having learned her lesson, she agrees to give up her evil habits, and the Buddha gives her back her child.

A new problem arises, however: what is she to eat instead of human flesh? How is she now to feed herself and her children? The Buddha's solution is noteworthy, and very much in line with that in the case of Kuntī above: every day, throughout Jambudvīpa, his disciples will make food offerings to her at the end of their own meal. In exchange, she is to promise to do two things: to protect Buddhist monasteries and the monks in them, and to help childless parents have offspring. Here too, then, an ogress converted by the Buddha is made into the beneficial object of a cult that is channeled through Buddhist monks. If the people of the community ensure that their monks have enough food, Hāritī and Kuntī will be fed and ensure everyone's prosperity.

The story of the dragon-like *nāga* king Apalāla is rather different. According to one version, in a previous life, Apalāla was a brahmin who, by virtue of his magical powers, was able to put an end to a drought by making it rain. The local ruler, however, failed to recompense him for this service, and, out of spite, he resolved to become a fierce nāga and ravage the crops in the area. He was then reborn as Apalāla. In the *Vinaya of the Mūlasarvāstivādins*, when the Buddha and Vajrapāṇi arrive in the region, Apalāla showers them with hail and dirt. The Buddha quickly enters into a meditation on loving-kindness and transforms the hailstones and dirt into a cloud of sweet perfumes. The *nāga* retreats to his abode at the bottom of a lake. The Buddha then resolves to ferret him out. He orders Vajrapāṇi to attack, and the *yakṣa*, with a few blows of his thunderbolt, crumbles the whole mountain top into the lake, and forces Apalāla to emerge from the waters. He is about to flee, but the Buddha is ready for him: he enters into the *samādhi* of fire and fills the whole valley with a mass of flames, leaving only a small space in front him, right at his feet, free from the conflagration. Apalāla, seeking a cool place, is forced to come there. The Buddha then grabs him by his hair and, in no uncertain terms, tells him to change his ways. If he repents, and ceases to plague the local community, he still has a chance to be reborn in heaven, but if he does not, he is destined for hell. Given that choice, Apalāla quickly makes up his mind: he takes refuge in the Triple Gem and agrees to stop harming the people in the region.

The violence of this encounter may surprise some in light of the Buddha's gentler tactics in the case of Kuntī, but it is actually not atypical. Similar scenarios could be cited in which the Buddha is presented as a master of magical means who does not hold back from using his powers to subdue troublemakers and force them to convert. As one scholar has put it, "the Buddha who elsewhere accepts the humility of lesser orders as a matter of course, appears [here] in the aggressive role of a conqueror" (Soper, 1949–50, pt 2, p. 318). The same scholar also compares the battle between the Buddha and Apalāla with various other Vedic and Persian stories of mythic combats between heroes and serpents.

There is an important way, however, in which Buddhist ethics have moderated this myth. Unlike some of the watery dragons slain by other heroes, Apalāla is not killed. He is subdued, he is converted, but he is left alive. He is, moreover, conquered in a way that is distinctly Buddhist. By filling the world with fire, the Buddha not only demonstrates his magical powers, he also forces his opponents to realize, graphically and concretely, the intolerable nature of *saṃsāra*. He uses his magic to make the world appear to them as it truly is: a place of suffering.

## ANOTHER DISTANT JOURNEY AND MORE DEMONS: THE BUDDHA IN SRI LANKA

It is interesting to compare the story of Apalāla with the story of the Buddha's dealings with the *yakṣas* of Sri Lanka. The Buddha is said by Sri Lankans to have made three visits to Sri Lanka, all of them by flying through the air, the first in the seventh month after his enlightenment, the second and third in the fifth and eighth years respectively, while he was dwelling at the Jetavana.

Here we shall focus only on the first part of the first visit, a sort of preliminary trip in which the Buddha prepares the island for the later establishment of Buddhism by ridding it of its demons (*yakṣas*). The episode is set as an interlude in the existing narrative of the Buddha's life. While he is in Uruvīlvā, about to convert the matted-haired brahmin Uruvilvā Kāśyapa, the Buddha has a spare moment and turns his thoughts southwards towards Sri Lanka. He knows that it is "filled with demons" and realizes that, before Buddhism can flourish there, these "must first be driven forth" (Geiger, 1912, p. 3). Accordingly, he flies to the island and, using his magical powers, he creates thick clouds, rain, cold winds, and darkness. The demons do not like this, and so he offers to make a fire for them, to bring them warmth; all they need to do is to give him a place where he can sit down and kindle it. They do, and there the Buddha spreads a carpet of hide. Sitting on it, he magically causes it to heat up so that there are flames all around it. He then gradually increases the size of its carpet, and with it, the circle of fire, which expands outwards so that it quickly spreads "insupportable heat over the [whole] island" (Oldenberg, 1879, p. 122). The demons, having asked for warmth, receive much more than they bargained for, and they quickly flee in all directions crying "where shall we go for safety and refuge?" The Buddha's solution is to give them "another island" named Giridīpa. It is situated "in the midst of the ocean and of the deep waters, where the waves incessantly break" and around it there is "a chain of mountains, towering, [and] difficult to pass" (Oldenberg, 1879, p. 122). Having brought this island, Giridīpa, near to Sri Lanka, the Buddha puts all of the demons on it and then returns it to its former place, far away. Having thus expelled the demons, he seeks to ensure that they will not return: he walks three times around the whole island of Sri Lanka, pronouncing a "spell of protection" (Oldenberg, 1879, p. 123). Lanka, he declares, is to be a place for human beings, a place for the Dharma, and he then returns to Uruvīlvā.

It is possible to contrast this scenario of the Buddha in Sri Lanka with that of his activities in Northwest India described above. In the case of his conversion of the *nāga* Apalāla, we have an example of what I call the "centripetal Buddha." The whole region is set on fire, except for one small spot at the Buddha's feet. Apalāla is thus forced to come to the Buddha and take refuge in him: conversion is his only option, but, as the stories of Kuntī and Hārītī make clear, this is a rather loose conversion in which the indigenous identities of divinities are allowed to continue under the aegis and sponsorship of Buddhism. In the case of the demons of Sri Lanka, we have, on the other hand, an example of what I call the "centrifugal Buddha." Here the fire emanates out from the Buddha; refuge from it is not to be found in the center, but beyond the periphery. The solution is not to convert the demons and make Buddhists out of them, but to chase them away, to send them into exile. This does not mean that there are no Sri Lankan examples in which the Buddha acts centripetally. In fact, on his very next visit, according to the *Chronicle of the Island (Dīpavaṃsa)*, he converts the *nāgas* in way that attracts them to him. In this first story of his dealing with the demons, however, a more exclusionist ideology seems to be at work.

## THE JOURNEY TO ŚROṆĀPARĀNTA: LEAVING FOOTPRINTS ON THE WAY

Finally, there is one more distant "apocryphal" journey of the Buddha to be considered here: the trip that he is said to take to the land of Śroṇāparānta at the invitation of his disciple Pūrṇa. After being converted and ordained by the Buddha at Śrāvastī, Pūrṇa returns to his native land, Śroṇāparānta, which is sometimes said to be located in Western India, but which in Southeast Asian traditions is commonly associated with a region of what is now Myanmar (Burma). Pūrṇa wants to give his compatriots, who have never had a chance to see the Buddha, an opportunity to do so. Hence he prepares a magnificent monastic hall for the Blessed One, and then invites him to come and stay there. The Buddha agrees and the next day, the gods prepare for the journey 501 special flying pavilions for him and his disciples, and have them ready and waiting at the gate of the Jetavana monastery. The Blessed One and 499 of his monks each mount a pavilion, and together they fly off in formation to Śroṇāparānta, one of the pavilions remaining empty. En route, they stop at a mountain called Saccabandha, where they meet a heretic teacher of the same name, who is leading people astray with his false doctrines. The Buddha, however, can see that Saccabandha is ripe for conversion so he preaches the Dharma, and instantaneously Saccabandha attains *arhat*ship and becomes ordained as a monk. He then mounts the empty pavilion which was intended for him all along, and the group proceeds on its way. In Śroṇāparānta they are cordially received by Pūrṇa and the entire population. The Buddha preaches there for seven days, converting eighty-four thousand people, before he decides to return home. On the way back, he makes two stops. He goes, first, to the Narmadā river where he is welcomed by a *nāga* king whom he also converts. When it comes time for him to leave, the *nāga* asks him for some sort of memento by which he can continue to honor him, and the Buddha obliges him by leaving the mark of his footprint on the riverbank. Depending on the height of the water, we are told, this relic is sometimes visible and sometimes not, and is venerated by humans or by *nāgas*. Leaving the Narmadā River, the Buddha then stops at Mount Saccabandha, where they leave off the now converted eponymous hermit. He too, however, asks for a relic which he can use as an object of veneration, and the Blessed One again obliges by impressing his footprint in the solid rock of the mountain.

These, of course, are not the only footprint relics left by the Buddha on his various journeys. The most famous one, perhaps, is the print still found today on Sri Pāda (also known as Adam's Peak) in south central Sri Lanka, but there are hundreds of others throughout the Buddhist world. The Narmadā and Saccabandha footprints, however, became famous in Thailand and Burma where they are still the object of local cults and pilgrimage. It has been argued by some that their popularity reflects Sri Lankan influence on the Buddhism of the area, but others have more convincingly shown that local indigenous Southeast Asian beliefs about mountains and rivers, about fertility and rainfall, have here influenced the Pali tradition. It would seem then, that we have here, in the story of this journey of the Buddha and footprints he left in distant lands, yet another example of the way in which the biography of the Buddha was developed to enhance indigenous Buddhism.

*The Buddha in* parinirvāṇa, *Aluvihare, Sri Lanka*

# 6 FINAL DAYS, THE *PARINIRVĀṆA*, AND THE *NIRVĀṆA* OF THE RELICS

After forty-five years of ministry, in India and beyond, the Buddha comes to be ready for death, for what is known as his "complete extinction" (*parinirvāṇa*). The importance of this event in the history of Buddhism is reflected in the fact that it denotes the beginning – year 1 – of the Buddhist era. Buddhist calendars measure time from the decease of their Master, unlike Christian calendars which count the years from the birth of theirs. But the *parinirvāṇa* should be thought of not so much as the death of the Buddha as his "last death," after which he will never have to die again, just as his birth in Lumbinī was his "last birth," after which he would never have to be reborn. With the parinirvāṇa, the Buddha escapes definitively from the round of *saṃsāra*.

Buddhist texts do not usually speak of the Buddha as "entering" or "attaining" *parinirvāṇa*; rather, they describe him as being "parinirvāṇized" – completely extinguished. The Buddha himself is said to have indicated that it was not fruitful to think about the ontological meaning of this; after death the saint was beyond imagining in terms of either being or non-being. As the great Buddhist philosopher Nagārjuna put it, it is wrong to say that the Buddha, after his *parinirvāṇa*, either is, or is not, or both is and is not, or neither is nor is not. And yet, as we shall see, though the Buddha is not reborn, though his life and death cease with his complete extinction, his biography does not stop: it continues on in the relics, in his teachings, and in the community he leaves behind after his body's cremation. Life is not always about ontology.

The *parinirvāṇa*, though it is called a "complete" extinction, is but the second of three *nirvāṇas* (extinctions) in the Buddhist tradition. First, there is the "*nirvāṇa with* a mind-body substratum remaining," which is equivalent to the Buddha's enlightenment at Bodhgaya, and might be thought of as the extinction of the *āśravas* (that is, of sensual desire, clinging to existence, speculative views, and ignorance) (see above, Chapter 3). Then there is the "*nirvāṇa without* a mind-body substratum remaining," which we shall consider in this chapter. This is the Buddha's *parinirvāṇa* which occurs at a town called Kuśinagarī and might be thought of as the extinction of the Buddha's karmic continuum, of his life and death. Finally, as we shall see, there is the "*nirvāṇa* of the relics" which can be thought of as the Buddha's truly final extinction, the end of his biography.

In this last chapter of the Buddha's lifestory, I want to examine in some detail the events leading up to the Buddha's *parinirvāṇa*. These center around the last journey that he makes over the course of several months, together with his attendant disciple Ānanda, from the city of Rājagṛha to the town of Kuśinagarī. Then I wish to consider the accounts of what took place on the Buddha's final deathbed – his last words, and wishes – as well as the actual event of his *parinirvāṇa*. To this I would like to add a consideration of the Buddha's funeral – the veneration of his body and its cremation. This is followed by the gathering and distribution of his relics. Finally, I conclude with a brief account of the ongoing life of his relics, and also of his teachings, their regathering and preservation, as well as their own projected disappearance, which is a part of the Buddha's biography that is yet to come.

## THE BUDDHA'S LAST JOURNEY

Any presentation of the Buddha's last journey – from Rājagṛha to Kuśinagarī – must ultimately be based on a canonical text known as the *Discourse on the Great Extinction (Mahāparinirvāṇa sūtra)*, which exists in several versions in Pali, Sanskrit, Chinese, and Tibetan.

It is possible to divide the Pali account of this journey into fourteen stages, each one featuring a stop in a given locality where the Buddha encounters different persons and preaches a number of sermons, some of them among the best known in the Buddhist tradition. The Buddha himself is portrayed as being old and unwell and his itinerary can sometimes be read as a sort of Buddhist *via dolorosa* – a way of suffering which ends by putting an end to suffering. It is worth recounting here in its entirety.

The journey starts at Vulture's Peak near Rājagṛha, a mountain retreat famous as the site of some of the Buddha's most significant sermons. The Buddha is visited by Varṣākāra, a minister of King Ajātaśatru, who has replaced his father Bimbisāra as ruler of Magadha. The king wants to wage war against the people of Vṛji and seeks the Buddha's evaluation of his prospects. The Buddha replies that the Vṛjis may be expected to prosper as long as they continue to do seven things: hold regular and frequent assemblies, meet in harmony, do not change the rules of their tradition, honor their elders, do not abduct women from other tribes, revere their shrines, and make provisions for holy men. The minister understands from this that it will not be possible for him to defeat the Vṛjis militarily as long as they do these things, and, thanking the Buddha, he soon departs. The Blessed One, however, then goes on to make parallel points about his own community, the *saṃgha*. The Buddhist *saṃgha*, he declares, may be expected to prosper as long as its members hold regular and frequent assemblies, meet in harmony, do not change the rules of training, honor their superiors who were ordained before them, do not fall prey to worldly desires, remain devoted to forest hermitages, and preserve their personal mindfulness. This is then followed by several more lists of "seven things" conducive to the well-being of the *saṃgha*. The point here is that the Buddha is beginning to turn his thoughts to the future and to how the community he has founded will manage to continue to live harmoniously in his absence. This is a theme he will return to several times in the events that follow.

The Buddha then proceeds, together with Ānanda and a large company of monks, to the town of Ambalaṭṭhikā. There, he repeats a sermon that he had also given at Vulture's Peak and that is called a "comprehensive discourse." It is a basic presentation of the Buddhist path, which he, in fact, will reiterate at virtually all the remaining stops along his way. Whatever else he says or does, this is a theme that he wants to hammer home:

> This is morality, this is [meditative] concentration, this is wisdom. Concentration, when imbued with morality, brings great fruit and profit. Wisdom, when imbued with concentration, brings great fruit and profit. The mind imbued with wisdom becomes completely free from the corruptions, that is the corruption of sensuality, of becoming, of false views and of ignorance. (Walshe, 1987, p. 234)

From Ambalaṭṭhikā, the Buddha goes on to Nālandā, a village which was to become famous in later Buddhist history for its great monastic university. In the *Great Story (Mahāvastu)*, it is said to be the hometown of Śāriputra, and indeed, it is Śāriputra who here comes to see the Buddha. He starts by praising his master: "It is clear to me, Lord, that there never has been, will be or is now another ascetic or Brahmin who is better or more enlightened than the Lord." Interestingly the Buddha, rather than accepting this as a compliment, takes it as a topic for debate. He asks Śāriputra on what grounds he can make such a statement. How can he be so sure? Does he know the minds of all the buddhas, past, present, and future? Śāriputra admits that he does not have direct knowledge of the minds of all buddhas, but nonetheless he stands by his statement based on what he can deduce from what he does know about *this* buddha. The whole interlude is noteworthy not only for its foreshadowing of debate traditions (that were to be featured at Nālandā University), but also as maintaining the importance of knowing things with certainty and not just taking them on faith, another theme that will reappear in the context of the Buddha's last sermons.

Next, the Buddha and Ānanda, along with other monks, move on to Pāṭaligrāma, on the banks of the Ganges. There he preaches a sermon to the villagers on the five dangers of immorality and the five benefits of morality. The real purpose of his stop, however, seems to be to make a prediction about the future. At this point, Varṣākāra, the same Magadhan general whom he met in the first episode above, is busy building a fort at Pāṭaligrāma, the first step in its eventual transformation into Pāṭaliputra, the great capital of the Mauryan Empire. In observing this, the Buddha also sees, with his divine eye, that many powerful deities are assembling and taking up lodging in the new city. The Buddha, accordingly, predicts the future greatness of Pāṭaliputra, and the next day, in his sermon to Varṣākāra, he shows how that can be assured: by making offerings to monks such as himself, laypeople such as Varṣākāra should transfer the merit of that offering to the local divinities. Thus revered and honored, they will in turn protect the place, the way a mother might protect her only son. This, of course, is the same solution as that proposed in the conversion of Kuntī (see Chapter 5), and the message in the present context is clear: the future greatness of the Mauryan capital will depend on the support its citizens offer to the Buddhist community.

From Pāṭaligrāma, the Buddha crosses the Ganges. As it is in flood (the Pali text tells us that it is so full of water that a crow, standing on the bank, can drink from it), various people are looking for boats or making rafts to get to the other side. The Buddha, however, does not need such a conveyance. As fast as a strong man might flex his arm, he uses his supernatural power to transport himself instantly to the other shore. This, of course, is symbolic of his having crossed over the stream of *saṃsāra*, a common metaphor in the Buddhist tradition, and a message which the Buddha makes explicit in a verse. But the Buddha's ability to cross the river is contrasted to the relative difficulties experienced by others, and here the variants are interesting. In the Pali text, where the Buddha reappears on the far side of the river, together with his monks, he merely distinguishes between those people who, wanting to cross, are busy finding a bridge or making a raft, and "the wise" who, like himself and his monks, have crossed already. In the Sanskrit, however, we find a number of further distinctions: "The Blessed One," it says, "has crossed over. The brahmin [presumably Varṣākāra who stays in Pāṭaligrāma] remains on the bank. The monks are swimming across. The disciples are building a raft" (Waldschmidt, 1950–51, p. 158). Interpreting, we can see here the germs of differentiation between different types of beings, and the ease with which they can transcend the sea of suffering. The Buddha has already transcended it. His immediate disciples will have a relatively easy time as they will depend on the Buddha's teaching, his Dharma, which is here likened to a raft. Ordinary monks, who will not be able to benefit directly from the Buddha's teaching (that is, after his death), will have a more difficult time: they will have to swim. Finally, some beings (for example, the brahmin) will not even try to cross the river but will be content with staying on the shore. Similar distinctions were to be made later in the Buddhist tradition between buddhas, *pratyekabuddhas*, and *śrāvakas* (*arhats*). Rather different, however, is the version of this verse found in one of the Chinese translations of the discourse, which refers to the Buddha as the Helmsman of the Great Vehicle who causes *all* beings, gods and men together, to cross over the sea of suffering on the bridge of Dharma.

The Buddha's next stop is the village of Kuṭigrāmaka, where he preaches a sermon on the Four Noble Truths and on the Path. At the same time, having just "crossed over" the stream of suffering, he makes this into a sort of re-affirmation of salvation, for he ends his sermon by declaring: "By virtue of not seeing the Four Noble Truths as they are, the road that you and I have wandered is long. These truths being seen, the thirst for existence is cut off, the round of rebirths is destroyed, rebirth is now no more" (Waldschmidt, 1950–51, p. 136).

From there, the Buddha and Ānanda and a large company of monks, proceed to a town called Nādikā where they stay in a place known as the "brick house." The Buddha is informed that many lay followers in town have recently died, and he comforts their relatives by telling them where they have each been reborn and what their individual fates will be. So-and-so will attain enlightenment without having to be reborn again; so-and-so is a stream-winner and will never have another unfortunate rebirth, and so on. We can see here part of the pastoral function of a great religious seer such as the Buddha, but after clarifying the karma of over a hundred individuals, he becomes weary of this and so he reveals to Ānanda a teaching known as the "Mirror of Dharma," whereby his followers can know for themselves that they will avoid unfortunate rebirths and when and whether they will attain enlightenment. There is nothing esoteric about this teaching; it consists of having unwavering faith (*prasāda*) in the Buddha, in the Dharma and in the *saṃgha*. People who have this will be able to see, as though they were looking in a mirror, that they will no longer be reborn in hell or in the animal or hungry-ghost realms, and that they are destined for enlightenment.

Next, the Buddha and his company reach the city of Vaiśālī, and there they stay outside of town in a mango grove known as "Āmrapālī's wood." Āmrapālī herself is a famous courtesan from Vaiśālī, and hearing that the Buddha is residing in her park, she drives out in a bullock cart to see him and to invite him to her house for a meal on the next day. He accepts. On her way back to town, however, she comes up against some young Licchavi lords who are also on their way to invite the Buddha, magnificently arrayed in their sumptuous carriages. So glorious are they that they are described as looking exactly like the gods of Indra's heaven. Āmrapālī, in a hurry to get back to start preparing for the Buddha's visit, and perhaps filled with pride at the privilege just shown her, refuses to give way to the Licchavi lords on the narrow road. They, maligning her as a "mango-woman," clearly think she, a woman of ill repute, should move aside and let them, her superiors, proceed. But she does not. In the Pali text, she meets them "axle to axle, wheel to wheel, yoke to yoke." In other versions, she is even more confrontational, smashing their banner-flags and parasols, and trying to drive through their ranks. "Let me through," she tells them, "the Blessed One is coming to *my* house." The Licchavis are upset by this news. They are on their way to invite the Buddha to *their* house, and so they offer to pay Āmrapālī a hundred thousand pieces of gold for the privilege of entertaining the Buddha in her stead. But she rejects their offer, telling them she would not give up this chance for the whole of Vaiśālī! The Licchavis, nonetheless, decide to try to outdo her. They go on to see the Buddha and still press him to come to their place on the morrow. The Buddha, however, quite properly, tells them that he cannot, as he has already accepted Āmrapālī's invitation. Indeed, the next day, along with his monks, he goes to her house where she not only serves him a fine meal, but also gives him the grove in which he is staying as a new Buddhist monastic park. In return, he preaches to her the Dharma.

The competition between Āmrapālī and the Licchavis is interesting since it pits lay supporters against one another, and it shows the Buddha's fair-mindedness in accepting invitations. As a courtesan, Āmrapālī is a woman of some ill repute; she is also very beautiful. Indeed, in some versions of this story, the Buddha begins by preaching to his monks a sermon on mindfulness. It is not clear, in the Pali text, whether or not this is related to Āmrapālī's coming, but that connection was perceived by the generally mysogynistic fifth-century Theravāda commentator Buddhaghosa, and it is clearly made in the Sanskrit where the Buddha cautions his monks to be attentive and mindful because Āmrapālī the harlot (along with a great number of her women-in-waiting) is coming. But apart from this, the Buddha here shows none of the bias which will soon portray him as telling Ānanda to have as little to do with women as possible, and, indeed, in a number of sources, the Buddha's sermon on mindfulness has nothing to do with Āmrapālī but is preached just prior to the arrival of the Licchavis, as a warning to his monks not to be taken in by all of their finery.

The Buddha decides to spend his final rains-retreat in the region of Vaiśālī, not at Āmrapālī's grove, but in a nearby village called Veṇugrāmaka. There is a famine in the area, and he chooses to stay in Veṇugrāmaka alone with Ānanda, advising the rest of the monks to spread out and find places in Vaiśālī or other parts of the region, so as not to burden any single community with their numbers. In Veṇugrāmaka, he becomes deathly ill, about to die. But, thinking he should not do so without taking leave of the community as a whole, he uses his powers of concentration to hold the disease in check. This is not easy. As he puts it to Ānanda, he is now eighty years old, and his body has become like an old cart, held together with straps. It is only when he withdraws his attention from outward things and cuts off sensory perceptions by entering a trance, that he manages to feel comfortable. Eventually, however, he recovers somewhat, and Ānanda prepares a seat for him outside, in front of their hut. There, he expresses his relief at the Buddha's recovery, especially because he has not yet made any statement about a successor. The Buddha is surprised. He tells Ānanda that he has not been a "closed fist" teacher who has kept certain doctrines back only to reveal them to individuals as esoteric truth. Rather he has revealed the Dharma equally to all, and there is no one of his monks who has any kind of special authority. All of his disciples should live "as islands unto themselves, being their own refuge, with no one else as their refuge," with the Dharma and none other as their sole resort. And if they are willing to learn and work hard, they can achieve enlightenment.

Still in the area of Vaiśālī, the Buddha decides, next, to spend an afternoon at the Cāpāla shrine. There, apparently as part of the aftermath of his successful overcoming of his illness by dint of concentration, he tells Ānanda that Tathāgatas, such as himself, because of their supernatural powers, are able to extend their lifetimes for as long as a whole aeon (or, less dramatically, to the end of a full life-span of one hundred years). Apparently, however, this is only if Tathāgatas are actually requested by someone to do so, and Ānanda fails to get the hint. So the Buddha tries a second time: a Tathāgata could, because of his supernatural powers, extend his lifetime for as long as a whole aeon. . . . Again Ānanda fails to ask him, and fails again when the Buddha repeats the statement a third time. He therefore dismisses his disciple and goes to sit down under a tree. There, Māra suddenly appears; always eager to get rid of the Buddha, he encourages him to pass immediately into complete extinction. But the Buddha replies that he is not ready to die – not until he is sure that he has monk-disciples who are accomplished and trained enough so as to be able to teach others and refute false doctrines. Māra replies that he already has such monks, and so should enter *parinirvāṇa*. The Buddha then argues that he wants to wait until he has nun-disciples . . . laymen disciples . . . laywomen disciples . . . who are accomplished and trained enough so as to be able to teach others and refute false doctrines, and again, Māra points out that this is already the case. Finally, the Buddha gives up; recognizing that his doctrine is now "successfully established . . . widespread, well-known . . . everywhere," he tells Māra that, in three months time, he will enter complete extinction.

This proclamation, definitively setting a term limit to the Buddha's life, is momentous enough to create a tremendous earthquake. Ānanda, understandably, inquires as to the cause of the earthquake, and this gives the Blessed One a chance to review his entire lifestory. There are eight reasons for earthquakes, he explains. The first is simply a naturalistic cause: the earth is established on water (we would say magma) and when the water moves, the earth quakes. The second is a quasi-naturalistic reason: when certain ascetics with psychic powers develop a very weak earth-consciousness but a very strong water-consciousness, the earth quakes. The last six reasons, however, are all connected to the biography of the Buddha. Earthquakes also occur when a buddha descends from Tuṣita Heaven, when he is born, when he attains enlightenment, when he preaches his first sermon, when he renounces the remainder of his possible lifespan, and finally, when he passes into *parinirvāṇa*. He then reveals to Ānanda that he has told Māra that he will pass away in another three months' time.

At last it dawns on his attendant-disciple to ask him to extend his lifespan for a whole aeon, but it is too late for that. Later, at the First Council after the Buddha's death, Ānanda was to be blamed for this by other monks in the *saṃgha*. More immediately, the Buddha reprimands him, and goes on to list no fewer than fifteen other times where, given the same hint, Ānanda failed to ask the Buddha to remain in the world. They then go together to an assembly of all the monks in the area and there the Buddha exhorts them all to further practice, and then announces publicly his imminent demise. In the Pali text, he ends with this verse:

> Ripe I am in years. My life-span's determined.
> Now I go from you, having made myself my refuge.
> Monks, be untiring, mindful, disciplined,
> Guarding your minds with well-collected thought.
> He who, tireless, keeps to law and discipline,
> Leaving birth behind will put an end to woe.
>
> (Walshe, 1987, pp. 253–54)

Having then said farewell to Vaiśālī, the Buddha goes on to Bhaṇḍagāma and several other villages, giving sermons on morality, meditation, wisdom, and liberation. Finally, he comes to the town of Bhoganagaraka, where, returning to the theme of how the monks will have to cope after his final death, he preaches on the four criteria for determining the authenticity of doctrine. Four possible scenarios are painted: a monk claims to have heard a teaching from the Buddha himself; a monk claims to have heard a teaching from an established community of monks; a monk claims to have heard a teaching from a number of monks who are learned; and a monk claims to have heard a teaching from a single monk who is learned. In each of these cases, one should proceed in the same way: suspending one's judgement as to the truth or the falsity of the teaching, one should carefully compare it to established discourses and/or review it in light of the accepted disciplinary code. If it is found to diverge from these, the conclusion should be: this is not the word of the Buddha. If, however, it is found to be in agreement with these, it may be accepted as the word of the Buddha.

Having thus set the criteria for the ongoing life of his Doctrine, the Buddha proceeds to the town of Pāpā, where he is hosted in a mango grove by a blacksmith named Cunda. Cunda invites him to his house, and prepares for him an elaborate meal, the main feature of which is a dish called "pig's delight" (*sūkaramaddava*). This is served, at the Buddha's own instructions, to him alone (and not to his monks). After the meal, the Buddha is "attacked by a severe sickness with bloody diarrhea, and with sharp pains as if he were about to die," even though he endures this with equanimity and without complaint (Walshe, 1987, p. 257).

Far too much ink has flowed over the identity of the food that the Buddha consumed on this, his last meal, for me to be able to address it fully here. Two points will suffice. First, it is important to note that, apart from the Pali version and one other text (on which see below) no account of the Buddha's last meal, whether in Sanskrit, Chinese, or Tibetan makes any reference whatsoever to the specific kind of food Cunda prepares for the Blessed One. The Pali text alone calls it "pig's delight". The other traditions appear uninterested in this question. Morevoer, the Pali term *sūkaramaddava* ("pig's delight") is ambiguous and can mean either a delightful part of a pig (some special pork dish) or something that pigs delight in. In the latter category, various kinds of mushrooms, roots, and truffles have been suggested. André Bareau has pointed out that pork was held in great contempt and disgust as an unclean dish in an India impregnated by brahmanical culture, and that it is unlikely it would ever be offered to the Buddha as a delicacy. He suggests some kind of textual error or even some kind of joke. And yet we know from a different source that at least one householder in Vaiśālī, Ugga, was said to be very fond of "pig's meat [*sūkara-maṃsa*] with jujubes" and that he offered such a dish to the Buddha. The Buddha accepted it and later praised Ugga as the foremost of laymen who give agreeable gifts.

The argument for mushrooms, on the other hand, seems to be supported by the only other text that actually identifies the kind of food served by Cunda. In a Chinese source translated in the early fifth century, it is said to be a kind of fungus named "sandalwood tree-ear." As one scholar has pointed out, however, that may be due to a later bias for vegetarianism.

Secondly, though all sources agree that the Buddha gets sick after eating at Cunda's, none of them establishes a direct link between his meal and his death. It is less the case that Cunda's food (which is praised as a special delicacy) is thought to be responsible for poisoning the Buddha than that it is seen as not sufficient to prevent him from getting ill. Indeed, one scholar, pointing to a list of Indian medicinal plants all having the word "pig" (*sūkara*) as their first element (*sūkara-kanda* ["pig-bulb"], *sūkara-pādika* [pig's foot], *sukareṣṭa* ["liked by pigs"]), suggests that Cunda's meal of "pig's delight," though not specifically listed in this pharmacopeia, may have been intended to be curative. The special nature of the food is further indicated by the fact that the Buddha instructs Cunda to bury the leftovers of his "pig's delight," because no one in this world of gods and humans, other than the Tathāgata, is capable of digesting that food. This is not, as some have thought, a measure intended to prevent the poisoning of others; it is rather because, as Cunda was preparing the "pig's delight," the gods added to it a subtle nutritive essence – a kind of elixir – intending to fortify the Buddha. This divine essence makes the meal indigestible to ordinary humans, but because it still contains gross human food as its base, it is also indigestible by the gods. We have already seen that the Buddha refused just such an elixir earlier in his career while he was undertaking strict asceticism. Here he seems to accept it, but it is not effective in sustaining him.

It should be remembered that the Buddha had already fallen deathly ill at Veṇugrāmaka during the rains-retreat, prior to coming to Cunda's house in Pāpā. At that time, he had staved off that illness by his powers of concentration. Having now decided to give up his life-force, however, it is understandable that that illness should recur, and it is also understandable that no special medicinal dish or divine elixir should be able to counter it.

All this appears to be confirmed later, in various versions of the story, when the Buddha declares that Cunda should not feel that his gift of food was not effective, or think that he reaped no merit from it, or that he is somehow to blame for the Buddha's demise. On the contrary, his meal is praised as especially meritorious and is compared to Sujātā's fortifying offering of milk-rice prior to the Buddha's enlightenment at Bodhgaya. The one dish led to *nirvāṇa*; the other will lead to *parinirvāṇa*, and both are praised as having much greater results than any other offerings.

From Cunda's house, the Buddha heads for Kuśinagarī, his final destination. Along the way, he gets tired and has Ānanda prepare a seat for him under a tree. There he asks his attendant disciple to get him some water from a nearby river. Ānanda tells him that a caravan of five hundred carts has just forded the river and churned up the water, making it dirty and undrinkable. He suggests that the Buddha wait until they reach another stream, which is not distant and has clean water. But the Buddha says he is thirsty and insists Ānanda bring him some water immediately, and finally, reluctantly, the disciple goes down to the nearby river. There, to his great astonishment, he finds that the water is clear and undisturbed. He is thus able to bring back a drink for his master.

At that moment, a man named Putkasa happens along and stops to greet the Buddha still sitting under his tree. Putkasa, it turns out, is a follower of the school of Ārāḍa Kālāma, the Buddha's first teacher before his enlightenment. He admiringly tells the Buddha of an occasion on which Ārāḍa, sitting in a trance, was oblivious to the passage right next to him of five hundred bullock carts, despite the fact that they covered his robes with dust. The Buddha, however, "one-ups" this with a story of his own, recalling that, while practicing walking meditation, he was once oblivious to a thunderstorm in which two farmers and four oxen were killed by lightning. Others might be disturbed by such a revelation, but Putkasa is tremendously impressed and, giving up the way of Ārāḍa, he converts to Buddhism. He then gives the Buddha a pair of magnificent robes made out of golden cloth, and departs. When Ānanda puts the robes on the Buddha, they pale next to his skin, which glows with an even more golden light. Ānanda marvels at this, and the Buddha explains that there are two occasions on which a buddha's skin appears particularly bright: on the day of his enlightenment, and on the day in which he attains *parinirvāṇa*. He then confides to his disciple, that, that very night, lying between two *śāla* trees in Kuśinagarī, he will pass into final extinction.

Master and disciple now proceed onwards. They reach the Hiraṇyavatī River, and there the Buddha takes his last bath. Then, tired, he lies down on his right side, in a posture that prefigures that which he will take at his *parinirvāṇa*, and it is at this point that, worried that the blacksmith Cunda might feel badly about his last meal, he clarifies for Ānanda the merit of that act. Then, having rested, he crosses the river and heads for Kuśinagarī.

## DEATH-BED DEEDS

At last the Buddha arrives at the site of his *parinirvāṇa*, a grove of *śāla* trees that belong to the Mallas and is located just outside their town of Kuśinagarī. There, between two trees, Ānanda prepares the Buddha's final bed. Mindful and aware, the Blessed One lies down on his right side, his head pointed towards the North, and his two feet carefully placed on top of each other in a posture made famous, iconographically, by representations of the Buddha in *parinirvāṇa*. The occasion is immediately marked by a number of supernatural manifestations: the *śāla* trees burst forth into untimely bloom and divine music resounds in the sky.

The sources recounting the Buddha's *parinirvāṇa* are basically the same as those telling of his last journey, but they exhibit, at this point, more divergence in the order in which they present the events. I shall here generally follow the order given in the Sanskrit text of the *Discourse on the Great Extinction (Mahāparinirvāṇa-sūtra)*. It may be divided into nine episodes.

The Sanskrit text begins with a touching account of an interaction between the Buddha and Ānanda. After helping the Buddha install himself on his death bed, Ānanda is suddenly overcome with emotion. Leaning against the couch, he exclaims:

> Too soon ... too soon the Blessed One will attain *parinirvāṇa*! Too soon the Eye of the World will be put out! In the past, monks from various regions used to come from all over to see and to venerate the Blessed One, and the Blessed One would preach the Dharma to them ... But from now on, those who used to come to listen to the Buddha will have heard that he has attained *parinirvāṇa*, and they will no longer make the journey. Thus the great rejoicing in the Dharma will cease. (Strong, 1995, p. 35)

The Pali text, which recounts this episode later, in a place that makes less sense, puts the reason for Ānanda's grief in more personal terms: he is upset because the Buddha is about to pass into *parinirvāṇa* and he, Ānanda, has not yet attained enlightenment. How will he do so without a teacher? In both instances, the Buddha's reaction is to comfort his disciple by praising him for his many services and remarkable qualities, and by reminding him of the law of impermanence, that all things and beings that are "born, living, fashioned, karmically constituted ... [and] dependently arisen [are also] subject to decay, to change, decline, destruction ... and dissolution" (Strong, 1995, p. 35).

Somewhat comforted, Ānanda is nonetheless still upset about something. He wants to know why the Buddha has chosen to die in Kuśinagarī, a miserable little town "in the boondocks" which he considers to be too insignificant and unimportant for such a grand occasion. Why did he not choose to pass away in a major city such as Śrāvastī or Sāketā, Campā or Benares, Vaiśālī or Rājagṛha? The Buddha replies with a lengthy historical discourse, revealing that, in ancient times, Kuśinagarī was the great glorious capital of the *cakravartin* king Mahāsudarśana. This discourse, moreover, is also a *jātaka* story, for Mahāsudarśana was none other than the bodhisattva in a previous life. He has, in this sense, come "home" to die.

Despite these "intimate" interchanges between the Buddha and Ānanda, it is clear that they are not alone in Kuśinagarī. Many other monks and, as we shall see, many divinities have assembled for the occasion. One of the monks is the Elder Upamāna who, according to one tradition at least, served as the Buddha's personal attendant before Ānanda. Upamāna is now standing by the Buddha's death bed, fanning him. According to some versions of the story, this upsets Ānanda, who complains that Upamāna has undertaken this task without asking his or the Buddha's permission. In others, however, it is the Buddha who gets upset with Upamāna, telling him rather abruptly to move, not to stand in front of him. Ānanda is surprised at this; in the twenty years and more that he has served the Buddha as his personal attendant, he has never seen him get irritated or heard him speak harshly to anyone like this. The Buddha then explains his reasons: "Right now," he says,

> myriads of deities are looking down from the sky and, upset, they are grumbling: "The appearance of fully enlightened Buddhas in the world is as rare an event as the blossoming of the udumbara tree, and today, this buddha is going to enter parinirvāṇa in the middle watch of the night. But this prominent monk is standing in front of him, so that we ... are unable to see the Blessed One, or to approach and pay homage to him." That is why I asked the Venerable Upamāna to move. (Strong, 1995, p. 36)

At this point, another protocol question occurs to Ānanda, and he asks the Buddha: "Lord, how should we pay homage to the Blessed One's body after his *parinirvāṇa*?" (Strong, 1995, p. 36.) The Buddha, at first, replies that Ānanda should not worry about this matter; the faithful brahmanical householders will take of care of the homage to the Buddha's body. Asked again, however, he replies that his remains should be treated in exactly the same way as those of a *cakravartin* king. We shall see, later on, just what such a funeral involves.

In the Sanskrit text, Ānanda's next step is to go and inform the Mallas of Kuśinagarī, of the arrival of the Blessed One in their community, and of his imminent demise. Upon learning the news, the Mallas all go to the *śāla* grove to pay their respects to the Buddha. Ānanda, in his role of protocol officer, realizes that there is not enough time for them individually to pay homage, so he has them approach the death-bed in groups. Even so the Buddha becomes exhausted.

It is understandable, then, that when a very old wandering ascetic named Subhadra appears and wants to see the Buddha, Ānanda refuses him access. Subhadra has questions about certain items of doctrine that he would like clarified, but Ānanda is adamant: "Enough! Subhadra," he says, "the Tathāgata is tired and weak." The Buddha, however, overhears this conversation and intervenes: "Enough, Ānanda," he says, "let Subhadra ask his questions." Subhadra, it turns out, wants to know which of the Buddha's contemporaries, the six great "heretical" teachers, have attained enlightenment and which have not, and whether, given the differences between them, they can all be enlightened or not. The Buddha, however, tells him not to worry about such things, and to listen to the Dharma, which he then teaches to him. Subhadra needs no more convincing. He converts to Buddhism, is ordained, and quickly becomes enlightened. He is the Buddha's last personal disciple. The Tibetan version of this story inserts prior to it an account of the conversion of the divine musician (*gandharva*) Sunanda. Taking a thousand-string lute, the Buddha plays for Sunanda a wonderful melody. Gradually, he cuts off all the strings on his instrument but one, but the music continues. Finally, he cuts off the last string, and still the music goes on. Sunanda, thoroughly impressed, listens to the Dharma and is converted.

At this point, the Buddha touches in rapid succession on a number of different questions, as though wrapping up some pieces of advice he was intending to give to his disciples on several different issues. These vary from one text to another. In the Sanskrit version, he first addresses the question of who will lead the monks after his death. "It may be," he says,

> that after I am gone some of you will think: Our Master has attained *parinirvāṇa*; we are now without a teacher, without hope of salvation! You should not see things in this way. The list of precepts [*prātimokṣa*] to be recited every fortnight, which I taught you, will henceforth be your Master and your salvation. (Strong, 1995, p. 36)

This, it should be noted, is somewhat different from the Pali text, which says that the Dharma (and *Vinaya*) will henceforth be their masters. But the Sanskrit text leads neatly into the next statement of the Buddha that the monks can, in due time, if they so wish, abolish certain minor precepts and secondary rules of conduct, for this will lead to their dwelling in harmony. Thirdly, with an eye perhaps on maintaining both order and harmony, the Buddha declares that henceforth junior monks should not address senior monks by their personal names or clan names, but call them "Reverend Sir" or "Venerable One." At the same time senior monks should be kind to junior monks and helpful to them in their training and practice. Finally, the Sanskrit text inserts here a passage that occurs much earlier in the Pali – namely the Buddha's identification of the four places of pilgrimage where future devotees will be able to recall his presence: the places of his birth, of his enlightenment, of his first sermon, and of his *parinirvāṇa*. The Sanskrit does not include a piece of advice that the Pali inserts after the description of the four places of pilgrimage: the passage in which Ānanda asks how to act with regard to women. The Buddha's response is not to look at them. "But if we [do] see them, how should we behave?" "Do not speak to them, Ānanda," comes the reply. "But if they speak to us?" pursues his disciple. "Practice mindfulness," is the Buddha's final advice (Walshe, 1987, p. 264).

At the end of all these quick admonitions, the Buddha then asks his monks, in both the Sanskrit and the Pali texts, whether they have any questions, any doubts or uncertainties that they would like to have elucidated. If they do, they should not worry about troubling him, even at this time. None of them, however, has any questions.

The time for the Buddha's *parinirvāṇa* has come. In the Pali text, satisfied that none of his disciples present has any doubts, he says these final words to all those assembled: "Now, monks, I declare to you: all conditioned things are of a nature to decay – strive on untiringly" (Walshe, 1987, p. 270). But the Pali has here omitted a significant passage which is found in most of the other versions of the story, and which relates these words specifically not to the Buddha's doctrine – his Dharma – but to his physical body – his *rūpa*. In the Sanskrit, this passage reads:

> Then the Blessed One took off his outer robe, and, baring his body said: "Monks, gaze now upon the body of the Tathāgata! Examine the body of the Tathāgata! For the sight of a completely enlightened buddha is as rare an event as the blossoming of the udumbara tree. Be still! All conditioned things are of a nature to decay." (Waldschmidt, 1950–51, pp. 392–94)

This is done so as to show, one last time, the thirty-two bodily marks of the great man. In this way, the Buddha has come full circle. The somatic signs of buddhahood which were first perceived at his birth in Lumbinī are now the last things to be seen in Kuśinagarī.

The rest of the story is quickly told: the Buddha, lying on his side, passes quickly through the eight levels of meditational trance and enters the sphere of cessation. At this point, Ānanda thinks he has passed away, but Aniruddha, who knows better, corrects him, and tells him he is not dead, but has only entered the sphere of cessation. From there, the Buddha soon goes back down through all eight meditational trance states and then back up to the fourth level – the highest state still in the realm of form. It was from this level that he originally attained enlightenment at Bodhgaya, and it is from this level that, finally, he passes away into *parinirvāṇa*.

## THE FUNERAL AND CREMATION

The first to react is the great earth: it quakes. Then the two *śāla* trees rain down blossoms upon the Buddha's body. Then the gods Indra and Brahmā utter verses on impermanence. Then the elders Aniruddha and Ānanda confirm in verse the Blessed One's demise. Many of the monks present enter into paroxysms of grief, rolling about on the ground, beating their breasts and crying out. Others, however, control their emotions, realizing that what the Buddha said – that all compounded things are impermanent – is true. In the morning, Ānanda goes to announce the death to the Mallas in Kuśinagarī, and they come *en masse* to honor the body of the Blessed One and to prepare it for cremation. They ask Ānanda what should be done, and Ānanda, who had asked the Buddha ahead of time how they should treat his corpse, is able to tell them. He outlines a particular sequence of ritual acts known as the "homage to the body" (*śarīra-pūjā*). The body of a buddha should be treated in the same manner as that of a *cakravartin* king. We can see here that the parallelism between the Buddha and kingship which marked his birth and early life surfaces again at his death. It should be wrapped in alternating layers of new cotton cloth and teased cotton wool (five hundred pieces of each). It should be placed in a sort of sarcophagus consisting of an iron vessel (*droṇī*) filled with oil which is then covered with another iron vessel acting as a lid. The body should then be cremated on a fire made with sweet-smelling woods. His relics should be collected, and a *stūpa* (funerary mound) should be erected for him at a crossroads.

All of these instructions are eventually followed, except perhaps for the last one which, as we shall see, is complicated by the dispute that ensues over the disposition of the Buddha's relics. In the meantime, however, the Mallas also honor the Buddha's body in their own manner. Approaching the Buddha's body between the two *śāla* trees, they make traditional offerings to it of garlands of flowers, cloth, perfumes, music, dance, lights, and so on. So caught up are they in their devotions that, by the time it occurs to them that they ought now to proceed with his cremation, they realize that "it is too late to cremate the Lord's body today. We shall do so tomorrow" (Walshe, 1987, p. 273). The next day, however, exactly the same thing happens, and the next and the next, until a whole week has passed. This, of course, is not the way funerals are generally carried out in India, where cremations are rarely delayed and are supposed to take place immediately, on the very day of death. Moreover, though some of the Buddha's disciples may have shown extreme sorrow at the passing of the Blessed One, the Mallas appear to use the occasion for merit-making and celebration, a feature that can readily be seen in bas-relief depictions of this scene. As Alfred Foucher has remarked, we seem to be dealing here with something resembling a village fair, a festival of the sort that was celebrated in honor of the relics of the Blessed One. Indeed, there are many aspects of the Buddha's funeral that can be understood as prefigurations of the cult of his relics.

In the midst of this fête, however, one scene is noteworthy for its strong expression of grief, as well as for the controversy it later created. The Buddha's disciple Ānanda, still acting as protocol officer, realizes that some Malla women, at the back of the crowd, have not had a chance to come forward and venerate the body of the Blessed One. He ushers them up to the front, therefore, and they break into lamentations, circumambulate the corpse, and make all sorts of offerings to it, except for one old widow who has nothing to give. Carried away with emotion, she bursts out crying, and her tears run down and wet the Buddha's feet.

Ānanda's willingness to espouse the cause of women in the *saṃgha* is well known, but here it gets him into trouble. The old woman's tears permanently stain the Buddha's feet, a discoloration that the Buddha's chief disciple, Mahākāśyapa, immediately notices when he comes to venerate those feet. We can see, here, the first signs of competition between Ānanda (or more precisely the factions within the *saṃgha* backing him) and Mahākāśyapa. Later, at the so-called "trial of Ānanda" at the First Buddhist Council (at which Mahākāśyapa was to preside), this point is brought up again as one of a series of faults committed by Ānanda. But this time, another more severe charge is added to it: not only did Ānanda allow the Buddha's feet to be stained by this old woman's tears, but more generally he showed the women who approached the body the Buddha's "sheath-encased penis." The Buddha's male organ was one of the thirty-two marks of the Great Man, and Ānanda seeks to justify his action by explaining that he hoped the women, upon seeing the Buddha's penis, would be ashamed of their female bodies and moved to plant roots of merit so as to be reborn as men. At the same time, there are some indications that the Buddha's body was washed, and one wonders whether this baring of the body of the Buddha may have been related to a rite of washing the corpse, normally undertaken in India, by women relatives.

A more immediate sign of the rivalry between Mahākāśyapa and Ānanda occurs in a final scenario of the veneration of the Buddha's body. Mahākāśyapa, it should be pointed out, is not present at the time of the *parinirvāṇa*, and does not find out about it until a week later, while he is on the road with some of his followers. In the meantime, in Kuśinagarī, the Mallas have ended their homage to the Buddha's body, and have now shrouded it in a thousand layers of cloth and encoffined it in its iron sarcophagus. They find, however, they are unable to light the cremation pyre. This is explained as being due to the gods, who do not want the fire to be lit until the arrival of Mahākāśyapa. Fortunately the latter, having learned of his master's demise, is not long in coming. Upon arrival, however, he first wants to be able to see the body of the Buddha and to venerate it one last time before consigning it to the flames. At this point the various accounts differ in exactly what happens, but all of them agree that either through Mahākāśyapa's own actions, or through the intervention of the gods, or by a miraculous post-mortem action of the Buddha himself, the Tathāgata's feet emerge from the coffin so that Mahākāśyapa is able to venerate them.

The miracle of the feet, moving of their own accord after the Buddha's death, is significant because it is the first graphic example of the Buddha's ongoing supernatural powers after his *parinirvāṇa*. The tradition as a whole, however, was not content with privileging Mahākāśyapa alone with such a miracle. Thus when the Chinese pilgrim Xuanzang visits Kuśinagarī, he is shown *stūpas* commemorating *three* post-mortem appearances of the Buddha while he was in his coffin. The first of these occasions is the story of the feet which we have just considered. The second appears to be connected to the rivalry between Mahākāśyapa and Ānanda. For just as the Buddha stuck his feet out for Mahākāśyapa to worship, he also later stuck his hand out in a farewell gesture to Ānanda. The third story is much more developed and features the Buddha actually sitting up in his coffin to greet his mother who has come down from Tuṣita Heaven to mourn. Xuanzang's retelling of it appears to be based on the *Discourse on Mahāmāyā (Mahāmāyā-sūtra)* and was later incorporated into popular Chinese biographies of the Buddha. Its theme is clearly filial piety. As soon as the Blessed One has been encoffined, Aniruddha goes up to heaven to inform Māyā of the death of her son. Hearing the news, she comes down to Kuśinagarī, where she loudly laments his passing. It is at this point that the miracle occurs: the lid of the Buddha's coffin opens, and the Blessed One himself sits up. He then tells his mother not to be overwhelmed by grief, that his passing away is in harmony with the law of all things, and that even with his extinction, there are still the refuges of the Dharma and the *saṃgha*. He then closes by explaining to Ānanda that he has done this as a lesson in proper filial conduct.

In the various versions of the *Discourse on the Great Extinction (Mahāparinirvāṇa-sūtra)*, this story about the Buddha's mother is not told and Mahākāśyapa's worship of his feet is generally presented as the last act prior to the igniting of the funeral pyre. This occurs by spontaneous combustion, in most versions of the story, although in some the action is undertaken by the Mallas, or alternatively by Mahākāśyapa, acting as the Buddha's "eldest son." The fire is eventually extinguished and, according to the Pali tradition, nothing is left of the Buddha's body – "neither skin, under-skin, flesh, sinew, or joint-fluid," not even ashes or soot – nothing at all except his relics.

## THE COLLECTION AND DISTRIBUTION OF THE RELICS

Our sources are, for the most part, agreed that the Mallas first collect the Buddha's relics, called *śarīra*. It is probable that we should not think of these relics as bits of bone, even though, later on, the tradition was to specify that certain teeth and certain actual bones were found in the remnants of the cremation fire. Rather, these *śarīra* collected by the Mallas are described as being like jasmine buds, washed pearls, and nuggets of gold, and as coming in various sizes (as big as mustard seeds, broken grains of rice, and split green peas). There is nothing surprising in this; to this day, Buddhist relics the world over appear more as jewel-like beads than as burnt bones.

The Mallas put these gem-like relics in a casket, put the casket on a litter, and transport it to the center of Kuśinagarī, where they enshrine the relics in a place that is variously described as a great building, a high tower, or their own assembly hall. What seems to be emphasized here is the defensive posture of the setting. The Pali text, for instance, specifies that the Mallas' assembly hall was then surrounded by "a lattice-work of spears," and encircled by a "wall of bows" (Walshe, 1987, p. 275). Clearly, the Mallas are not expecting their possession of the Buddha's relics to go unchallenged. And indeed, it is not long before King Ajātaśatru of Magadha, learning of the demise of the Buddha, sends a message to the Mallas, saying: "The Blessed One was a *kṣatriya*, and so am I. I am worthy of building a *stūpa* and paying homage to the relics of the Blessed One" (Walshe, 1987, pp. 275–76). He then backs up his demand by setting out himself to Kuśinagarī along with a great army.

Much the same sequence of emotions are felt and demands are then made by six other kings or communities besides Ajātaśatru and the Magadhans. The Licchavis of Vaiśālī, the Śākyas of Kapilavastu, the Mallas of Pāvā, the Bulakas of Calakalpa, the Krauḍyas of Rāmagrāma, and the brahmins of Viṣṇudvīpa all want to have at least a share in the Buddha's relics and declare themselves ready to take it by force. The Mallas of Kuśinagarī, however, are not about to co-operate.

In the depiction of these events on two bas-reliefs at Sanchi, it is clear from the scenes of armies engaging in combat that the so-called "war for the relics" was actually thought to have taken place. In our texts, however, hostilities never quite break out, and instead the matter is resolved by the arbitration of the brahmin Dhūmrasagotra, also known as Droṇa. Droṇa goes about his task in an apparently equitable and satisfactory fashion, dividing the relics of the Buddha into eight equal shares, each one of which is then taken away to be enshrined in a *stūpa* in the recipient's home country. When this process is finished, Droṇa asks the assembled kings for the urn in which he measured out the relics, and he is accorded that. He resolves to build a *stūpa* over it. Finally, to close the episode, a young brahmin of Pippalāyana arrives belatedly; finding that all the relics have already been distributed, he asks for and is given the embers of the cremation fire, which he takes away to enshrine in a *stūpa* as well. Later traditions were to suggest that other relics (such as four teeth of the Buddha) were acquired by other persons including various divinities on this occasion, or that Droṇa was involved in stealing some of the relics. For the present, however, we have a situation in which what was left of the body of the Buddha has been divided into eight shares and enshrined in different localities throughout North India.

## THE LIFE AND FINAL EXTINCTION OF THE DHARMA AND THE RELICS

One way of thinking of the death and *parinirvāṇa* of the Buddha is that it is an event which saw the separation of the body of his doctrine (his *dharmakāya*) from his physical body (his *rūpakāya*). This bifurcation was further exacerbated by the fact that what was left of both his doctrine (the memory of his teachings), and of his body (his relics) was in danger of being scattered far and wide throughout the world. In order for the memory of the Buddha to be preserved, in order for Buddhism to be established as a religion, steps had to be taken to re-collect both the doctrinal corpus and the relics.

The former task fell to the monks (although this does not mean that the Dharma was solely intended for them). According to tradition, shortly after the *parinirvāṇa*, the Buddha's disciple Mahākāśyapa, fearing the dissipation of the Buddha's teachings, assembled five hundred elders at Rājagṛha and held what is commonly known as the First Buddhist Council. The chief purpose of the meeting was the recitation, or gathering, of the Buddha's discourses (*sūtras*) and of his rules of the Discipline (*Vinaya*). Ānanda was asked to recite the former, and Upāli was asked to recite the latter.

Much the same thing happened in the case of the relics. Sometime after the division of the physical remains of the Buddha and their enshrining in various kingdoms, Mahākāśyapa began to worry about their dispersal, and, together with King Ajātaśatru, he took steps to collect them so that there could be "a single enshrinement of the relics" (Jayawickrama, 1971, p. 44). This too took place near Rājagṛha. Later, King Aśoka discovered the spot and undertook the orderly redistribution of these relics into eighty-four thousand *stūpas* all over his empire, so that today Buddha relics may be found throughout the Buddhist world.

This is not the place to trace the ongoing fortune either of the Buddha's Dharma or of his bodily relics. That would be more or less equivalent to recounting the whole history of Buddhism. Suffice it to illustrate quickly some ways in which the life, or at least the presence, of the departed master was thought somehow to continue on in both of these dimensions. According to a number of accounts, as soon as Ānanda began to recite the discourses of the Buddha at the First Council, all the elders in attendance exclaimed: "What? Is it possible? The Buddha has come back to earth and is still teaching! It is the Buddha whom we hear speaking thus!" (Przyluski, 1926, pp. 84, 70.) There could hardly be a more graphic statement of an understanding that came to be established throughout the Buddhist world that one who sees (or in this case hears) the Dharma sees (or hears) the Buddha. There are many stories of monks and others who claim to have met or seen the Buddha, even after his death, by seeing or understanding his Doctrine.

This vision in the dharmalogical dimension has its parallel, however, in what might be called the rupalogical dimension of the relics. Here again many examples could be given. The most graphic, perhaps, is from the *Great Chronicle (Mahāvaṃsa)*. King Aśoka's son, the elder Mahinda, who is in Sri Lanka, complains that it has been a long time since he has seen the Buddha. The Sri Lankan king is astonished. "I thought you told me the Buddha had passed away into *parinirvāṇa*" he says. And Mahinda quickly explains that he meant it had been a long time since he had been able to worship the relics of the Buddha, for "when we behold the relics, we behold the Conqueror" (Geiger, 1912, p. 116).

Both the Dharma and the relics, then, provide focal points for an ongoing relationship with the Buddha, even after his death. They also, however, provide focal points for lessons in impermanence. Neither Gautama's teachings nor his relics can last forever. Jan Nattier has studied a variety of traditions about the gradual decline of the Dharma as it goes through different phases from a period of the True Dharma, during and shortly after the Buddha's lifetime, to an age of the Final Dharma, when enlightenment and understanding are no longer possible. Eventually, according to some texts, the Dharma will disappear altogether, only to be rediscovered and reintroduced by the future Buddha Maitreya. A similar tradition developed about the disappearance of the relics. Over the millennia, we are told, following the *parinirvāṇa* of the Buddha, various aspects of the Buddha's religion will be lost. The first thousand years will see the disappearance of the possibility of enlightenment; the next thousand, the loss of the practice of meditation and the keeping of the precepts. The next millennium (in which presumably we find ourselves now?) will see the slow disappearance of Buddhist texts. Then, the outward signs of the religion will gradually vanish; monks will eventually give up the wearing of robes and return to lay life. Finally, in the last thousand years, we will see the "*parinirvāṇa* of the relics." And here we come to the final chapter of the story of the Buddha Gautama.

The *parinirvāṇa* of the relics is foretold in a number of Pali and Sanskrit sources. Some time prior to the advent of the next Buddha Maitreya, all the relics of Gautama – all of his jewel-like *śarīra*, and bones, and other bits and pieces, including those not only in our world but in the world of the *nāgas* and the realm of the gods – will come together at Bodhgaya. None, not even those that are but the size of a mustard seed, will be lost en route. At Bodhgaya they will reassemble and take on once more the form of the Buddha, complete with the thirty-two major and eighty minor marks of the great man. Then, elevating itself into mid-air, this relic-body of the Buddha will perform once again the miracle of the double appearance of both fire and water that was displayed at Śrāvastī. No human will be present at that time, but the gods will be there, and they will lament: "Today, the Buddha will enter complete extinction; from now on, there will be darkness." Then a great fire, emanating from within the relic-body itself, will completely consume all of the relics, and the body of the Buddha will be seen no more.

# SOURCES AND FURTHER READING

## PREFACE (pp. ix–x)

There have been numerous popular presentations of the life of the Buddha and it is impossible to list them all here. In my view, two classics of the genre still stand among the most comprehensive and useful: Thomas, 1927, and Foucher, 1987. The latter was originally written in 1949. An English translation (Foucher, 1963) was published, but as it was a rather significant abridgement, I shall make use, in this book, of the revised French edition of 1987. Both Thomas and Foucher are willing to make use of early and later textual materials, Thomas generally emphasizing Pali sources, and Foucher Sanskrit ones. A number of biographies, however, have sought to limit themselves to canonical texts. Among these, the following are worthy of note: Nakamura, 1977, which exploits the full scope of canonical literature, and Carrithers, 1983, which limits itself to Pali sources. Creative rewritings of the life of the Buddha as a historical novel may be found in Kalupahana and Kalupahana, 1982 and Nhat Hanh, 1991.

## INTRODUCTION (pp. 1–14)

For a variety of positions on the question of the date of the Buddha's death, see Bechert, 1995, and the important article by Gombrich, 1992. On the development and history of the study of the Buddha's life in the West, see Almond, 1988, pp. 54–79, and de Jong, 1997, pp. 28–34. The most frequently cited examples of nineteenth-century solar mythological approaches to the life of the Buddha are works by Senart, 1882, and Kern, 1882–84. The historicist reaction may be seen in the work of Oldenberg, 1882.

**Textual sources (pp. 4–5)** For an example of a recent reformulation of the life of the Buddha, see Ambedkar, 1957. On the question of when a full biography of the Buddha was first formulated, see the different positions taken by Frauwallner, 1956, and Lamotte, 1988, p. 655. Lamotte's classification of sources is spelled out in his 1988, pp. 648ff., and used also in Reynolds and Hallisey, 1987.

The "Discourse on the Noble Quest (*Ariyapariyesana-sutta*)" has been translated in Horner, 1954–59, 1, pp. 207–19. For Chinese parallels, see Bareau, 1963, pp. 13 ff., and Chau, 1964, pp. 153ff. Other canonical biographical fragments include: the "Discourse on Wonderful and Marvellous Things (*Acchariyabbhutadhamma-sutta*)" (Horner, 1954–59, 3, pp. 163–69), a Pali text which contains an account of the marvels accompanying the Buddha's conception and birth; the "Discourse to Mahā-saccaka (*Mahā-saccaka-sutta*)" (Horner, 1954–59, 1, pp. 291–305), an "autobiographical" account of the Buddha's practice of austerities; the "Discourse on Exertion (*Padhāna-sutta*)", a short text in the Pali *Collection of Discourses (Sutta Nipāta)*, which recounts the bodhisattva's resistance to Māra's wiles prior to his enlightenment (Fausbøll, 1901, pp. 68–71); the first sections of the "Great Division (*Mahāvagga*)" of the Pali *Book of the Discipline (Vinaya-piṭaka)* (Horner, 1938–52, 4, pp. 1ff.), which reviews the first events following the Buddha's enlightenment; the Sanskrit *Discourse on the Fourfold Assembly (Catuṣpariṣat-sūtra)* (Kloppenborg, 1973), which also recounts events immediately following the Buddha's enlightenment up to the conversion of Śāriputra and Maudgalyāyana; and the *Discourse on the Complete Extinction (Mahāparinirvāṇa-sūtra)* (Walshe, 1987, pp. 231–77, Waldschmidt, 1950–51, and Weller, 1939–40), which recounts the final events of the Buddha's life, including his death and the distribution of his relics. Studies of these as well as other texts and their parallels in the Chinese Buddhist canon may be found in a series of works by André Bareau (1963, 1970–71, 1974).

Among the autonomous "lives" of the Buddha, the *Great Story (Mahāvastu)* has been translated in Jones, 1949–56. Various translations of the *Acts of the Buddha (Buddhacarita)* are also available: Cowell, 1894, from the Sanskrit; Johnston, 1936 and 1937, from the Sanskrit and the Tibetan; and Beal, 1883, from the Chinese. Other autonomous biographies include: The *Discourse on Going Forth (Abhiniṣkramaṇa-sūtra)*, an incomplete life ending with the Buddha's return to Kapilavastu, translated from the Chinese in Beal, 1875; The *Living out of the Game (Lalitavistara)*, an incomplete life in Sanskrit and Tibetan ending with the first sermon, translated into French by Foucaux, 1884, and from French into English by Bays, 1983; *The Clarifier of Sweet Meaning (Madhuratthavilāsinī)*, a Pali commentary on the *Buddha Chronicle (Buddhavaṃsa)* which contains in its last chapter an incomplete life ending with the first sermon (see Horner, 1978, pp. 387–425); the *Discourse on the Great Legend (Mahāvadāna Sūtra)*, an incomplete life of the past Buddha Vipaśyi ending with his enlightenment, translated from the Pali in Walshe, 1987, pp. 199–222, and into German from the Chinese (with edition of the Sanskrit text) in Waldschmidt, 1953–56; the "Introduction" (*Nidāna-kathā*) to the Pali *Jātaka Commentary (Jātakaṭṭhakathā)*, an incomplete life ending with the dedication of the Jetavana monastery (see Jayawickrama, 1990); a complete life of the Buddha contained within the "historical sections" of the *Vinaya (Book of the Discipline) of the Mūlasarvāstivādins*, edited in part in Gnoli, 1977–78. An abridged English translation of the Tibetan version appears in Rockhill, 1907.

For examples of late and vernacular lives of the Buddha, see the following: Hardy, 1853, pp. 98–358, a life of the Buddha consisting of translations of a medley of Sinhalese sources, mostly dating from the thirteenth to fourteenth centuries. Bigandet, 1866, an English translation of a late Burmese life of the Buddha known as the *Mālālankāra-vatthu*; a different translation may be found in Edwardes, 1959. Alabaster, 1871, pp. 76–244, an English translation of one of the most popular Thai biographies of the Buddha. A French translation of a Khmer version of the same text may be found in Leclère, 1906, pp. 13–114. Gray, 1894, an English translation of the *Jīnālaṃkāra (Embellishments on the Victorious One)*, a Pali poem written in Sri Lanka and attributed to Buddharakkhita. It is sometimes assigned an impossibly early date, but should probably be placed in the twelfth century C.E. It retells in two hundred and fifty stanzas (which sometimes feature displays of literary prowess such as alliteration and palindromes) the whole lifestory of the Buddha, praising him profusely as it goes along. Rouse, 1904–05, an English translation of the thirteenth-century Pali work by the Sinhalese author Medhankara, the *Jinacarita* (Acts of the Victorious One). Wieger, 1913, a French translation of a popular Ming-dynasty Chinese biography of the Buddha attributed to Bao zhong, and illustrated by a hundred and fifty woodblock prints. Poppe, 1967, an English translation of a Mongolian abbreviated version of the *Living out of the Game* (*Lalitavistara*).

**Lifestory and pilgrimage (pp. 5–8)** For the Buddha's advocacy of visits to the four sites of pilgrimage, see Walshe, 1987, pp. 263–64. On the eight places of pilgrimage, see the "Stanzas on the Eight Commemorative Shrines" (*Aṣtamahāsthānacaitya-stotra*) translated in Strong, 1995, pp. 4–6, and Cook, 1994, pp. 3–132. The eight were commonly represented in art on steles (see Huntington, 1985–86 and 1987, and Snellgrove, 1978, p. 308). Foucher uses the notion of cycles of stories organized around particular sites in his 1987. The list of particular sites in the Lumbinī–Kapilavastu cycle is taken from the *Aśokāvadāna*, translated in Strong, 1983, pp. 246–47. Foucher's speculation on the use of guidebooks by biographers comes from his 1987, p. 109. The *Living out of the Game (Lalitavistara)* story of Gautama's arrow may be read in Bays, 1983, p. 233. Faxian's description of the "Spring of the Arrow" may be found in Legge, 1886, p. 65, Xuanzang's in Li, 1996, p. 179. On the Buddha's apocryphal tour of the Northwest, see Strong, 1992, p. 25, and for narratives of his visits to Sri Lanka, see Geiger, 1912, pp. 3, 6 and 8. Often, such travels of the Buddha are associated with stories that feature his making predictions about certain sites or his leaving of relics (e.g. footprints) of himself in these places (on which see Hazlewood, 1986, and Strong, forthcoming: chapter 3).

**Lifestory and art (pp. 8–9)** For representations in art of the Buddha and his life, see Snellgrove, 1978, and Cummings, 1982, and, for more specialized discussions, Narain, 1985. On the use of symbols in early Buddhist art, see Huntington, 1990. Lamotte's list of biographical episodes depicted at Sanchi may be found in his 1988, pp. 405–06. For the Sanchi representation of the offering of honey, see Marshall, 1955, p. 64. For an example from Sarnath, see Huntington, 1985–86, pt IV, p. 30. Lamotte's discussion of the origin of the Buddha's webbed fingers (1988, pp. 666–67) is based on arguments by Foucher, 1905–18, 2, pp. 306–12, which are echoed in Banerjea, 1930 and Coomaraswamy, 1931.

**Lifestory and ritual (p. 10)** On the use of the Buddha biography in image consecrations, see Swearer, forthcoming. The account of the gods dressing up the bodhisattva prior to his great departure is from

Jayawickrama, 1990, p. 80. Similar symbioses may be found between the story of the Buddha's descent from heaven at Sāṃkāśya and annual celebrations of the end of the rains-retreat (see Strong, 1992, p. 152), and between the account of the bodhisattva, in his past life, lying down in the road at the feet of the previous Buddha Dīpaṃkara and the ritual practice of laypersons offering their prostrate selves for monks to walk over (see Bizot, 1976, p. 1).

**Lifestories and buddhology (pp. 10–14)** For stories of bodhisattvas who are now walking the path to future buddhahood, see Saddhatissa, 1975. For the "Discourse on the Great Legend (*Mahāvadāna-sūtra*)," see Walshe, 1987, p. 204 and Waldschmidt, 1953–56. The list of ten indispensible actions is from the *Divyāvadāna* (see Burnouf, 1876, pp. 151–52). The Tibetan list of the Twelve Great Acts may be found in Obermiller, 1931–32, 2, pp. 7ff., and is used in the Mongolian biography in Poppe, 1967. The Pali list of thirty obligatory deeds comes from Horner, 1978, pp. 429–30. An example of the *Great Story (Mahāvastu)*'s understanding of the docetic nature of the Buddha may be found in Jones, 1949–56, 1, pp. 132–33. The *Living out of the Game (Lalitavistara)* is translated in Bays, 1983. For an example of the incorporation of the Buddha's lifestory into a greater Mahāyāna scheme of the bodhisattva path, see Conze, 1975, p. 177. For a specific study of how changes in notions of the Buddha are reflected in changes in the biographical tradition, see Bareau, 1969.

## 1 PREVIOUS LIVES OF THE BUDDHA (pp. 15–34)

Almost all of the Pali *Jātaka Commentary* has been translated in Cowell, 1895–1907. Other anthologies of *jātakas* in English include: The *Basket of Conduct (Cariyapiṭaka)* (trans. in Horner, 1975, part 2). This is a Pali canonical collection of thirty-five *jātakas* intended to illustrate the practice of different perfections by the bodhisattva. The *Buddha-Chronicle (Buddhavaṃsa)* (trans., Horner, 1975, part 1; see also Horner, 1978). This is another Pali canonical collection of *jātakas* featuring Gautama's renewal of his vow for buddhahood under twenty-four past Buddhas. The *Buddha-Legends (Buddhāvadāna)*. Part of the *Vinaya (Book of the Discipline) of the Mūlasarvāstivādins*, this recounts *jātakas* explaining negative things about the Buddha's last life as Gautama. It has been translated into French in Hofinger, 1990. The *Discourse of the Wise Man and the Fool (Damamūkanidāna-sūtra)*, a collection of *jātakas* and other tales known as the *ḥDsangs blun* in Tibetan and the *Xian yu jing* in Chinese: the Mongolian version has been translated in Frye, 1981. The *Fifty Birth Stories (Paññāsa-Jātaka)*, a Pali collection of fifty "extra-canonical" jātakas, especially popular in Southeast Asia; see Horner and Jaini, 1985–86. *A Garland of Birth-Stories (Jātakamālā)*. This is a Sanskrit collection of thirty-four *jātakas* compiled and written by the poet Āryaśūra; two English translations are available in Khoroche, 1989 and Speyer, 1895. Two other "garlands of birth stories" compiled by Haribhaṭṭa and Gopadatta (see Hahn, 1985). The *Praise of the Birth-Stories (Jātakastava)*, a Khotanese collection that recounts certain *jātakas* in order to praise the Buddha, translated in Dresden, 1955. For examples of the use of *jātakas* as "flashbacks" in biographical texts, see Jones, 1949–56 and Gnoli, 1977–78.

For discussions and representations of the *jātakas* in art, see Brown, 1997; Wray, Rosenfeld and Baily, 1972; and Cummings, 1982, pp. 15–104. Davids's discussion of the "Ass in the Lion's Skin" may be found in his 1880, p. v. For an illustration of that *jātaka*, see Cummings, 1982, pp. 30–34; for a translation, see Cowell, 1895–1907, 2, pp. 76–77. For sources on the Rhampsinitus-like *jātaka* of the clever thief, see Huber, 1904 and Strong, 1992, p. 338 n. 37. On the Buddhist reworking of the Rāma story, see Reynolds, 1991, p. 53. For a translation of the Pali text of it, see Cowell, 1895–1907, 4, pp. 78–82. For the Chinese Buddhist version of it, see Willemen, 1994, pp. 6–9.

**Adding karmic depth (pp. 16–19)** A translation of the *Somanassa jātaka* may be found in Cowell, 1895–1907, 4, pp. 275–80. For references to Māyā's advanced age when she gave birth to the Buddha, see Malalasekera, 1937, 2, p. 609. For Milinda's discussion of Devadatta's karma, see Davids, 1890–94, 1, pp. 283–93. On Devadatta, see also Ray, 1994, pp. 162–73.

**The path to buddhahood (pp. 19–27)** Table 1.1 and much of the description of the lineage of the twenty-four past buddhas is based on Horner, 1975, part 1, and Horner, 1978. The story of Sumedha and Dīpaṃkara is from Horner, 1975, part 1, pp. 9–25. Other versions of the tale may be found in Jones, 1949–56, 1, pp. 188ff. (the story of Megha); Strong, 1995, pp. 19–23 (the story of Sumati); and Bareau, 1966–74. For an illustration in art, see Snellgrove, 1978, p. 187.

On the duration of an "incalculable" and the various types of aeons, see Childers, 1909, pp. 59, and 185–86. The division of the Buddha's life into three periods is spelled out in Jayawickrama, 1990, p. 2. The earlier periods of the "very distant" and "great" causes are described in Jayawickrama, 1968, pp. 7–12, and in the Sinhalese *Ornament of the Good Teaching (Saddharmālaṃkāraya)* (see Gombrich, 1972, p. 79). The different resolves in these different periods are spelled out most clearly in Malalasekera, 1971, p. 359. Table 1.2 is based on these three sources. A slightly different version of this scenario is also known in the Sanskrit tradition (see La Vallée Poussin, 1980, 3, pp. 227–28, and Lamotte, 1949–80, pp. 247–49). The hard-line orthodox position on the requisites for making a vow for buddhahood is spelled out in Jayawickrama, 1990, p. 18. The earliest "epoch of the first arousing of thought" is described in Jayawickrama, 1968, pp. 3–7, Hardy, 1853, pp. 90–93, and Reynolds, 1997. The story of the shipwrecked bodhisattva saving his mother is also found in Gombrich, 1972, pp. 90–91. The tale of the starving tigress will be dealt with below. The story of the bodhisattva's birth as a princess is discussed in Reynolds, 1997, p. 29. The specification that only a male human can make a vow for buddhahood is found in Jayawickrama, 1990, p. 18. For another tale of a long-ago previous life of the Buddha as a woman, see Ohnuma, 2000.

**The practice of perfections (pp. 27–32)** The *Jataka Commentary*'s suggestions for classifying its tales according to the perfections can be found in Jayawickrama, 1990, pp. 58–61. The list of perfections varies according to tradition; in some contexts only six are listed instead of ten. For a full study of the variants, see Dayal, 1932, pp. 165–269.

On Āryaśūra's purported plan for the *Garland of Birth Stories*, see Chimpa and Chattophadhyaya, 1980, p. 135 and Khoroche, 1989, p. xii. For the tale of the hungry tigress, see Khoroche, 1989, pp. 5–9; other versions may be found in Frye, 1981, pp. 13–16, and Emmerick, 1970, pp. 85–97, with a discussion in Schlingloff, 1987, p. 145; see also Cummings, 1982, pp. 85–94. For an analysis of such "gifts of the body," see Ohnuma, 1998. Faxian's account of the "four great *stūpas*" may be found in Legge, 1886, pp. 30–32. In China, the same four *jātakas* were commonly depicted on the four sides of reliquary monuments (see Soper, 1940, pp. 641, 647, 654). On the *jātaka* of King Śibi, see Frye, 1981, pp. 10–11, and Schlingloff, 1987, pp. 86–92. Other sources may be found listed in Lamotte, 1949–80, pp. 255–56. On the gift of the eyes, see Khoroche, 1989, pp. 10–17, Cowell, 1895–1907, 4, pp. 250–56; and Parlier, 1991. On Candraprabha's gift of the head, see Frye, 1981, pp. 105–14, and other sources listed in Lamotte, 1949–80, p. 144. On the *jātaka* of the hare, see Khoroche, 1989, pp. 32–38; Schlingloff, 1987, pp. 123–29; and Willemen, 1994, pp. 39–40. For the story of Kṣāntivādin, see Khoroche, 1989, pp. 193–204; Cowell, 1895–1907, 3, pp. 26–29; and Schlingloff, 1987, pp. 219–21. For the monkey *jātaka*, see Khoroche, 1989, pp. 186–92; Cowell, 1895–1907, 3, pp. 225–27; Schlingloff, 1987, pp. 250–51, and, for illustrations of the story from Bharhut and Sanchi, Cummings, 1982, pp. 50–55. The story of Sutasoma may be found in Khoroche, 1989, pp. 221–36, and Cowell, 1895–1907, 5, pp. 246–79. See also Schlingloff, 1987, pp. 93–112. For the *Mahā Ummagga jātaka*, see Cowell, 1895–1907, 6, pp. 156–246. Finally, on the tale of Viśvantara, see Khoroche, 1989, pp. 58–73; Cone and Gombrich, 1977; Schlingloff, 1987, pp. 146ff.; and for an interesting close reading, Collins, 1998, pp. 497–554. For an extensive listing of other sources, see Lamotte, 1949–80, pp. 713–14; 2251. Milinda's discussion of Viśvantara is found in Davids, 1890–94, 2, pp. 114–32.

The relationship between the marks of the great man and the *jātakas* is spelled out in Davids, 1899–1924, 3, pp. 139ff. For later Mahāyāna sources on this, see Makranski, 1997, p. 120; Conze, 1975, pp. 659–61; and Lamotte, 1949–80, p. 668.

**Gautama's imperfections (pp. 32–34)** The story of the bodhisattva's loss of magical powers in the *Saṃkappa-jātaka* may be found in Cowell, 1895–1907, 2, p. 191, and is discussed in Strong, 1983a. On the whole tradition of the Buddha's negative karma, see Walters, 1990 and Hofinger, 1990. See also Lamotte, 1949–80, pp. 507–509n. Table 1.3 is based primarily on Hofinger.

## 2 ANCESTRY, BIRTH AND YOUTH (pp. 35–48)

**The Śākya lineage (pp. 35–38)** The presentation of the Śākya lineage is based on the account in Gnoli, 1977–78, 1, pp. 14–35; see also Rockhill, 1907, pp. 9–15. Other versions of the lineage may be found in Jones, 1949–56, 1, pp. 293–302; Geiger, 1912, pp. 10–13, and Oldenberg, 1879, pp. 129–33; see also Malalasekera, 1937, 1, pp. 461–62. The story of Mahāsammata, found in Gnoli, 1977, 1, pp. 7–15, is also told in Davids, 1899–1924, 3, pp. 77–94. For additional references, see Lamotte, 1949–80, pp. 933–34n. For a discussion of different types of *cakravartins*, see Strong, 1983, pp. 44–56. The four sons of Virūḍhaka are said to marry their half-sisters in Jones, 1949–56, 1, p. 296, their actual sisters in Davids, 1899–1924, 1, p. 115, something that occasionally resulted in their being accused of incest (see Cowell, 1895–1907, 5, p. 219, and the discussion in Bollée, 1970, p. 80). The story of the Koliyas being descendant from a Śākya princess who was sent away because of her leprosy and who eventually married the sage Kola is found in Jones, 1949–56, 1, pp. 298–302. It is told somewhat differently in the Pali commentaries (see Malalasekera, 1937, 1, pp. 689–90).

There is some confusion over the identity of the Buddha's maternal grandfather, Suprabuddha, who, in some sources, is apparently confused with another Suprabuddha who was a nephew of the Buddha's father, Śuddhodana (see Gnoli, 1977–78, 1, p. 32). In any case, the Pali tradition (see Geiger, 1912, pp. 274–75) presents this part of the genealogy dealing with the Buddha's parents somewhat differently; in it, Śuddhodana and Māyā are said to be cousins, sharing, in fact, two sets of grandparents.

**The Buddha's birth (pp. 38–40)** Canonical accounts of the Buddha's birth may be found in Bareau, 1974, pp. 203–209. For a discussion of the belief that birth trauma wipes out memory of past lives see Hara, 1980. See also Johnston, 1936, p. 3. The *Living out of the Game*'s chapters on the bodhisattva's life in Tuṣita Heaven may be found in Bays, 1983, 1, pp. 5–119. On the conception dream of the six-tusked white elephant, see Foucher, 1987, p. 37, and Cummings, 1982, pp. 106ff. The elephant *jātaka* itself may be found in Cowell, 1895–1907, 5, pp. 20–31, and Willemen, 1994, pp. 37–39. See also Foucher, 1917a, pp. 185–204, and Feer, 1895. The bodhisattva's life *in utero* is described in Bays, 1983, pp. 102–16. The Emperor Aśoka's inscription at Lumbinī may be read in Nikam and McKeon, 1959, p. 69. The Pali story of Māyā trying to get home to give birth is in Jayawickrama, 1990, p. 69, while the tale of her mother being named Lumbinī can be found in Gnoli, 1977–78, 1, p. 33. Doubts about Lumbinī being the actual birthplace are expressed in Bareau, 1987. For representations of the Buddha's birth in art, see Snellgrove, 1978, pp. 26–27, 30, 64, 65, 176, 309, and Cummings, 1982, pp. 115–22. The thirty-two portents that occur at the moment of his birth are listed in Jayawickrama, 1990, p. 68. Lists of the seven co-natals may be found in Horner, 1978, p. 395, and Jayawickrama, 1990, p. 71; see also Davids, 1880, p. 68n. Foucher, 1987, pp. 52–53 mentions their possible connection to the gems of the *cakravartin*. For a study of the first words of the Buddha, see Irwin, 1981; for an interpretation of his seven steps, see Mus, 1935, 1, pp. 457ff., and Foucher, 1987, pp. 50–52.

**Signs of the Great Man (pp. 41–43)** Canonical accounts of the infant Buddha being examined by soothsayers may be found in Bareau, 1974, pp. 209–13. For varying lists of the signs of the great man, see Jones, 1949–56, 2, p. 26; Bays, 1983, pp. 155–56; and Davids, 1899–1924, 3, pp. 139–67. See also the discussion in Burnouf, 1852, pp. 553–647. Bibliographies on some of the particular signs may be found in Lamotte, 1949–80, pp. 271ff. The examples of parallelism between the two careers of buddha and *cakravartin* come from the Pali "Discourse on the Signs (*Lakkhaṇa-sutta*)" (Davids, 1899–1924, 3, pp. 139–67). The story of Kauṇḍinya holding up one finger is from Jayawickrama, 1990, pp. 74–75. Three versions of the tale of Asita may be found in Jones, 1949–56, 2, pp. 27–30; Bays, 1983, 1, pp. 162–63, and Johnston, 1936, pp. 11–17. For a study of the episode as a whole see de Jong, 1954, pp. 322–23.

The tale of the Buddha being presented in the temple to the goddess Abhayā is from Jones, 1949–56, 2, pp. 22–23. A comparable story about Kaḷadeva may be found in Jayawickrama, 1990, p. 72. Śuddhodana's reaction to these events is recalled in Strong, 1983, pp. 246–47, and Bays, 1983, 1, pp. 175–76, while the tradition of his three prostrations is highlighted in Durt, 1979, pp. 375–76.

**Upbringing in the palace (pp. 43–46)** Bareau, 1974, pp. 251–53, raises doubts about the death of the Buddha's mother seven days after his birth. The various explanations of her death are found in Foucher, 1987, pp. 65–69, and Johnston, 1936, p. 23. Canonical traditions about the number of his nurses are presented in Bareau, 1974, p. 216. For another account of his school lesson, see Beal, 1875, pp. 69–70. His recollections of his life of luxury are found in Woodward and Hare, 1932–36, 1 p. 128, and in Jones, 1949–56, 2, p. 111.

Xuanzang's account of the elephant pit is found in Li, 1996, p. 175. The bodhisattva's feats in wrestling and archery are described in Bays, 1983, 1, pp. 216–38, as well as in Beal, 1875, pp. 83–92. The relationship between the Buddha and Devadatta has been characterized by some as a traditional cross-cousin rivalry (see Hocart, 1923 and Mitra, 1924). For a study of traditions about Yaśodharā, see Bareau, 1982. Two distinct versions of the story of her betrothal to the bodhisattva can be found in Jayawickrama, 1990, p. 78, and Beal, 1875, pp. 78–83. The account of his three wives is contained in Gnoli, 1977–78, 1, pp. 62–78. See also Péri, 1918.

**Turning away from kingship (pp. 46–48)** For canonical accounts of the bodhisattva's dissatisfaction with life in the palace, see Bareau, 1974, p. 218, and Foucher, 1987, p. 92. An account of his meditation under the jambu tree may be found in Jayawickrama, 1990, pp. 76–77. For a study of the episode as a whole, see Durt, 1982, who cites the Chinese account of the series of deaths occasioned by the ploughing (p. 109); see also Beal, 1875, pp. 72–78. Other versions of the four signs story may be found in Jayawickrama, 1990, pp. 78–79; Jones, 1949–56, 2, pp. 145–51; Johnston, 1936, pp. 37ff.; and Beal, 1875, pp. 115–23. The story of the signs being seen after exiting the four city gates in the different directions is recounted in Bays, 1983, pp. 284–90. Bareau's comment on it is from his 1974, p. 241. Bareau's conclusion that this portion of the Buddha's life exhibits exaltation and exemplification is in his 1974, p. 266.

## 3 QUEST AND ENLIGHTENMENT (pp. 49–76)

The "Discourse on the Noble Quest" has been translated in Horner, 1954–59, 1, pp. 203–19. For parallel passages in other canonical sources, see Bareau, 1963, pp. 13ff.

**Incitements to leave home (pp. 51–53)** The account of the bodhisattva's adornment by the gods prior to his great departure may be found in Jayawickrama, 1990, p. 80. The story of Kisāgotamī is told in Jayawickrama, 1990, p. 81; her verse, however, is my own translation from Fausbøll, 1877–96, p. 60. In the *Vinaya of the Mūlasarvāstivādins*, Kisāgotamī is called "Mṛgajā," and the bodhisattva's action is enough actually to make her one of his three wives (see Gnoli, 1977, 1, p. 78). In the *Great Story (Mahāvastu)*, where she is called Mṛgī, the bodhisattva neither looks at nor speaks to her, and his indifference peeves her (see Jones, 1949–56, 2, p. 153). The account of the gods reworking the words of the songs of the harem women may be found in Bays, 1983, pp. 246–69. For other presentations of the harem scene, see Jayawickrama, 1990 p. 82, and Jones, 1949–56, 2, pp. 154–55. The latter source also explicitly compares the harem to a burial ground. For a further discussion of this point, see Wilson, 1996, pp. 65–70.

**The great departure (pp. 53–60)** Śuddhodana's dreams are recounted in Jones, 1949–56, 2, p. 129, and Beal, 1875, pp. 111–15. The details about the gods putting the citizens of Kapilavastu to sleep and about the difficulty in waking Chandaka are from Strong, 1995, p. 11. Chandaka and Kaṇṭhaka's failure to be heard when they give the alarm is from Jones, 1949–56, 2, pp. 155–56. In Bays, 1983, pp. 316–27, Chandaka has a long conversation with the bodhisattva in which he reminds the latter of all the pleasures of the palace and all the duties of kingship. For other versions of the conversation between the bodhisattva and his father, see Jones, 1949–56, 2, pp. 141–44, and Johnston, 1936, pp. 67–69, where Śuddhodana does not grant his blessing. Instead, he increases the guard and seeks to tempt his son further with women and other pleasures. The same role is taken by his friend Udāyin in Beal, 1875, pp. 124–25, and Johnston, 1938, pp. 53–55. Alfred Foucher's speculations about filial piety are in his 1987, p. 100. At ordination ceremonies to this day, candidates are asked whether or not they have the permission of their parents (see Warren, 1896, p. 399). For representations in art of the bodhisattva's farewell to his wife and son, see Cummings, 1982, p. 148, and Snellgrove, 1978, p. 65.

The alternative tradition from the *Vinaya of the Mūlasarvāstivādins* in which the bodhisattva makes love to Yaśodharā on the night of the great departure is presented and discussed in Strong, 1997. Corroborative sources are listed in 1997, p. 125 nn. 6–7, to which should be added Willemen, 1994, pp. 240–45. For an account of the ordination ceremony in which the question "are you a male?" is posed, see Warren, 1896, p. 399. For a further discussion of the import of this provision, see Zwilling, 1995, p. 205. The preceptor's verification of a candidate's masculinity at the time of ordination is described in Takakusu, 1896, p. 96. For the bodhisattva's five dreams, see Strong, 1997, p. 115. See also Jones, 1949–56, 2, pp. 131–32; Bays, 1983, pp. 296–97; and Woodward and Hare, 1932–36, 3, pp. 175–77. For other versions of Yaśodharā's dreams, see Bays, 1983, pp. 293–96; Beal, 1875, p. 128; and Jones, 1949–56, 2, pp. 129ff. In the latter text (1, pp. 189–90) her relationship with the bodhisattva and her agreement not to hinder him in his quest goes all the way back to the time of his vow under Dīpaṃkara. On the five ascetics actually being Śākya agents, see Strong, 1997, p. 116, and Jones, 1949–56, 2, pp. 197, 220. For Yaśodharā's ascetic practices, the development of her pregnancy, and the birth of Rāhula, see Strong, 1997, pp. 117–19, and Jones, 1949–56, 2, p. 197. For the Śākyas' reaction to her being pregnant, see also Willemen, 1994, pp. 140–45.

On the actual great departure through or over the city gates, see Jayawickrama, 1990, p. 84; Strong, 1995, p. 12; and Johnston, 1936, p. 78. For the story of the city goddess asking him to turn back, see Jones, 1949–56, 2, p. 159. For the episode of Māra trying to block his way, see Jayawickrama, 1990, p. 84. For the encounter with Mahānāman, see Gnoli, 1977, 1, p. 87. For ritual repetitions of these events, see Wells,

1960, p. 140, and Leclère, 1899, p. 406. For representations of the great departure in art, see Cummings, 1982, pp. 144, 146, 150, and Snellgrove, 1978, pp. 80, 166. For the episode of the deities crying, see Strong, 1995, p. 12. The detail of Kaṇṭhaka not being able to get through the mass of flowers is from Jayawickrama, 1990, pp. 85–86. On the ritual connections of these events, see Wells, 1960, pp. 137–38 and 140 n.1. On the different distances of the Anomiya river from Kapilavastu, see Foucher, 1987, p. 105.

**The making of a monk (pp. 60–62)** For different versions of the story of the bodhisattva's acquisition of his robes, see Jayawickrama, 1990, p. 87, and Strong, 1995, p. 13. The former source also mentions the provisions of the other requisites for a monk. Representations of the bodhisattva cutting his own hair may be seen in Snellgrove, 1978, pp. 160, 166, 307. On the relics of the hairknot and clothes in heaven, see Strong, forthcoming, ch. 2, and Snellgrove, 1978, p. 29. On Chandaka's reluctance to leave the bodhisattva, see Gnoli, 1977, 1, p. 91; Johnston, 1936, pp. 81–88; and Foucher, 1987, pp. 105–07. On the horse Kaṇṭhaka, see Jayawickrama, 1990, p. 87, and Jones, 1949–56, pp. 182–83. Foucher, 1987, pp. 119–20, discusses the theme of the dismissal of the gods. Bareau, 1963, pp. 33–41, presents sources on the dangers of the forest. The bodhisattva's subsequent refusal of divine help is exemplified in Jones, 1949–56, 2, p. 126, and Bays, 1983, p. 406. Two rather different accounts of the meeting with Bimbisāra may be found in Johnston, 1936, pp. 141–48, and Jayawickrama, 1990, pp. 87–88; see also the discussion in Foucher, 1987, pp. 126–28. For canonical sources on his studies with Ārāḍa and Udraka, see Bareau, 1963, pp. 13–27. See also the chapter in Johnston, 1936, pp. 166–87. On their identities as teachers of *saṃkhya* and of yoga, see Foucher, 1987, p. 133. For a presentation of the eight levels of trance in Buddhist meditation, see Conze, 1956, pp. 113–18. On the trance of cessation, see Griffiths, 1986.

**The practice of austerities (pp. 62–66)** A translation of the autobiographical "Discourse to Saccaka" which includes descriptions of the bodhisattva's breath control and fasting may be found in Horner, 1954–59, 1, pp. 291–305. For a discussion of parallel canonical texts, see Bareau, 1963, pp. 45–54. For a representation in art of the bodhisattva practicing austerities, see Snellgrove, 1978, p. 106. The obscuring of his thirty-two marks as a result of his fast is mentioned in Jayawickrama, 1990, p. 89. For accounts of the false rumor of his death, see Jayawickrama, 1990, pp. 89–90, and Jones, 1949–56, 2, p. 198. For a study of the Jain practice of fasting to death, see Jaini, 1979, pp. 227–33. On Mahāvīra's austerities, see ibid., pp. 25–27. On his decision to resume eating, see Horner, 1954–59, 1, p. 301; Jones, 1949–56, 2, pp. 125–26; and Bays, 1983, p. 386, where it is his meeting with his mother that convinces him to do so. On the importance of "seeing the body as bones," see Strong, 1992, pp. 83–84, 88, and Wilson, 1996. For a discussion of his covering himself with a shroud, see Foucher, 1987, pp. 139–40. The use of the *tacapañcaka* in Buddhist ordination is described in Warren, 1896, p. 396, and discussed in Strong, 1992, p. 88.

**The abandonment of austerities (pp. 66–67)** The story of the lute player is found in Swearer, forthcoming, ch. 5; see also Rockhill, 1907, p. 73.

**The offering of milk-rice (pp. 67–70)** The *Great Story (Mahāvastu)* version of the Sujāta episode is found in Jones, 1949–56, 2, pp. 195–97. For the version in the "Introduction" to the *Jātaka Commentary*, see Jayawickrama, 1990, pp. 90–91. For a representation of Sujāta's offering in art, see Snellgrove, 1978, p. 29. For the *Living out of the Game (Lalitavistara)*story of the collection of bathwater relics, see Bays, 1983, p. 409. On the number of riceballs (forty-nine), specified in Jayawickrama, 1990, p. 93, see Swearer, forthcoming, ch. 4, and Porée-Maspero, 1962–69, 2, pp. 335–37. Jayawickrama, 1990, p. 93 also contains the information that the bodhisattva will not eat or defecate for seven weeks. The description of his procession to the bodhi tree may be found in Bays, 1983, pp. 415–39. His encounter with the *nāga* Kālika is in Jones, 1949–56, 2, pp. 356–60, and Strong, 1983, p. 121. The story of Svastika and the search for the right spot is recounted in Jayawickrama, 1990, pp. 93–94, the multiplication of bodhi trees is in Bays, 1983, pp. 437–38. A bas-relief depicting the Svastika episode may be found in Snellgrove, 1978, p. 160.

**The defeat of Māra (pp. 70–73)** On Māra in general, see Ling, 1962, and Boyd, 1975. On Māra's attempts to get the bodhisattva to go home, see Fausbøll, 1901, pp. 68–71, and Jones, 1949–56, 2, pp. 224–27. Māra's thirty-two bad dreams are listed in Bays, 1983, pp. 459–61. His bragging is described in Jones, 1949–56, 2, p. 252. For Māra's assault in the "Introduction" to the *Jātaka Commentary*, see Jayawickrama, 1990, pp. 96–97. For a representation in art, see Snellgrove, 1978, p. 329. The bodhisattva's calling the earth to witness is described in Jones, 1949–56, 2, p. 366, and Jayawickrama, 1990, p. 98. On the Earth-goddess wringing out her hair, see Guthrie, 1996, p. 7; for depictions of the scene in art, see Cummings, 1982, p. 168, and Snellgrove, 1978, p. 320. The thirty-two kinds of feminine wile are described in Bays, 1983, p. 484. For the different female forms taken on by the daughters of Māra, see Jones, 1949–56, 3, pp. 270–71. Māra's final defeat is described in Bays, 1983, pp. 485–511.

**Enlightenment (pp. 73–76)** Canonical accounts of the acquisition of the three knowledges are presented in Bareau, 1963, pp. 75–91. For a text featuring realization of the *six* knowledges, see Kloppenborg, 1973, pp. 1–4. On the preliminary entrance into the fourth trance, see Bareau, 1963, pp. 67–71. The listing of the six superknowledges is taken from Van Zeyst, 1961, p. 98. For canonical accounts of the experiences in the first two watches of the night, see Bareau, 1963, pp. 75–79; Jayawickrama, 1990, p. 99; and Strong, 1995, p. 17. In Jones, 1949–56, 2, pp. 265–66, and Bays, 1983, pp. 516–17, the order of the first two experiences is reversed. The same texts also contain descriptions of the third watch, on which see also Horner, 1954–59, 1, p. 29. On the dharmalogical realization of the third watch as being the understanding of interdependent origination, see Foucher, 1987, pp. 163–75; see also Jones, 1949–56, p. 267, and Strong, 1995, p. 100. Declarations of enlightenment are also found in canonical accounts of this scene, presented in Bareau, 1963, pp. 75–79. The declaration of enlightenment in the "Introduction" to the *Jātaka Commentary* is actually a quote from the *Dhammapada* (see Thanissaro, 1998, pp. 43–44).

## 4 TEACHINGS AND COMMUNITY (pp. 77–99)

**The weeks following enlightenment (pp. 77–81)** For accounts of week 1, see Jayawickrama, 1990, p. 103, and Jones, 1949–56, 3, pp. 261ff. A source that features the Buddha formulating the law of interdependent origination during this time is Horner, 1938–52, 4, p. 1. See also Bareau, 1963, pp. 93–97. For weeks 2, 3, and 4, see Jayawickrama, 1990, p. 104. For week 5, see ibid., p. 105. In Jones, 1949–56, 3, p. 269, the Buddha encounters Māra's daughters while walking back and forth on his meditation walkway. In Bays, 1983, pp. 572–73, he turns Mara's daughters into old hags and they are forced to take refuge in him in order to get their youth back. In Horner, 1938–52, 4, p. 6, no mention is made of Māra's daughters; instead, while sitting under the goatherd's banyan, the Buddha encounters a haughty "murmuring brahmin." For an account of week 6, see Jayawickrama, 1990, p. 107. Depictions of the scene featuring the Buddha sitting under Mucilinda's hood became particularly popular in the iconographic tradition (see Cummings, 1982, pp. 174–77, and Snellgrove, 1978, pp. 77, 144, 151). In the *Great Story (Mahāvastu)*, the Buddha spends one week (the fourth) in the abode of a *nāga* named Kāla, and another (the fifth) with Mucilinda. For an account of week 7, see Jayawickrama, 1990, p. 107, where we are told that, during this time, he is visited by the god Indra who brings him a medicinal myrobalan (to prepare his digestive track for the meal that follows?) See also Bareau, 1963, p. 1.

The Trapuṣa and Bhallika episode is recounted in Jayawickrama, 1990, pp. 107–108. For the full development of their legend, see Strong, 1998. See also Bigandet, 1866, 1, pp. 108–10. For a representation of the story in art, see Snellgrove, 1978, p. 81. On the Buddha's wondering whether or not he should preach, see Horner, 1954–59, 1, pp. 211–212, and Jones, 1949–56, 3, p. 303. For two studies of *pratyekabuddha* traditions, see Kloppenborg, 1974 and Wiltshire, 1990. Canonical accounts of Brahmā's imploring him to do so are presented in Bareau, 1963, pp. 135–43.

The more narrative account of the seven weeks is found in Gnoli, 1977, 1, pp. 121–30 (see also Rockhill, 1907, pp. 33–35), and Kloppenborg, 1973, pp. 6–19. Table 4.1, column 2 is based on the latter. Column 1 is based on Jayawickrama, 1990, pp. 103–108. Xuanzang's account of these sites may be found in Li, 1996, p. 250. For Faxian's, see Legge, 1886, pp. 88–89.

**The first sermon: the Middle Way and the Four Noble Truths (pp. 81–84)** On the decision to go to Benares, see Jayawickrama, 1990, pp. 108–09, Kloppenborg, 1973:18–19; Bareau, 1963, pp. 144–54; Bays, 611–14; and Jones, 1949–56, 3, p. 312. On the encounter with Upaka, see Bareau, 1963, p. 155, and Jones, 1949–56, 3, pp. 316ff. The flight across the Ganges is described in Jones, 1949–56, 3, pp. 319–20. For canonical sources on his re-encounter with the five ascetics, see Bareau, 1963, pp. 161ff. For a comparative study of canonical versions of the first sermon, see Bareau, 1963, pp. 172–82. Other versions may be found in Jones, 1949–56, 3, pp. 322–28; Johnston, 1937, pp. 28–35; Beal, 1875, pp. 251–56; and Kloppenborg, 1973, pp. 24–26. On the Eightfold Noble Path, see Rahula, 1959, pp. 45ff. The presentation of the Four Noble Truths is that found in the *Great Story (Mahāvastu)* (see Strong, 1995, pp. 32–33). For a commentary on the doctrine, see Rahula, 1959, and Robinson and Johnson, 1997, pp. 34–42.

**The second sermon at Benares: non-self and impermanence (pp. 84–85)** For canonical sources on the second sermon, see Horner, 1938–52, 4, pp. 20ff., and Davids and Woodward, 1917–30, 3, pp. 59ff; see also Bareau, 1963, pp. 190–98. For a discussion of non-self, see Collins, 1982. For a discussion of impermanence in the context of the three marks of existence, see Conze, 1967, pp. 31–46, and 134ff. On the enlightenment of the five monks at the end of this sermon, see Horner, 1938–52, 4, p. 21.

**Other teachings to the group of five (pp. 85–86)** For the Buddha's third sermon at Benares, see Horner, 1954–59, 1, pp. 217–19, and Bareau, 1963, p. 193.

**Further conversions in Benares: Yaśa and his family (pp. 86–88)** In addition to the stories of Yaśa found in Horner, 1938–52, 4, pp. 21–26, and Kloppenborg, 1973, pp. 31–40, see Bareau, 1963, pp. 199ff.; Beal, 1875, pp. 258–66; and Johnston, 1937, pp. 36–37 (where the tale is much reduced). On the preliminary discourse, see Lamotte, 1988, p. 77. For the identification of Yaśa as Sujāta's son, see Strong, 1995, pp. 48–49. The stories of Yaśa's four friends and of his fifty friends are recounted in Horner, 1938–52, 4, pp. 26–28; Kloppenborg, 1973, pp. 40–43; and Bareau, 1963, pp. 223–28. For other versions of the Buddha's instructions to his disciples, see Horner, 1938–52, 4, pp. 28–30, and Bareau, 1963, p. 243.

**The return to Magadha (pp. 88–91)** For an alternative account of the conversions of the thirty friends, and of the Kāśyapa brothers, see Kloppenborg, 1973, pp. 45–74. For a representation of the Buddha and the Kaśyapas in art, see Snellgrove, 1978, p. 189. On the Buddha's appearance together with the Kāśyapas in front of Bimbisāra, see Kloppenborg, 1973, pp. 75–90. For other accounts of the conversion of Śāriputra and Maudgalyāyana, see Bareau, 1963, pp. 343–47, and Kloppenborg, 1973, pp. 91–98. For a bibliography, see Lamotte, 1949–80, p. 623 n.2. On the legend of Śariputra, see Nyanaponika and Hecker, 1997, pp. 1–66, and Migot, 1954. On the legend of Maudgalyāyana, see Nyanaponika and Hecker, 1997, pp. 67–106.

**The return to Kapilavastu: the conversion of the Śākyas (pp. 91–99)** On the episode of the Buddha's return home, see Foucher, 1987, pp. 231–37; Jones, 1949–56, 3, p. 6; Jayawickrama, 1990, pp. 115–24; Beal, 1875, pp. 349ff.; and Horner, 1938–52, 4, pp. 103–05. The detail about Śuddhodana abdicating the throne is from Gnoli, 1977–78, 1, pp. 198–99. Mahāprajāpatī's attainment of the first level of enlightenment is mentioned in Jones, 1949–56, 3, pp. 245–46. On her, see also Walters, 1994. The story of the founding of the order of nuns is from Strong, 1995, pp. 52–56. On this, see also Murcott, 1991, pp. 13–19; Tsomo, 1996, pp. 19ff.; Horner, 1930, pp. 95–117; and Wijayaratna, 1991, pp. 21–32. On Śuddhodana's rule, see also Gnoli, 1977–78, 1, p. 200, and Rockhill, 1907, p. 53, and on his worry that the *saṃgha* is dominated by brahmins, see Jones, 1949–56, 3, p. 171. On the story of Aniruddha and Mahānaman, see ibid., pp. 172–73, and contrast Gnoli, 1977–78, 1, pp. 200–02 and Rockhill, 1907, pp. 53–54. On Aniruddha more generally, see Nyanaponika and Hecker, 1997, pp. 183–210. On the ordination of Upāli, see Horner, 1938–52, 5, p. 25; Jones, 1949–56, 3, pp. 175–77; and Gnoli, 1977, 1, pp. 204–07. On Ānanda's youthfulness, see Gnoli, 1977, 1:119–20, 2, p. 30, and on his ordination, ibid., 2, pp. 53–57, and Rockhill, 1907, p. 57. For a more general account of his life, see Nyanaponika and Hecker, 1997, pp. 137–82. The story of the tricking of Devadatta into ordination is recalled in Gnoli, 1977, 1, pp. 202–03, and Rockhill, 1907, p. 54. On the Buddha calling Devadatta a "drooler of snot" see Lamotte, 1970. On Devadatta more generally, see Ray, 1994, pp. 162–73; Mukherjee, 1966 and Bareau, 1991. The brief mention of Sundara-Nanda as not being ordained may be found in Jones, 1949–56, 3, p. 171. The whole saga of his story is found, however, in Johnston, 1928; Burlingame, 1921, 1, pp. 217–25; and Beal, 1875, pp. 369–78. See also Lamotte, 1949–80, p. 118 for a bibliography. References to Yaśodharā's attempt to seduce the Buddha may be found in Strong, 1997, p. 121, and Foucher, 1987, p. 234. Her emotional worship of her husband is described in Jayawickrama, 1990, p. 122. The story of "Bimbā's lament" is presented in Swearer, 1995, pp. 541–52. Her talk of suicide is also found in Strong, 1997, p. 121. The ordination of Rāhula and the consequent rule about ordaining children only with their parents' permission are described in Jayawickrama, 1990, pp. 123–24; see also Strong, 1997, pp. 120–21. The final account of Yaśodharā's loss of her son is from Jones, 1949–56, 3, pp. 249–59. For reference to Yaśodharā's eventual enlightenment, see Strong, 1997, p. 121. For the story of Pāṭacārā, see Strong, 1995, pp. 56–59. On her more generally, see Nyanaponika and Hecker, 1997, pp. 293–300.

## 5 DAILY ROUTINES, MIRACLES, AND DISTANT JOURNEYS (pp. 100–123)

The Buddha is called a world wanderer (*lokassa cārin*) in Oldenberg, 1879, p. 124.

**Settling down (pp. 101–104)** The rules on rains-retreats are described in Wijayaratna, 1990, p. 20. Table 5.1 is based on Horner, 1978, p. 4. Sukumar Dutt, 1962, pp. 53–58, has been among those emphasizing the importance of the rains-retreats in the formation of monasticism. For translations of different versions of the "Prātimokṣa" for monks, see Thanissaro, 1994, and Prebish, 1975; for that for nuns, see Tsomo, 1996. This account of the story of the monks of Kauśāmbī is from Burlingame, 1921, 1, pp. 176–83; for a somewhat different version, see Horner, 1938–52, 4, pp. 483ff. For another account of the Buddha's withdrawal to the Pārileyyaka forest, see Woodward, 1935, pp. 49–50. On the meaning of unintentionally violating the rules, see Thanissaro, 1994, p. 489.

**The Jetavana monastery (pp. 104–105)** The statement about the Buddha settling in Śrāvastī is from Jayawickrama, 1968, p. 49. The story of the founding of the Jetavana may be found in Horner, 1938–52, 5, pp. 222–23. For a depiction of its offering in art, see Snellgrove, 1978, p. 60. The story of the founding of the Pūrvārāma is in Burlingame, 1921, 2, p. 81. On the Buddha's splitting his time between Anāthapiṇḍada's and Viśākhā's house, see ibid., p. 80, and also Falk, 1990.

**Daily Routine (pp. 105–107)** The entire description of a normal day in the life of the Buddha, taken from Buddhaghosa's commentary on the *Dīgha Nikāya*, may be found in Warren, 1896, pp. 92–95.

**The Great Miracle at Śrāvastī (pp. 107–112)** On the depiction of the Great Miracle in art, see Foucher, 1917; Snellgrove, 1978, pp. 152, 241; and Cummings, 1982, pp. 185–92. The Pali account of it in the *Commentary on the Dharma Stanzas* may be found in Burlingame, 1921, 3, pp. 35–47. On the story of Piṇḍola, see Strong, 1979. On the "mango trick" in Indian magic, see Siegel, 1991, pp. 165–68 and plates 3 and 4. For the Sanskrit account of the Great Miracle, from the "Discourse on the Miracle" in the *Divyāvadāna,* see Burnouf, 1876, pp. 144–68. See also Lamotte, 1966–74, p. 122. On the injunction to "Start Now! Leave Home!" see also Strong, 1983, p. 202. For Foucher's stress on the multiplication of images, see his 1917, pp. 153–54. Mus's discussion of the three elements of hut, tree, and walkway, may be found in his 1935, 2, pp. 412–14. For other discussions of the Great Miracle by Mus, see also his 1934, pp. 198–213. For the argument that the "double appearance" in the miracle refers not to fire and water but to the Buddha and the twin image he creates, see Foucher, 1917, pp. 156–57, and Davids, 1880, pp. 105 n.4. On the inability of *arhats* to converse with images of their own creation, see Burnouf, 1886, p. 167. For the coming together of two buddhas in the *Lotus Sūtra*, see Kern, 1884, pp. 227–54 and Snellgrove, 1978, p. 213. On the ceremony of entrance into the rains-retreat, see Wells, 1960, pp. 163–68. The "teachings to be remembered" (*sārāniya dhamma*) that are to be recited on that occasion may be found in Horner, 1954–59, 1, p. 384.

**The rains-retreat in Trāyastriṃśa Heaven (pp. 112–115)** The account of the Buddha's preaching in the Trāyastriṃśa Heaven is taken primarily from Burlingame, 1921, 3, pp. 47–52. For a description of the Pali and Sanskrit books of the *Abhidharma*, see Frauwallner, 1995, pp. 13–96. The tradition that only the preaching of the *Abhidharma* can repay one's debt to one's mother is mentioned in Wells, 1960, p. 104. For Xuanzang and Faxian's account of the first Buddha image at Śrāvastī, see Li, 1996, p. 160 and Legge, 1886, pp. 56–57. Somewhat similar tales may be found in Gombrich, 1978 and Bizot, 1994, pp. 103–04. On the sentiment of filiality found in the episode of the Buddha's preaching to his mother, see also Willemen, 1994, pp. 19–20.

**The descent from Trāyastriṃśa Heaven (pp. 115–117)** On the representation of the descent of the Buddha in art, see Lamotte, 1988, pp. 339 n.; Snellgrove, 1978, pp. 30, 303, 310; and Huntington, 1986–87, part III. For its connection to ritual, see Tambiah, 1972, p. 61; p. 159 n. and Wells, 1960, pp. 104–105. For Foucher's description of the Sāṃkāśya region, see his 1987, pp. 274–75. For a textual account of the descent from heaven, see Burlingame, 1921, 3, pp. 52–56. Faxian's account of Sāṃkāśya may be found in Legge, 1896, pp. 50; see also Li, 1996, p. 137. Foucher's relating the miracle to irrigation ramps in the region is found in his 1987, p. 276. On p. 376, he give a drawing of such a ramp. On the importance of "seeing the gods" on the occasion of the Buddha's descent, see Strong, 1992, pp. 151–52. The Pali tradition's emphasis on Śāriputra's welcoming the Buddha may be found in Burlingame, 1921, 3, p. 55. On the story of Utpālavarṇā, see Strong, 1983, p. 262, and Rockhill, 1907, p. 81. For the tradition in which she is reprimanded by the Buddha, see Lamotte, 1949–80, pp. 634–35 n.

On the ceremonies marking the end of the rains-retreat, see Wijayaratna, 1990, pp. 38–39, 126; Holt, 1981, pp. 131–37 and

DeSilva, 1974, pp. 150–51. On the Buddha's celebration of the *pravāraṇā* just prior to his descent, see Burlingame, 1921, 3, p. 53. Wells's account of the reenactment of the Buddha's sermon is found in his 1960, p. 104.

**Distant journeys: the visit to the Northwest (pp. 117–120)** For a general account of the Buddha's missionary activities in Northwest India, see Przyluski, 1914. Lamotte's doubting of the historicity of this voyage is found in his 1988, p. 335. For his identification of the different stages of this journey, see his 1966–74, pp. 133ff. On the story of Kuntī, see Strong, 1992, p. 35. On the cult of Hārītī, see Péri, 1917 and Strong, 1992, p. 36. For a bibliography on the *nāga* Apalāla, see Lamotte, 1949–80, p. 188 n. The tale of Apalāla's past life is from Przyluski, 1914, pp. 559–62. The story of his taming by the Buddha and Vajrapāṇi may be found in ibid., pp. 410–512 and Lamotte, 1966–74, p. 130. For a discussion of such "violent" methods of conversion, see Strong, 1992, pp. 26–27. Alexander Soper's comparisons of this story to Vedic and other examples is in his 1949–50, pt 1, pp. 263–72.

**Another distant journey and more demons: the Buddha in Sri Lanka (pp. 120–122)** For one account of the three voyages of the Buddha to Sri Lanka, see Geiger, 1912, pp. 3, 6, 8. For the *Dīpavaṃsa*'s account of the Buddha's conversion of the *nāgas* in Sri Lanka, see Oldenberg, 1879, pp. 124–27.

**The journey to Śroṇāparānta: leaving footprints on the way (pp. 122–123)** On the legend of Pūrṇa, see Tatelman, 1999. On his association with Myanmar and for the story of the Buddha's visit to that country, see Duroiselle, 1905. On the footprint on Adam's Peak, see Hazlewood, 1986 and Strong, forthcoming, chapter 6. The argument that the Pūrṇa story reflects Sri Lankan influences may be found in Duroiselle, 1905, p. 153. The counterclaim that it reflects indigenous Southeast Asian beliefs is maintained in Porée-Maspero, 1962–69, p. 734.

## 6 FINAL DAYS, THE *PARINIRVĀṆA*, AND THE *NIRVĀṆA* OF THE RELICS (pp. 125–148)

For Nāgārjuna's view of *nirvāṇa*, see Garfield, 1995, p. 75.

**The Buddha's last journey (pp. 126–137)** For different versions of the *Discourse on the Great Extinction*, see Walshe, 1987, pp. 231–77; Bareau, 1970–71; Waldschmidt, 1944–48 and 1950–51; and Weller, 1939–40. The fourteen episodes of this section of the chapter all make use of these sources. For the Buddha's advice to Varṣākāra, see Walshe, 1987, pp. 231–34; and also Waldschmidt, 1950–51, pp. 102–06; Weller, 1939–40, pp. 40–50; Bareau, 1970–71, 1, pp. 7–39; and Waldschmidt, 1944–48, pp. 34–47. For other sources on the Buddha's "comprehensive discourse," see Bareau, 1970–71, 1, pp. 41–42; Waldchmidt, 1944–48, pp. 47–51; and Rockhill, 1907, p. 126. His discussion with Śāriputra is found in Walshe, 1987, pp. 234–5. See also Jones, 1949–56, 3, p. 56; Bareau, 1970–71, 1, pp. 43–44; and Waldschmidt, 1944–48, pp. 51–52. The account of the Buddha in Pāṭaligrāma is based on Walshe, 1987, pp. 236–38; see also Waldschmidt, 1950–51, pp. 134–54; Weller, 1939–40, pp. 51–57; Bareau, 1970–71, 1, pp. 49–72; Waldschmidt, 1944–48, pp. 52–60; and Rockhill, 1907, pp. 126–28. The Pali version of his crossing the Ganges is found in Walshe, 1987, p. 239. For the Sanskrit version, see Waldschmidt, 1950–51, p. 158. See also Bareau, 1970–71, 1, pp. 72–77; Waldschmidt, 1944–48; and Willemen, 1978, p. 75. On the differentiation between the way buddhas, *pratyekabuddhas*, and disciples "cross the stream," see Emmerick, 1968, pp. 187–89. For the view of the Buddha as the great helmsman, see Weller, 1939–40, p. 57. On the Buddha's sermon at Kuṭigrāmaka see also Walshe, 1987, pp. 239–40; Weller, 1939–40, p. 58; Bareau, 1970–71, 1, pp. 79–85; and Waldschmidt, 1944–48, pp. 67–69. On the Buddha's teachings at the Brick House in Nādikā, see Walshe, 1987, pp. 240–42; Waldschmidt, 1950–51, pp. 160–70; Weller, 1939–40, pp. 59–62; Bareau, 1970–71, 1, pp. 85–93; Waldschmidt, 1944–48, pp. 69–72; and Rockhill, 1907, p. 128. The Pali version of Āmrapālī's encounter with the Licchavis may be found in Walshe, 1987, p. 243. For other versions, see Bareau, 1970–71, 1, p. 114. For Buddhaghosa's warnings about Āmrapālī's seductive ways, see Davids, 1899–1924, 2, p. 102 n. For the Sanskrit text's, see Waldschmidt, 1950–51, p. 172; see also Rockhill, 1907, pp. 128–29. For warnings about the Licchavis, see Bareau, 1970–71, 1, p. 117 and Weller, 1939–40, p. 65. On Āmrapālī more generally, see Lamotte, 1949–80, pp. 990ff. On the Buddha's illness in Veṇugrāmaka, and his advice to his disciples to be self-sufficient, see Walshe, 1987, p. 245. See also Waldschmidt, 1950–51, pp. 190–202; Weller, 1939–40, pp. 72–78; Bareau, 1970–71, 1, pp. 137–47; Waldschmidt, 1944–48, pp. 96–99; and Rockhill, 1907, pp. 130–31. On the Buddha's setting of the duration of the rest of his lifespan see, in addition to the passage cited from Walshe, 1987; Waldschmidt, 1950–51, pp. 202–24; Weller, 1939–40, pp. 78–84; 406–14; Bareau, 1970–71, 1, pp. 147–207; and

Waldschmidt, 1944–48, pp. 99–125. On the, view that a "*kalpa*" here refers to a hundred years and not an aeon, see Bareau, 1970–71, 1, p. 152n., and Walshe, 1987, p. 569 n.400. On the accusation made against Ānanda at the First Council, see Przyluski, 1926, pp. 257ff. On the four criteria for determining the authenticity of doctrine, see Walshe, 1987, pp. 255–56; Waldschmidt, 1950–51, pp. 238–53; Weller, 1939–40, pp. 416–19; Bareau, 1970–71, 1, pp. 222–39; and Waldschmidt, 1944–48, pp. 132–40. On the nature of the Buddha's last meal, see Bareau, 1970–71, 1, pp. 265–73; Waley, 1931–32, pp. 343–54; and Wasson, 1982. On the identity of "pig's delight," see Davids, 1899–1924, 2, p. 137, where he settles on truffles after discarding his earlier "tender pork" (see Davids, 1890–94, 1, p. 244). Bareau's comments on pork in India are in his 1970–71, 1, p. 267. On the meal of pork offered to the Buddha by Ugga, see Woodward and Hare, 1932–36, 3, p. 41. The identification of the meal as consisting of "sandalwood tree-ears" is made in Weller, 1939–40, p. 420. A Pali commentary from about the same period also suggests mushrooms as a possibility, although it finally opts for pork (see Thomas, 1927, p. 149n.). Waley, 1931–32, p. 350 makes the point about a bias towards vegetarianism, and also cites the listing of medicines involving pork (pp. 345–46). The Buddha's instructions to Cunda to bury the remains of the "pig's delight" is found in Walshe, 1987, pp. 256–57. Bareau, 1971, p. 4 discusses the addition of divine nutritive essence. The Buddha's praise of Cunda's offering is found in Bareau, 1970–71, 1, pp. 301–10. This is also intended to free Cunda from any blame or thought that he might be responsible for the Buddha's demise. The same point is made to King Milinda in Davids, 1890–94, 1, pp. 242–46. This entire scenario is further complicated by an episode found in all the versions of the story *except* the Pali: the mysterious and confused account of the "bad monk" who steals the bowl of food originally intended for the Buddha (thus forcing Cunda to prepare a second special meal), or who steals a bowl containing the leftovers of the meal (see Bareau, 1970–71, 1, pp. 258–64). On Ānanda's getting the Buddha some water, and on the conversion of Putkasa, see Walshe, 1987, pp. 257–60; Waldschmidt, 1950–51, pp. 264–82; Weller, 1939–40, pp. 425–32; Bareau, 1970–71, 1, pp. 276–99; Waldschmidt, 1944–48, pp. 148–62; and Rockhill, 1907, pp. 133–35. On the Buddha's last bath, see Walshe, 1987, pp. 260–62; Waldschmidt, 1950–51, pp. 282–86; Weller, 1939–40, pp. 432; Bareau, 1970–71, 1, pp. 300–310; Waldschmidt, 1944–48, pp. 163–68; and Rockhill, 1907, p. 135.

**Death-bed deeds (pp. 137–141)** For representations in art of the death of the Buddha, see Snellgrove, 1978, pp. 123, 188, 194, 299, 392 and Cummings, 1982, pp. 202, 210. On the Buddha's comforting of Ānanda, see Strong, 1995, p. 35; Walshe, 1987, pp. 265; Bareau, 1970–71, 2, pp. 54–71; and Rockhill, 1907, pp. 135–36. On the status of Kuśinagarī, see Walshe, 1987, p. 266; Bareau, 1970–71, 2, pp. 72–76; Rockhill, 1907, p. 136; and especially Waldschmidt, 1950–51, pp. 304–54 which incorporates the entire text of the *Mahāsudarśana-sūtra*. The Pali canon preserves that discourse in a separate sūtra in the *Dīgha Nikāya* (see Walshe, 1987, pp. 279–90). On the episode of Upamāna, see also Walshe, 1987, pp. 262–63; Weller, 1939–40, pp. 141–42; Bareau, 1970–71, 2, pp. 231–290; and Rockhill, 1907, p. 136. The Buddha's instructions as to how his body should be treated may also be found in Walshe, 1987, pp. 264–65; Bareau, 1970–71, 2, pp. 35–53 and Rockhill, 1907, p. 137. See also Schopen, 1997, pp. 99–113. On the visit of the Mallas, see Waldschmidt, 1950–51, pp. 360–66; Walshe, 1987, pp. 266–67; Bareau, 1970–71, 2, pp. 76–92; and Rockhill, 1907, pp. 137. For the conversion of Subhadra, the Buddha's last disciple, see Waldschmidt, 1950–55, pp. 366–86. See also Walshe, 1987, pp. 267–69; Bareau, 1970–71, 2, pp. 92–131; and Rockhill, 1907, pp. 138–40. On the story of the divine musician Sunanda, see Obermiller, 1931–32, 2, p. 59. On the Buddha's authorization of the abolition of minor precepts, see Bareau, 1970–71, 2, p. 139. On the identification of the four places of pilgrimage, see Strong, 1995, pp. 36–37 and also Bareau, 1970–71, 2, pp. 131–44; 29–32. For the Buddha's advice on women, see Walshe, 1987, pp. 264. On the Buddha's instructions to gaze upon his body, see also Bareau, 1970–71, 2, pp. 147 and Obermiller, 1931–32, 2, p. 61. On his final passing into *parinirvāṇa*, see Waldschmidt, 1950–51, pp. 390–96; Walshe, 1987, pp. 270–71 and Bareau, 1970–71; 2, pp. 144–56.

**The Funeral and cremation (pp. 141–144)** For an interesting interpretation of the śāla trees raining down blossoms, see Vaudeville, 1964. For a study of the various verses uttered by different beings at the moment of the Buddha's death, see Przyluski, 1920, pp. 5–46. For a discussion of the nature of the "homage to the body" (*śarīra-pūjā*), see Schopen, 1997, pp. 99–113. Various views on the wrapping of the Buddha in five hundred double layers of cloth are discussed in Strong, forthcoming, ch. 4, as is the peculiar nature of the Buddha's coffin, on which see also Przyluski, 1935–36. On the inclusion of the gathering of relics in this ritual sequence, see Waldschmidt, 1944–48, pp. 214–15 and Bareau, 1970–71, 2, p. 46. On the specification that a *stūpa* should be constructed, see Schopen, 1994, p. 39. For a representation in art of the Mallas' festivities, see Snellgrove, 1978, p. 31. Foucher's likening of this to a village fair is from his 1987, p. 317. On various other reasons for the delay in Buddha's cremation, see Bareau, 1970–71, 2, pp. 187–92. The scene in which the mourning Malla woman cries over the Buddha's feet may be found in Waldschmidt, 1944–48, pp. 267–70 and Bareau, 1970–71, 2, pp. 185–86. Bareau, 1970–71, 2 pp. 249–51; Weller, 1939–40, p. 197; and Jones, 1949–56, 1, p. 55 state that her tears stained the feet. On Ānanda being blamed for allowing this to happen, see Lamotte, 1949–80, pp. 94–96 n. On Ānanda showing the Buddha's private parts to the women, see Lamotte, 1949–80, p. 96; Li, 1993, p. 104; Przyluski, 1923, p. 325 and 1926, pp. 15, 233; and Rockhill, 1907, p. 154. The washing of the Buddha's body is mentioned in Weller, 1939–40, p. 434, and Waldschmidt, 1944–48, p. 296. See also Schopen, 1994, pp. 38–39. For discussions of Mahākāśyapa's late arrival, see Waldschmidt, 1944–48, pp. 185–89 and Bareau, 1970–71, 2, pp. 215–22. For explanations of the Mallas' failure to light the cremation fire, see Waldschmidt, 1950–51, pp. 424–27 and Bareau, 1970–71, 2, p. 235. On the emergence of the feet from the coffin and Mahākāśyapa's worship of them, see ibid., pp. 241–42, and Waldschmidt, 1944–48, pp. 297–305. Xuanzang's account of the three post-mortem movements of the Buddha may be found in Li, 1996, p. 191 and 1995, p. 84. On his hand appearing to Ānanda, see also Durt, 1992. On his sitting up to greet his mother come down from heaven, see Li, 1996, pp. 189–90; Durt, 1992, pp. 1–4; and Wieger, 1913, pp. 246–53, which also contains a woodblock illustration of the episode. For various accounts of the lighting of the cremation pyre, see Bareau, 1970–71, 2, pp. 254ff. and Waldschmidt, 1944–48, pp. 305ff. The Pali account of what is left when the fire goes out may be found in Walshe, 1987, p. 275. In other traditions, it is said that two of the thousand shrouds enveloping the body of the Buddha were left unburned (see Bareau, 1970–71, 2, pp. 261–62 and, for a discussion, Strong, forthcoming, ch. 4).

**The Collection and Distribution of the Relics (pp. 144–146)** On the relics being likened to pearls, nuggets of gold, etc., see Stede, 1886–1932, 2, pp. 603–04, and Jayawickrama, 1971, p. 34, and 1968, pp. 52–53. On the Mallas' initial enshrinement of the relics, see also Waldschmidt, 1944–48, p. 309; Rockhill, 1907, p. 145; and Bareau, 1970–71, 2, pp. 262–63. On Ajātaśatru's claim to a share of the relics, see also Waldschmidt, 1944–48, pp. 313–21; Bareau, 1970–71, 2, pp. 265–88; and Li, 1996, p. 191. On the various kings and communities who want portions of the relics, see Bareau, 1970–71, 2, pp. 284–85; and Waldschmidt, 1967. For representations in art of the "war for the relics," see Marshall, 1955, p. 53, plate IV and Srivastava, 1983, p. 99, plates XV–XVI. On Droṇa's division of the relics, see Bareau, 1970–71, 2, pp. 288–303, and Waldschmidt, 1944–48, pp. 321–24. On the relics of the urn and of the ashes, see Waldschmidt, 1944–48, pp. 324–28, and Bareau, 1970–71, 2, pp. 303–08. On Droṇa's possible theft of relics, see Li, 1996, pp. 87, 192, 209, and Trainor, 1992.

**The life and final extinction of the Dharma and the relics (pp. 146–148)** On the theory of the Buddha's two bodies, see Strong, 1992, pp. 105–06, and 317 n.59. For discussions of the First Council, see Przyluski, 1926, and Lamotte, 1988, pp. 124–26. On Ajātaśatru's collection of the relics, see also Strong, forthcoming, ch. 5, and, for his redistribution of the relics into eighty-four thousand *stūpas*, Strong, 1983, pp. 109–19. For stories of persons who claim to have seen the Buddha after "seeing" his Dharma, see Strong, 1992, pp. 105–06. For examples of how the relics are also equated with the Buddha, see Schopen, 1997, pp. 125ff., 258ff. For a study of the doctrine of the decline of the Dharma, see Nattier, 1991; her discussion of the five stages of decline is on p. 57. For various accounts of the *parinirvāṇa* of the relics, see Walleser and Kopp, 1924–56, 1, p. 91; Stede, 1886–1932, 3, p. 899; Coedès, 1956, pp. 5ff.; Reynolds and Reynolds, 1982, pp. 330–31; and Lévi and Chavannes, 1916, p. 13.

# GLOSSARY OF SANSKRIT NAMES AND TERMS WITH PALI EQUIVALENTS

| | |
|---|---|
| Ajataśatru (Pali: Ajatasattu) | King of Magadha; son of Bimbisāra |
| Amrapālī (Pali: Ambapālī) | A courtesan of Vaiśālī who invites the Buddha to a meal towards the end of his life |
| Amṛtodana (Pali: Amitodana) | Uncle of the Buddha |
| Ānanda (Pali: *idem)* | A cousin and disciple of the Buddha; his personal attendant |
| Anāthapiṇḍada (Pali: Anāthapiṇḍika) | Important lay disciple of the Buddha; donor of the Jetavana monastery |
| Anavatapta (Pali: Anotatta) | A lake said to be located in the Himālayas |
| Aniruddha (Pali: Anuruddha) | A cousin and disciple of the Buddha |
| Anomiya (Pali: Anomā) | A river some distance from Kapilavastu where the bodhisattva first stops on the night of his great departure |
| Apalāla (Pali: *idem)* | A nāga king who is converted by the Buddha in Northwest India |
| Ārāḍa Kālāma (Pali: Āḷāra Kālāma) | First teacher of the bodhisattva after his great departure |
| Asita (Pali: *idem)* | Soothsayer who examines the signs on the Buddha's body at birth |
| Aśoka (Pali: Asoka) | Third-century B.C.E. king of the Mauryan dynasty who rules over most of the Indian subcontinent and converts to Buddhism |
| Aśvajit (Pali: Assaji) | An early disciple of the Buddha; one of the group of five ascetics |

| | |
|---|---|
| Bhadrika (Pali: Bhaddiya) | A cousin of the Buddha; a Śākyan who becomes a monk |
| Bimbisāra (Pali: *idem)* | King of Magadha; important ruler at the time of the Buddha |
| Bodhi Tree | Name given to the tree (ficus religiosus) under which the Buddha attains enlightenment |
| bodhisattva (Pali: bodhisatta) | A "Buddha-to-be" – epithet of the Buddha prior to his enlightenment |
| Brahmā (Pali: *idem)* | Name of an important divinity |
| cakravartin (Pali: cakkavatti) | A universal "wheel-turning" monarch who, like the Buddha, possesses the thirty-two marks of the mahāpuruṣa |
| Chandaka (Pali: Channa) | The bodhisattva's groom who accompanies him on the great departure |
| Cunda (Pali: *idem)* | Worker in metals who serves the Buddha his last meal |
| Devadatta (Pali: *idem)* | The Buddha's cousin, rival, and jealous maligner |
| Devadṛśa (Pali: Devadaha) | A Śākyan town close to Kapilavastu and said to have been the home of the Buddha's mother |
| Dīpaṃkara (Pali: Dīpankara) | Name of a past buddha |
| Droṇa (Pali: Doṇa) | The brahmin who distributes the Buddha's relics after his death. He was also called Dhūmrasagotra |
| Faxian (Fa-hsien) | Chinese pilgrim who visited India in early fifth century C.E. |
| Gautama (Pali: Gotama) | Clan name of the Buddha |
| Gopā (Pali: N/A) | A wife of the bodhisattva (in the Sanskrit tradition) |
| Hārītī (Pali: *idem)* | An ogress who is converted by the Buddha |
| Indra, aka Śakra (Pali: Sakka) | King of the gods who often intervenes in the affairs of humans |
| Jetavana (Pali: *idem)* | A monastic park in Śrāvastī, given to the Buddha by the rich lay merchant Anāthapiṇḍada. The Buddha spent many rains-retreats there, especially in the latter half of his life |

| | |
|---|---|
| Kaṇṭhaka (Pali: Kanthaka) | The bodhisattva's horse |
| Kapilavastu (Pali: Kapilavatthu) | Hometown of the Buddha |
| Kauṇḍinya (Pali: Kondañña) | The Buddha's first monastic disciple. The leader of the group of five ascetics. Also the name of a soothsayer who predicts the Buddha's destiny at his birth |
| Kauśāmbī (Pali: Kosambī) | One of the chief cities of North India during the Buddha's lifetime |
| Kisāgotamī | Śākyan woman who sees the Buddha prior to his enlightenment |
| Koliya (Pali: *idem)* | Name of a tribe closely related to the Śākyas |
| kṣatriya (Pali: khattiya) | A member of the ruling or warrior caste |
| Kuntī (Pali: *idem)* | An ogress who is converted by the Buddha |
| Kuśinagarī (Pali: Kusinārā) | A city of the Mallas where the Buddha attained parinirvāṇa |
| Licchavi (Pali: *idem)* | A powerful tribe at the time of the Buddha; their capital was Vaiśālī |
| Lumbinī (Pali: *idem)* | Site of the Buddha's birth |
| Magadha (Pali: *idem)* | One of the chief kingdoms in North India at the time of the Buddha |
| Mahākāśyapa (Pali: Mahākassapa) | A chief disciple of the Buddha, who presides over the First Buddhist Council after the Buddha's death |
| [Mahā]Maudgalyāyana (Pali: [Mahā]Moggallāna) | One of the chief disciples of the Buddha |
| Mahānāman (Pali: Mahānāma) | A cousin of the Buddha; a Śākyan noble |
| Mahāprajāpatī (Pali: Mahāpajāpatī) | The Buddha's aunt and stepmother; the leader of the order of nuns |
| Mahāpuruṣa (Pali: Mahāpurisa) | A "great man"; one destined to become either a buddha or a universal monarch |
| Mahāsammata (Pali: *idem)* | Name of mythic first king |
| Maitreya (Pali: Metteyya) | Name of the future buddha |
| Malla (Pali: *idem)* | Name of the people who rule the area around Kuśinagarī, and who carry out the Buddha's funeral ceremonies. A branch of the tribe also ruled the land of Pāvā |

| | |
|---|---|
| Māra (Pali: *idem)* | Chief god of the realm of desire, who consistently tries to thwart the Buddha's career |
| Māyā, aka Mahāmāyā (Pali: *idem)* | Mother of the Buddha |
| Mucilinda (Pali: Mucalinda) | A nāga king under whose hood the Buddha sheltered shortly after his enlightenment |
| nāga (Pali: *idem)* | A snake or snake-like supernatural being |
| Nanda (Pali: Nanda), aka Sundara-Nanda | Handsome half-brother of the Buddha who is ordained against his will |
| Nandā and Nandabalā | Two sisters who, in the Sanskrit tradition, offer milk-rice to the Buddha. See also Sujātā |
| Narmadā (Pali: Nammadā) | Name of a river where the Buddha leaves a footprint |
| Nigrodhārāma (Pali: *idem)* | Monastic park near Kapilavastu |
| Prasenajit (Pali: Pasenadi) | King of Kosala |
| pratyekabuddha (Pali: paccekabuddha) | One who attains enlightenment like the Buddha but then does not preach the Dharma |
| Pūrṇa (Pali: Puṇṇa) | A disciple of the Buddha |
| Pūrvārāma (Pali: Pubbārāma) | Monastery in Śrāvastī, given to the Buddha by the laywoman Viśākhā |
| Rāhula (Pali: *idem)* | The Buddha's son |
| Rājagṛha (Pali: Rājagaha) | Capital of the land of Magadha, visited several times by the Buddha. It was the residence of King Bimbisāra |
| Śākya (Pali: Sākiyā) | Name of tribe to which the Buddha belonged |
| Śākyamuni (Pali: Sakyamuni) | The "Sage of the Śākyas" – an epithet of the Buddha |
| Sāṃkāśya (Pali: Sankassa) | City on the Ganges where the Buddha came down from the Trāyastriṃśa Heaven after spending a rains-retreat there |
| Śāriputra (Pali: Sāriputta) | One of the chief disciples of the Buddha |
| Siddhārtha (Pali: Siddhattha) | The Buddha's personal name |
| Śrāvastī (Pali: Sāvatthi) | The capital of the kingdom of Kosala, where the Buddha performed a great miracle. It was the site of the Jetavana and Pūrvārāma monasteries |

| | |
|---|---|
| Śroṇāparānta (Pali: Sunāparanta) | A land variously located in Western India or Southeast Asia and associated with the Buddha's disciple Pūrṇa |
| Subhadra (Pali: Subhadda) | A wandering ascetic who visits the Buddha on his deathbed and becomes his last personal disciple |
| Śuddhodana (Pali: Suddhodana) | The Buddha's father |
| Sujātā (Pali: *idem)* | Name of the woman who offered the milk-rice to the Buddha prior to his enlightenment. See also Nandā and Nandabalā |
| Sumedha (Pali: *idem)* | Name of the bodhisattva at the time of Dīpaṃkara |
| Suprabuddha (Pali: Suppabuddha) | The Buddha's maternal grandfather (in the Pali tradition, the name also of his father-in-law) |
| Svastika (Pali: Sotthiya) | Grass-cutter who provides grass for the seat of enlightenment |
| Tathāgata (Pali: *idem)* | An epithet of the Buddha meaning "he who has come thus," i.e., in the same manner as past buddhas |
| Trapuṣa and Bhallika (Pali: Tapassu and Bhallika) | Two merchants who are the first to make an offering of food to the Buddha after his enlightenment |
| Trāyastriṃśa (Pali: Tāvatiṃsa) | Heaven of the thirty-three gods over whom Indra presides |
| Tuṣita (Pali: Tusita) | The heaven in which the bodhisattva resides in his last past life, just prior to his final birth on earth |
| Udāyin (Pali: Kāḷudāyī) | Childhood friend of the Buddha who becomes a monk |
| Udraka Rāmaputra (Pali: Uddaka Rāmaputta) | Second teacher of the bodhisattva after his great departure |
| Upāli (Pali: *idem*) | Śākyan barber who became a chief disciple of the Buddha |
| Uruvilvā (Pali: Uruvela) | Locality near Bodhgaya where the bodhisattva practiced asceticism for a period of six years |
| Uruvilvā Kāśyapa (Pali: Uruvela Kassapa) | An ascetic who lived in Uruvilvā; one of three brothers converted by the Buddha |

| | |
|---|---|
| Utpālavarṇā (Pali: Uppalavaṇṇā) | A nun and one of the chief female disciples of the Buddha; she is the first to greet him upon his return from the Trāyastriṃśa Heaven |
| Vaiśālī (Pali: Vesāli) | Capital city of the Licchavis; home of the courtesan Āmrapālī |
| Vajrapāṇi (Pali: Vajirapāṇi) | A yakṣa who sometimes accompanies the Buddha and serves as his strong-armed assistant |
| Varṣākāra (Pali: Vassakāra) | Brahmin prime minister of King Ajātaśatru who is anxious to wage war against the Vṛjis |
| Veṇuvana (Pali: Veḷuvana) | The "bamboo grove" – a monastic park in Rājagṛha given to the Buddha by King Bimbisāra |
| Vipaśyi (Pali: Vipassi) | Name of a past buddha |
| Viśākhā (Pali: Visākhā) | Important laywoman disciple of the Buddha |
| Viśvantara (Pali: Vessantara) | Name of a prince, the bodhisattva in his penultimate past life |
| Vṛji (Pali: Vajji) | Name of a country and its people in North India at the time of the Buddha |
| Xuanzang (Hsüan-tsang) | Chinese pilgrim who visited India in the seventh century C.E. |
| yakṣa (Pali: yakkha) | A class of supernatural beings, generally thought of as powerful and demonic, but capable of being converted to the cause of Buddhism |
| Yaśa (Pali: Yasa) | An early convert of the Buddha |
| Yaśodharā (Pali: Yasodharā) | The wife of the bodhisattva; the mother of Rāhula |

# BIBLIOGRAPHY


Alabaster, Henry, 1871. *The Wheel of the Law. Buddhism Illustrated from Siamese Sources.* London, Trübner and Co.

Almond, Philip C., 1988. *The British Discovery of Buddhism.* Cambridge, Cambridge University Press

Ambedkar, B.R., 1957. *The Buddha and His Dhamma.* Bombay, Siddharth College Publications

Banerjea, J.N., 1930. "The Webbed Fingers of Buddha." *Indian Historical Quarterly*, 6, pp. 717–27

Bareau, André, 1963. *Recherches sur la biographie du Buddha dans les sūtrapiṭaka et les vinayapiṭaka anciens: de la quête de l'éveil à la conversion de Śāriputra et de Maudgalyāyana.* Paris, Ecole Française d'Extrême-Orient

—1966–74. "Le *Dīpaṃkarajātaka* des Dharmaguptaka." In *Mélanges de sinologie offerts à Monsieur Paul Demiéville.* Paris, Institut des Hautes Etudes Chinoises, 2 volumes, 1, pp. 10–16

—1969. "The Superhuman Personality of the Buddha and its Symbolism in the Mahāparinirvāṇasūtra of the Dharmaguptaka." In *Myths and Symbols: Studies in Honor of Mircea Eliade*, ed. Joseph M. Kitagawa and Charles H. Long. Chicago, University of Chicago Press, pp. 9–21

—1970–71. *Recherches sur la biographie du Buddha dans les sūtrapiṭaka et les vinayapiṭaka anciens: II. Les derniers mois, le parinirvāṇa et les funérailles.* Paris, Ecole Française d'Extrême-Orient, 2 volumes

—1971. "La transfomation miraculeuse de la nourriture offerte au Buddha par le brahmane Kasibhāradvaja". In *Etudes tibétaines dédiées à la mémoire de Marcelle Lalou.* Paris, pp. 1–10

—1974. "La jeunesse du Buddha dans les sūtrapiṭaka et les vinayapiṭaka anciens." *Bulletin de l'Ecole Française d'Extrême-Orient*, 61, pp. 199–274

—1982. "Un personage bien mystérieux: l'épouse du Buddha." In *Indological and Buddhist Studies: Volume in Honour of Professor*

*J.W. de Jong on his Sixtieth Birthday*, ed. L.A. Hercus, *et al.* Delhi, Satguru Publications, pp. 31–59

—1987. "Lumbinī et la naissance du futur Buddha." *Bulletin de l'Ecole Française d'Extrême-Orient*, 76, pp. 69–81

—1991. "Les agissements de Devadatta selon les chapitres relatifs au schisme dans les divers *vinayapiṭaka*." *Bulletin de l'Ecole Française d'Extrême-Orient*, 78, pp. 87–132

Bays, Gwendolyn, 1983. *The Voice of the Buddha: the Beauty of Compassion.* Berkeley, Dharma Publishing. 2 volumes. Translated from the French of Foucaux, 1884

Beal, Samuel, 1875. *The Romantic Legend of Śākya Buddha: A Translation of the Chinese Version of the Abhiniṣkramaṇasūtra.* London, Trübner and Co.

—1883. *The Fo-sho-hing-tsan-king: A Life of Buddha.* Oxford, The Clarendon Press

Bechert, Heinz (ed.), 1995. *When Did the Buddha Live? The Controversy on the Dating of the Historical Buddha.* Delhi, Sri Satguru Publications

Bigandet, Paul, 1866. *The Life or Legend of Gaudama, the Buddha of the Burmese.* Reprint edition, Delhi, Bharatiya Publishing House, 1979, 2 volumes

Bizot, François, 1976. *Le figuier à cinq branches: recherches sur le bouddhisme khmer.* Paris, Ecole Française d'Extrême-Orient

—1994. "La consécration des statues et le culte des morts." In *Recherches nouvelles sur le Cambodge.* Paris, Ecole Française d'Extrême-Orient, pp. 101–39

Bollée, W.B., 1970. *Kuṇālajātaka.* London, Pali Text Society

Boyd, James, 1975. *Satan and Māra: Christian and Buddhist Symbols of Evil.* Leiden, E.J. Brill

Brown, Robert L., 1997. "Narrative as Icon: the Jātaka Stories in Ancient Indian and Southeast Asian Architecture." In Schober, 1997, pp. 64–109

Burlingame, E.W., 1921. *Buddhist Legends.* Cambridge, Harvard University Press, 3 volumes

Burnouf, Eugène, 1852. *Le Lotus de la Bonne Loi.* Paris, Imprimerie Nationale

—1876. *Introduction à l'histoire du buddhisme indien.* 2nd edn, Paris, Maisonneuve

Carrithers, Michael, 1983. *The Buddha.* Oxford, Oxford University Press

Chau, Thich Minh, 1964. *The Chinese Madhyama Āgama and the Pāli Majjhima Nikāya (A Comparative Study)*, Saigon, Institute of Higher Buddhist Studies

Childers, Robert Caesar, 1909. *A Dictionary of the Pali Language.* London, Kegan Paul, Trench, Trübner and Co.

Chimpa (Lama) and Chattopadhyaya, Alaka, 1980. *Tāranātha's History of Buddhism in India.* Calcutta, K.P. Bagchi and Co.

Coedès, Georges, 1951. "Le 2.500ème anniversaire du Bouddha." *Diogène*, 15, pp. 1–16

Collins, Steven, 1982. *Selfless Persons*. Cambridge, Cambridge University Press
—1998. *Nirvana and other Buddhist Felicities*. Cambridge, Cambridge, University Press
Cone, Margaret and Gombrich, Richard, 1977. *The Perfect Generosity of Prince Vessantara*. Oxford, The Clarendon Press
Conze, Edward, 1956. *Buddhist Meditation*. New York, Harper and Row
—1967. *Buddhist Thought in India*. Ann Arbor, University of Michigan Press
—1975. *The Large Sutra on Perfect Wisdom*. Berkeley, University of California Press
Cook, Elizabeth, 1994. *Holy Places of the Buddha*. Berkeley, Dharma Publishing
Coomaraswamy, A.K. "The Webbed Fingers of Buddha." *Indian Historical Quarterly*, 7, pp. 365–66
Cowell, E.B. (ed.), 1894. "The Buddha-carita of Aśvaghosha." Part 1 of *Buddhist Mahāyāna Texts*. Oxford, Clarendon Press
—1895–1907. *The Jātaka or Stories of the Buddha's Former Births*. London, Pali Text Society, 6 volumes
Cowell, E.B. and Neil, R.A. (eds.), 1886. *The Divyāvadāna: A Collection of Early Buddhist Legends*. Cambridge, Cambridge University Press
Cummings, Mary, 1982. *The Lives of the Buddha in the Art and Literature of Asia*. Ann Arbor, MI, Center for South and Southeast Asian Studies, University of Michigan
Davids, T.W. Rhys, 1880. *Buddhist Birth-Stories or Jātaka Tales*. London, Trübner and Co.
—1890–94. *The Questions of King Milinda*. Reprint edn, 1963. New York, Dover, 2 volumes
—1899–1924. *Dialogues of the Buddha*. London, Pali Text Society, 3 volumes
Davids, C.A.F. Rhys and Woodward, F.L., 1917–30. *The Book of Kindred Sayings*. London, Pali Text Society, 5 volumes
Dayal, Har, 1932. *The Bodhisattva Doctrine in Buddhist Sanskrit Literature*. London, Routledge and Kegan Paul
de Jong, J.W., 1954. "L'épisode d'Asita dans le Lalitavistara." In *Asiatica-Festschrift Friedrich Weller*. Leipzig, O. Harrassowitz, pp. 312–25
—1997. *A Brief History of Buddhist Studies in Europe and America*. Tokyo, Kōsei Publishing
DeSilva, Lynn, 1974. *Buddhism: Beliefs and Practices in Sri Lanka*. Battaramulla, SIOLL School of Technology
Dresden, Mark J., 1955. "The Jātakastava or Praise of the Buddha's Former Births." *Transactions of the American Philosophical Society*, n.s. 45, pp. 397–588
Duroiselle, Charles, 1905. "Notes sur la géographie apocryphe de la Birmanie: à propos de la légende de Pūrṇa." *Bulletin de l'Ecole Française d'Extrême-Orient*, 5, pp. 146–67
Durt, Hubert, 1979. "Chōrai." In *Hōbōgirin: dictionnaire encyclopédique du bouddhisme d'après les sources chinoises et japonaises*. Paris, Adrien Maisonneuve, 5, pp. 371–80

—1982. "La 'visite aux laboureurs' et la 'méditation sous l'arbre *jambu*' dans les biographies sanskrites et chinoises du Buddha." In *Indological and Buddhist Studies. Volume in Honour of Professor J.W. de Jong on his Sixtieth Birthday*, ed. L.A. Hercus, *et al.* Delhi, Satguru Publications, pp. 95–120

—1992. "Récit de l'apparition du Buddha, sortant du cercueil, à sa mère, Mahāmāyā." Paper delivered at the Scuola di Studi sull'Asia Orientale, Kyoto, Japan

Dutt, Sukumar, 1962. *Buddhist Monks and Monasteries of India.* London, George Allen and Unwin

Edwardes, Michael, 1959. *A Life of the Buddha from a Burmese Manuscript.* London, The Folio Society

Emmerick, R.E., 1968. *The Book of Zambasta.* London, Oxford University Press

—1970. *The Sūtra of Golden Light.* London, Luzac & Co.

Falk, Nancy Auer, 1990. "Exemplary Donors of the Pāli Tradition." In *Ethics, Wealth, and Salvation: A Study in Buddhist Social Ethics*, ed. Russell F. Sizemore and Donald K. Swearer. Columbia SC, University of South Carolina Press

Fausbøll, V. (ed.), 1877–96. *The Jātaka Together with Its Commentary.* London, Pali Text Society, 6 volumes

—1901. *The Sutta-Nipāta–A Collection of Discourses.* In *Sacred Books of the East*, American Edition. New York, Charles Scribner's Sons, volume 12

Feer, Léon, 1895. "Le Chaddantajātaka." *Journal asiatique.* pp. 31–85, 189–223

Foucaux, Ph. Ed., 1884. *Le Lalita Vistara – Développement des jeux.* Paris, Ernest Leroux

Foucher, Alfred, 1905–18. *L'art gréco-bouddhique du Gandhara.* Paris, E. Leroux, 2 volumes

—1917. "The Great Miracle at Śrāvastī." In *The Beginnings of Buddhist Art.* Paris, Paul Geuthner, pp. 147–84

—1917a. "The Six-Tusked Elephant." In *The Beginnings of Buddhist Art.* Paris, Paul Geuthner, pp. 185–204

—1963. *The Life of the Buddha According to the Ancient Texts and Monuments of India.* Translated by Simone Brangier Boas. Middletown, CT, Wesleyan University Press

—1987. *La vie du Bouddha d'après les textes et les monuments de l'Inde.* Paris, Adrien Maisonneuve

Frauwallner, Erich, 1956. *The Earliest Vinaya and the Beginnings of Buddhist Literature.* Rome, Istituto Italiano per il Medio ed Estremo Oriente

—1995. *Studies in Abhidharma Literature and the Origins of Buddhist Philosophical Systems.* Translated by Sophie Kidd. Albany, State University of New York Press

Frye, Stanley, 1981. *The Sūtra of the Wise and the Foolish (mdo bdsans blun) or the Ocean of Narratives (üliger-ün dalai).* Dharmsala, Library of Tibetan Works and Archives

Garfield, Jay L., 1995. *The Fundamental Wisdom of the Middle Way.* New York, Oxford University Press
Geiger, Wilhelm, 1912. *The Mahāvaṃsa or the Great Chronicle of Ceylon.* London, Pali Text Society
Gnoli, Raniero, 1977–78. *The Gilgit Manuscript of the Sanghabhedavastu.* Rome, Istituto Italiano per il Medio ed Estremo Oriente, 2 volumes
Gombrich, Richard, 1972. "Feminine Elements in Sinhalese Buddhism." *Wiener Zeitschrift für die Kunde Südasiens*, 16, pp. 67–93
—1978. "Kosala-Bimba-Vaṇṇanā." In *Buddhism in Ceylon and Studies on Religious Syncretism in Buddhist Countries*, ed. Heinz Bechert. Göttingen, Vandenhoeck & Ruprecht, pp. 281–303
—1992. "Dating the Buddha: A Red Herring Revealed." In *The Dating of the Historical Buddha–Die Datierung des historischen Buddha*, ed. Heinz Bechert. Göttingen, Vandenhoeck and Ruprecht, 2, pp. 237–59
Gray, James, 1894. *Embellishments of Buddha.* London, Luzac and Co.
Griffiths, Paul J., 1986. *On Being Mindless: Buddhist Meditation and the Mind-Body Problem.* La Salle, IL, Open Court
Guthrie, Elizabeth, 1996. "The Provenance of Neang Kanghing." International Conference on Khmer Studies, 26–30 August 1996
Hahn, Michael, 1985. *Haribhaṭṭa and Gopadatta. Two authors in the Succession of Āryaśūra: On the Rediscovery of Parts of their Jātakamālās.* Tokyo
Hara Minoru, 1980. "A Note on the buddha's Birth Story." In *Indianisme et bouddhisme*. Louvain, Institut Orientaliste, pp. 142–57
Hardy, R. Spence, 1853. *A Manual of Buddhism in its Modern Development.* New Delhi, Munshiram Manoharlal. Reprint edition, 1995
Hazlewood, Ann Appleby, 1986. *In Praise of Mount Samanta.* London, Pali Text Society
Hocart, A.M., 1923. "Buddha and Devadatta." *Indian Antiquary*, 52, pp. 267–72
Hofinger, Marcel, 1990. *Le congrès du Lac Anavatapta. II Légendes du Bouddha (Buddhāvadāna).* Louvain-la-neuve, Institut Orientaliste
Holt, John C., 1981. *Discipline: The Canonical Buddhism of the Vinayapiṭaka.* Delhi, Motilal Banarsidass
Horner, I.B., 1930. *Women under Primitive Buddhism.* London, Routledge and Kegan Paul
—1938–52. *The Book of the Discipline.* London, Pali Text Society, 6 volumes
—1954–59. *The Collection of the Middle Length Sayings.* London, Pali Text Society, 3 volumes
—1975. *The Minor Anthologies of the Pali Canon, Part III: Chronicle of Buddhas and Basket of Conduct.* London, Pali Text Society
—1978. *The Clarifier of the Sweet Meaning.* London, Pali Text Society
Horner, I.B. and Jaini, Padmanabh S., 1985–86. *Apocryphal Birth-Stories (Paññāsa-jātaka).* London: Pali Text Society, 2 volumes
Huber, Edouard, 1904. "Le trésor du roi Rhampsinite." *Bulletin de l'Ecole Française d'Extrême-Orient*, 4, pp. 701–07

Huntington, John C., 1985–86. "Sowing the Seeds of the Lotus: A Journey to the Great Pilgrimage Sites of Buddhism." *Orientations (Hong Kong)*, 16, 11, pp. 46–61 (Part I); 17, 2, pp. 28–43 (Part II); 17, 3, pp. 32–46 (Part III); 17, 7, pp. 28–40 (Part IV); and 17, 9, pp. 46–58 (Part V)

—1987. "Pilgrimage as Image: the Cult of the *Aṣṭamahāprātihāry.*" *Orientations (Hong Kong)*, 18, 4, pp. 55–63 (Part I); 18, 8, pp. 56–68 (Part II)

Huntington, Susan L., 1990. "Early Buddhist Art and the Theory of Aniconism." *The Art Journal*, 49, pp. 401–8

Irwin, John, 1981. "The Mystery of the (Future) Buddha's First Words." *Annali del Istituto Universitario Orientale*, 41, pp. 623–53

Jaini, Padmanabh S., 1979. *The Jaina Path of Purification.* Berkeley, University of California Press

Jayawickrama, N.A., 1968. *The Sheaf of Garlands of the Epochs of the Conqueror.* London, Pali Text Society

—1971. *The Chronicle of the Thūpa and the Thūpavaṃsa.* London, Pali Text Society

—1990. *The Story of Gotama Buddha: the Nidāna-kathā of the Jātakaṭṭha-kathā.* London, Pali Text Society

Johnston, E.H., 1928. *The Saundarananda of Aśvaghoṣa.* Reprint edition, Delhi, Motilal Banarsidass, 1975

—1936. *The Buddhacarita or Acts of the Buddha.* Calcutta, Baptist Mission Press

—1937. "The Buddha's Mission and Last Journey (Buddhacarita xv to xxviii)." *Acta Orientalia*, 15, pp. 26–62, 85–111, 231–92

Jones, J.J., 1949–56. *The Mahāvastu.* London, Pali Text Society

Kalupahana, David J. and Kalupahana Indrani, 1982. *The Way of Siddhartha: A Life of the Buddha.* Lanham, MD, University Press of America

Kern, Hendrik, 1884. *Saddharma-Puṇḍarīka or The Lotus of the True Law.* Oxford, The Clarendon Press

—1882–84. *Der Buddhismus und seine Geschichte in Indien.* Translated by Hermann Jacobi. Leipzig, O. Schulze

Khoroche, Peter, 1989. *Once the Buddha was a Monkey: Ārya Śūra's Jātakamālā.* Chicago, The University of Chicago Press

Kloppenborg, Ria, 1973. *The Sūtra on the Foundation of the Buddhist Order (Catuṣpariṣatsūtra).* Leiden, E.J. Brill

—1974. *The Paccekabuddha: A Buddhist Ascetic.* Leiden, E.J. Brill

La Vallée Poussin, Louis de, 1980. *L'Abhidharmakośa de Vasubandhu.* Reprint edition: Brussels, Institut Belge des Hautes Etudes Chinoises

Lamotte, Etienne, 1949–80. *Le traité de la grande vertu de sagesse.* Louvain, Institut Orientaliste, 5 volumes.

—1966–74. "Vajrapāṇi en Inde." In *Mélanges de sinologie offerts à Monsieur Paul Demiéville.* Paris, Institut des Hautes Etudes Chinoises, 1, pp. 113–59

—1970. "Le Bouddha insulta-t-il Devadatta?" *Bulletin of the School of Oriental and African Studies*, 33, pp. 107–15

—1988. *History of Indian Buddhism*. Translated by Sara Webb-Boin. Louvain-la-neuve, Institut Orientaliste

Leclère, Adhémard, 1899. *Le buddhisme au Cambodge*. Paris, E. Leroux

—1906. *Les livres sacrés du Cambodge*. Paris, E. Leroux

Legge, James, 1886. *A Record of Buddhistic Kingdoms*. Oxford, The Clarendon Press

Lévi, Sylvain and Chavannes, Edouard, 1916. "Les seize arhat protecteurs de la loi." *Journal asiatique*, 8, pp. 5–48, 189–304

Li Rongxi, 1993. *The Biographical Scripture of King Aśoka*. Berkeley, The Numata Center for Buddhist Translation and Research

—1995. *A Biography of the Tripiṭaka Master of the Great Ci'en Monastery of the Great Tang Dynasty*. Berkeley, Numata Center for Buddhist Translation and Research

—1996. *The Great Tang Dynasty Record of the Western Regions*. Berkeley, Numata Center for Buddhist Translation and Research

Ling, Trevor O., 1962. *Buddhism and the Mythology of Evil*. London, Allen and Unwin

Makransky, John J., 1997. *Buddhahood Embodied*. Albany, State University of New York Press

Malalasekera, G.P., 1937. *Dictionary of Pāli Proper Names*. London, Pali Text Society, 2 volumes

—1971. "Buddha." In *Encyclopaedia of Buddhism*, ed. G.P. Malalasekera. Colombo, Government of Ceylon Press, 3, pp. 357–80

Marshall, John, 1955. *A Guide to Sāñchī*. Calcutta, Government of India Press

Migot, André, 1954. "Un grand disciple du Buddha: Śāriputra." *Bulletin de l'Ecole Française d'Extrême-Orient*, 46, pp. 405–554

Mitra, Kalipada, 1924. "Cross-Cousin Relation between Buddha and Devadatta." *Indian Antiquary*, 53, pp. 125–28

Mukherjee, Biswadeb, 1966. *Die Überlieferung von Devadatta, dem Widersacher des Buddha, in den kanonischen Schriften*. Munich, J. Kitzinger

Murcott, Susan, 1991. *The First Buddhist Women*. Berkeley, Parallax Press

Mus, Paul, 1934. "Barabuḍur, Sixième partie: Genèse de la bouddhologie mahāyāniste." In *Bulletin de l'Ecole Française d'Extrême-Orient*, 34, pp. 175–400

—1935. *Barabuḍur: esquisse d'une histoire du bouddhisme fondée sur la critique archéologique des textes*. Hanoi, Imprimerie d'Extrême-Orient, 2 volumes

—1998. *Barabuḍur: Sketch of a History of Buddhism Based on Archaeological Criticism of the Texts*. Translated by Alexander W. MacDonald. New Delhi, Indira Gandhi National Centre for the Arts

Nakamura Hajime, 1977. *Gotama Buddha*. Los Angeles, Buddhist Books International

Narain, A.K. (ed.), 1985. *Studies in Buddhist Art of South Asia*. New Delhi, Kanak Publications

Nattier, Jan, 1991. *Once Upon a Future Time: Studies in a Buddhist Prophecy of Decline.* Berkeley, Asian Humanities Press
Nhat Hanh, Thich, 1991. *Old Path White Clouds.* Berkeley, Parallax Press
Nikam, N.A. and McKeon, Richard, 1959. *The Edicts of Aśoka.* Chicago, University of Chicago Press
Nyanaponika Thera and Hecker, Hellmuth, 1997. *Great Disciples of the Buddha.* Boston, Wisdom Publications
Obermiller, E., 1931–32. *History of Buddhism (Chos-hbyung) by Bu-ston.* Heidelberg, O. Harrassowitz, 2 volumes
Ohnuma, Reiko, 1998. "The Gift of the Body and the Gift of Dharma." *History of Religions*, 37, pp. 323–59
—2000. "The Story of Rūpāvatī: A Female Past Birth of the Buddha." *Journal of the International Association of Buddhist Studies*, 23, pp. 103–45
Oldenberg, Hermann, 1879. *The Dīpavaṃsa: An Ancient Buddhist Historical Record.* Reprint edition, New Delhi, Asian Educational Services, 1982
—1882. *The Buddha: His Life, his Order, his Doctrine.* Translated by William Hoey, London
Parlier, Edith, 1991. "La légende du roi des Śibi: du sacrifice brahmanique au don du corps bouddhique." *Bulletin d'études indiennes*, 9, pp. 133–60
Péri, Noël, 1917. "Hārītī la mère-de-démons." *Bulletin de l'Ecole Française d'Extrême-Orient*, 17, pp. 1–102
—1918. "Les femmes de Śākya-muni." *Buletin de l'Ecole Française d'Extrême-Orient*, 18, pp. 1–37
Poppe, Nicholas, 1967. *The Twelve Deeds of Buddha.* Wiesbaden, Otto Harrassowitz
Porée-Maspero, Eveline, 1962–69. *Etude sur les rites agraires des Cambodgiens.* Paris, Mouton, 3 volumes
Prebish, Charles S., 1975. *Buddhist Monastic Discipline.* University Park, PA, Pennsylvania State University Press
Przyluski, Jean, 1914. "Le Nord-ouest de l'Inde dans le Vinaya des Mūlasarvāstivādin et les textes apparentés." *Journal asiatique*, 4, pp. 493–568
—1920. *Le parinirvāṇa et les funérailles du Buddha.* Paris, Paul Geuthner
—1923. *La légende de l'empereur Açoka dans les textes indiens et chinois.* Paris, Paul Geuthner
—1926. *Le concile de Rājagṛha.* Paris, Paul Geuthner
—1935–36. "Le partage des reliques du Buddha." *Mélanges chinois et bouddhiques*, 4, pp. 341–67
Rahula, Walpola, 1959. *What the Buddha Taught.* New York, Grove Press
Ray, Reginald A., 1994. *Buddhist Saints in India.* New York, Oxford University Press
Reynolds, Frank E., 1976. "The Many Lives of Buddha: A Study of Sacred Biography and Theravada Tradition." In *The Biographical Process*, ed. Frank E. Reynolds and Donald Capps. The Hague, Mouton

1993. "*Rāmāyaṇa*, *Rāma Jātaka*, and *Ramakien*: A Comparative Study of Hindu and Buddhist Traditions." In *Many Rāmāyaṇas*, ed. Paula Richman. Berkeley, University of California Press, pp. 50–63

—1997. "Rebirth Traditions and the Lineages of Gotama: A Study in Theravāda Buddhology." In Schober, 1997, pp. 19–39

Reynolds, Frank E. and Hallisey, Charles, 1987. "Buddha." *Encyclopedia of Religion*, ed. Mircea Eliade. New York, MacMillan, 2, pp. 319–32

Reynolds, Frank E. and Reynolds, Mani, 1982. *Three Worlds According to King Ruang*. Berkeley, Asian Humanities Press

Robinson, Richard and Johnson, Willard, 1997. *The Buddhist Religion*. 4th edn, Belmont, CA, Wadsworth

Rockhill W. Woodville, 1907. *The Life of the Buddha*. London, Kegan Paul, Trench, Trübner

Rouse, W.H.D. 1904–05. "Jinacarita."*Journal of the Pali Text Society*, pp. 1–65

Saddhatissa, H., 1975. *The Birth-Stories of the Ten Bodhisattas and the Dasabodhisattuppattikathā*. London, Pali Text Society

Schlingloff, Dieter, 1987. *Studies in the Ajantā Paintings: Identifications and Interpretations*. Delhi, Ajanta Publications

Schober, Juliane (ed.), 1997. *Sacred Biography in the Buddhist Traditions of South and Southeast Asia*. Honolulu, University of Hawai'i Press

Schopen, Gregory, 1994. "Ritual Rights and Bones of Contention: More on Monastic Funerals and Relics in the *Mūlasarvāstivāda-Vinaya*." *Journal of Indian Philosophy*, 22, pp. 31–80

—1997. *Bones, Stones, and Buddhist Monks*. Honolulu, University of Hawai'i Press

Senart, Emile, 1882. *Essai sur la légende du Buddha*. 2nd edition, Paris, E. Leroux

Shway Yoe [James George Scott], 1882. *The Burman: His Life and Notions*. Reprint edn, New York, The Norton Library, 1963

Siegel, Lee, 1991. *Net of Magic. Wonders and Deceptions in India*. Chicago, University of Chicago Press

Snellgrove, David L. (ed.), 1978. *The Image of the Buddha*. Tokyo, Kodansha International

Soper, Alexander, 1940. "Japanese Evidence for the History of the Architecture and Iconography of Chinese Buddhism." *Monumenta Serica*, 4, pp. 638–78

—1949–50. "Aspects of Light Symbolism in Gandhāran Sculpture." Parts 1–3. *Artibus Asiae*, 12, pp. 252–83, 314–30; 13, pp. 63–85

Speyer, J.S., 1895. *The Jātakamālā or Garland of Birth-Stories of Āryaśūra*. London

Srivastava, A.L., 1983. *Life in Sanchi Sculpture*. Atlantic Highlands, NJ, Humanities Press

Stede, W. (ed.), 1886–1932. *Sumangala Vilāsinī, Buddhaghosa's Commentary on the Dīgha-Nikāya*. London, Pali Text Society, 1886–1932, 3 volumes

Strong, John S., 1979. "The Legend of the Lion-Roarer: A Study of the Buddhist Arhat Piṇḍola Bhāradvāja." *Numen*, 26, pp. 50–88

—1983. *The Legend of King Aśoka*. Princeton, Princeton University Press

—1983a. "Wenn der magische Flug misslingt." In *Sehnsucht nach dem Ursprung*, ed. Hans Peter Duerr. Frankfurt, Syndikat, pp. 503–18

—1992. *The Legend and Cult of Upagupta*. Princeton, Princeton University Press

—1995. *The Experience of Buddhism: Sources and Interpretations*. Belmont, Wadsworth Publishing

—1997. "The Buddha, Yaśodharā, and Rāhula in the *Mūlasarvastivāda Vinaya*." In *Sacred Biography in the Buddhist Traditions of South and Southeast Asia*, ed. Juliane Schober. Honolulu, University of Hawai'i Press, pp. 113–28

—1998. "Les reliques des cheveux du Bouddha au Shwe Dagon de Rangoon." *Aséanie*, 2, pp. 79–107

—forthcoming. *Relics of the Buddha's Body*

Swearer, Donald K., 1995. "Bimbā's Lament." In *Buddhism in Practice*, ed. Donald S. Lopez, Jr. Princeton, Princeton University Press, pp. 541–52

—forthcoming. *Opening the Eyes of the Buddha: the Ritual of Buddha Image Consecration in Northern Thailand*

Takakusu, Junjiro, 1896. *A Record of Buddhistic Religion as Practiced in India and the Malay Archipelago*. Reprint edn, Delhi, Munshiram Manoharlal, 1966

Tambiah, Stanley J., 1992. *Buddhism and the Spirit Cults in North-east Thailand*. Cambridge, Cambridge University Press

Tatelman, Joel, 1999. *The Glorious Deeds of Pūrṇa*. London, Curzon Press

Thanissaro Bhikkhu [Geoffrey DeGraff], 1994. *The Buddhist Monastic Code*. Valley Center, CA, Metta Forest Monastery

—1998. *Dhammapada: A Translation*. Barre, MA, Dhamma Dana Publications

Thomas, E.J., 1927. *The Life of Buddha as Legend and History*. London, Routledge and Kegan Paul

Trainor, Kevin, 1992. "When is a Theft not a Theft? Relic Theft and the Cult of the Buddha's Relics in Sri Lanka." *Numen*, 39, pp. 1–26

Tsomo, Karma Lekshe, 1996. *Sisters in Solitude: Two Traditions of Buddhist Monastic Ethics for Women*. Albany, State University of New York Press

Van Zeyst, H.G.A., 1961. "Abhiññā." In *Encyclopaedia of Buddhism*, ed. G.P. Malalasekera. Colombo, Government of Ceylon Press, 1, pp. 97–102

Vaudeville, Charlotte, 1964. "La légende de Sundara et les funérailles du Buddha." *Bulletin de l'Ecole Française d'Extrême-Orient*, 52, pp. 73–91

Waldschmidt, Ernst, 1944–48. *Die Überlieferung vom Lebensende des Buddha: Eine vergleichende Analyse des Mahāparinirvāṇasūtra und seiner Textentsprechungen*. Göttingen, Vandenhoeck & Ruprecht, 2 volumes

—1950–51. *Das Mahāparinirvāṇasūtra*. Berlin, Akadmie Verlag, 3 parts

—1953–56. *Das Mahāvadānasūtra: ein kanonischer Text über die sieben letzten Buddhas*. Berlin, Akademie Verlag

—1967. "Der Buddha preist die Verehrungswürdigkeit seiner Reliquien." *Vom Ceylon bis Turfan*. Göttingen, Vandenhoeck und Reprecht, pp. 417–27

Waley, Arthur, 1931–32. "Did Buddha Die of Eating Pork?" *Mélanges chinois et bouddhiques*, 1, pp. 343–54

Walleser, Max and Kopp, Hermann, 1924. *Manoratha-pūraṇī: Commentary on the Anguttara Nikāya*. London, Pali Text Society, 5 volumes

Walshe, Maurice, 1987. *Thus Have I Heard: The Long Discourses of the Buddha*. London, Wisdom Publications

Walters, Jonathan S., 1900. "The Buddha's Bad Karma: A Problem in the History of Theravāda Buddhism." *Numen*, 37, pp. 70–95

—1994. "A Voice from the Silence: The Buddha's Mother's Story." *History of Religions*, 33, pp. 358–79

Warren, Henry Clarke, 1896. *Buddhism in Translations*. Cambridge, MA, Harvard University Press

Wasson, R. Gordon, 1982. "The Last Meal of the Buddha." *Journal of the American Oriental Society*, 102, pp. 591–603

Watanabe, K., 1909. "The Story of Kalmāṣapāda and its Evolution in Indian Literature." *Journal of the Pali Text Society*, pp. 329–47

Weller, Friedrich, 1939–40. "Buddhas letzte Wanderung." *Monumenta Serica* 4, pp. 40–84, 406–40; 5, pp. 141–207

Wells, Kenneth E., 1960. *Thai Buddhism: Its Rites and Activities*. Bangkok, The Police Printing Press

Wieger, Leon, 1913. "Les vies chinoises du Buddha: Récit de l'apparition sur terre du Buddha des Sakya." In *Buddhisme*, Sien Hsien, Imprimerie de la Mission Catholique

Wijayaratna, Mohan, 1990. *Buddhist Monastic Life According to the Texts of the Theravāda Tradition*. Translated by Claude Grangier and Steven Collins. Cambridge, Cambridge University Press

—1991. *Les moniales bouddhistes: naissance et développement du monachisme féminin*. Paris, Edition du Cerf

Willemen, Charles, 1978. *The Chinese Udānavarga*. Bruxelles, Institut Belge des Hautes Etudes Chinoises

—1994. *The Storehouse of Sundry Valuables*. Berkeley, Numata Center for Buddhist Translation and Research

Wilson, Liz, 1966. *Charming Cadavers: Horrific Figurations of the Feminine in Indian Buddhist Hagiographic Literature*. Chicago, University of Chicago Press

Wiltshire, Martin G., 1990. *Ascetic Figures before and in Early Buddhism: the Emergence of Gautama as the Buddha*. Berlin, Mouton de Gruyter

Winternitz, Maurice, 1933. *History of Indian Literature*. Calcutta, University of Calcutta, volume 2

Woodward, F.L., 1935. *The Minor Anthologies of the Pali Canon, Part II*. London, Pali Text Society

Woodward, F.L. and Hare, E.M., 1932–36. *The Book of the Gradual Sayings*. London, Pali Text Society, 5 volumes

Wray, Elizabeth, Rosenfeld, Clare and Baily, Dorothy, 1972. *Ten Lives of the Buddha: Siamese Temple Painting and Jātaka Tales*. Tokyo, Weatherhill

Zwilling, Leonard, 1995. "Homosexuality as seen in Indian Buddhist Texts." In *Buddhism, Sexuality and Gender*, ed. José Ignacio Cabezón. Albany, State University of New York Press, pp. 203–14

# INDEX

Page numbers in *italics* refer to tables.